Springer Series on Death and Suicide

Robert Kastenbaum, PhD, Series Editor

Bert Hayslip, Jr., PhD, received his doctorate in Experimental Developmental Psychology from the University of Akron in 1975. After teaching at Hood College in Frederick, MD for three years, he joined the faculty at the University of North Texas, where he is now Regents Professor of Psychology. Dr. Hayslip is a Fellow of the American Psychological Association, the Gerontological Society of America, and The Association for Gerontology in Higher Education, and has held research grants from the National Institute on Aging, The Hilgenfeld Foundation, and the National Endowment for the Humanities. He is currently Associate Editor of *Experimental Aging Research* and Editor of *The International Journal of Aging and Human Development*. His published research deals with cognitive processes in aging, interventions to enhance cognitive functioning in later life, personality-ability interrelationships in aged persons, grandparents who raise their grandchildren, grief and bereavement, hospice care, death anxiety, and mental health and aging. He is coauthor of *Hospice Care, Psychology and Aging: An Annotated Bibliography, Grandparents Raising Grandchildren: Theoretical, Empirical, and Clinical Perspectives* (Springer, 2000), *Adult Development and Aging, Working with Custodial Grandparents* (Springer, 2003), and *Diversity Among Custodial Grandparents* (Springer, In Press).

Cynthia A. Peveto, PhD, graduated from the University of Texas School of Allied Health Sciences with a degree in Occupational Therapy, completed a doctorate in Human Anatomy at the University of Texas Medical Branch at Galveston, a Master's Degree in Clinical and Counseling Psychology at Southern Methodist University, and a PhD in Counseling Psychology at the University of North Texas. She is a licensed psychologist specialized in college counseling and bereavement therapy.

Cultural Changes in Attitudes Toward Death, Dying and Bereavement

Bert Hayslip, Jr., PhD
Cynthia A. Peveto, PhD

SP *Springer Publishing Company*

Springer Publishing Company, Inc.
11 W 42nd Street
New York, NY 10036

Acquisitions Editor: Helvi Gold
Production Editor: Janice Stangel
Cover design by Joanne Honigman

05 06 07 08 09 / 5 4 3 2 1

Library of Congress Cataloging-in-Publication Data

Hayslip, Bert.
   Cultural changes in attitudes toward death, dying, and bereavement / Bert Hayslip, Jr., Cynthia A. Peveto—1st ed.
       p. cm. — (The Springer series on death and suicide)
   Includes bibliographical references and index.
   ISBN 0-8261-2796-7 (alk. paper)
   1. Death—Social aspects. 2. Death—Psychological aspects. 3. Mourning customs. 4. Bereavement. I. Peveto, Cynthia A. II. Title. III. Series.

   GT3150.H38 2005
   306.9—dc22

                                                            2004023927

Printed in the United States of America by Integrated Book Technology.

To my wife Gail, for her friendship and unwavering faith in me.

—BH

To my husband Rod, for his love, support, and encouragement.

—CP

Contents

Foreword

"Tell me what you really think about something you really don't want to think about!"

Social psychologist Richard A. Kalish and anthropologist David K. Reynolds (1976) did not use those precise words, but they did take the risk of asking people to share their personal views on death at a time when such a request was still considered beyond the borders of gentility. Nevertheless, respondents classified as "Black Americans," "Japanese Americans," Mexican Americans," and "White Americans" did respond. This community survey of more than four hundred Los Angeles area residents became foundational for the study of death attitudes within the general U.S. population. A carefully developed and detailed survey it was: the survey included more than a hundred questions and had been refined through eight versions before its use in the final study. The Kalish and Reynolds study was also notable in its inclusion of three subpopulations who had so often been underrepresented in academic research. The results would therefore look more like America than previous (and most subsequent) studies.

The Kalish-Reynolds contribution was welcomed by the growing number of researchers, educators, and service providers who were becoming interested in death-related issues. Basic facts popped out of the data to support the mission of the still-emerging death awareness movement. Perhaps the most persuasive finding was that most adults had experienced personally significant deaths in their lives, often recently. That about two thirds of the diverse responder sample had attended at least one funeral in the previous two years suggested that there was much to learn about the way in which such experiences influenced ongoing lives.

New questions also emerged along with the findings. Why, for example, did the four subpopulations studied have such different patterns of grave visitation—what did this suggest about their overall beliefs and values? And, for another example, what were the implications of the areas of agreement across Black, Caucasian, Japanese, and Mexican heritage populations? Physicians at that time were mostly hesitant to level with terminally ill patients: did they realize that regardless of ethnicity, most people believed that doctors had the responsibility to tell them the truth?

Fast forward to the present time. Controversies prefigured in the Kalish-Reynolds study have become more salient issues; hospice care has had another quarter of a century to establish itself, peer support groups, grief counseling, and death education courses are no longer rarities. Furthermore, the conditions of life have altered with the emergence of new technologies, changing economic circumstances, the continued "graying" of the population and emerging threats to security. With every passing year the Kalish-Reynolds data have acquired more of an archival status. It was reasonable to suppose that some of the basic patterns discovered in the mid-70's would still be evident today, but also reasonable to suppose that there would be notable changes as well.

Meanwhile, another generation of service providers and scholars have entered the scene with limited exposure to the pioneering contributions in thanatology. Specifically, the Kalish-Reynolds monograph has not been readily available for some time now. One is fortunate to find a brief summary here and there, but is unlikely to have the original source with all its wealth of data at hand. Why doesn't "somebody" do a real follow-up study? How much longer must we wait to learn how and how much American attitudes toward death have been changing?

Psychologists Bert Hayslip, Jr. and Cynthia A. Peveto have risen to this challenge. Follow-up studies have been infrequent, and especially so when the original work was complex and even its quasi-replication a daunting enterprise. Fortunately, seasoned researchers Hayslip and Peveto have applied the necessary skill, effort, and stamina to accomplish this difficult task.

On these pages we will find a generously detailed summary and discussion of the Kalish-Reynolds study. This is a valuable contribution in and of itself. We then find an equally well detailed and clearly presented account of their follow-up research project. Readers will find much occasion for reflection. Why, for example, would people today report thinking less about death on a daily basis than respondents a quarter of a century ago-despite the fact that they were more likely to have spoken to or visited dying persons? What are we to make of the finding that Caucasians now report the highest frequency of paranormal death experiences although this subpopulation had the lowest frequency in the original study? Plenty of questions to stimulate re-thinking. Plenty of data to draw upon for course preparation, research planning, and program development.

The follow-up study was guided by several hypotheses that were variously supported and not supported by the results. These propositions, though, well served their purpose of highlighting key questions. The authors' useful discussions stay close to their data. I don't know how they could exercise such admirable restraint in avoiding airy speculations (I would surely have succumbed to the temptation). The careful interpretations they do offer are well worth our attention, while leaving the way open for those who care to find longer limbs to climb out on. (Alternative formulation for residual grammarians: longer limbs out on which to climb.)

The publication of this book does have one disconcerting effect: it makes previous discussions of death attitudes in the United States somewhat outdated and incomplete. Hayslip and Peveto have done the heavy lifting. Now it's our turn for the rewarding exercise of incorporating their findings into our understanding. Sociologists, anthropologists and other students of culture will also find much of value here even if they have not already been enchanted by death-related issues.

ROBERT KASTENBAUM

REFERENCES

Kalish, R. A., & Reynolds, D. K. (1976). *Death and ethnicity: A psychocultural study.* Los Angeles: The University of Southern California Press.

1

Introduction

Each generation and each society has constructed its own solutions to the problem of death and has enshrined them in a complex web of beliefs and customs which, at first glance, seem so diverse as to be impossible to digest. Yet there are common themes that run through all of them. (Parkes, Laungani, & Young, 1997, p. 8)

D eath and grief are universal and natural experiences that occur within a social milieu and are deeply embedded within each person's reality. The meaning of the dying experience, the locus of death, and the response of other people to dying and death are shaped by the values and institutions of the culture and society (Moller, 1996). Consequently, there are a multitude of factors that affect the way people grieve and react to death. This is particularly true when each is examined in a multicultural context. Myths and mores that characterize both the dominant and nondominant cultural groups directly affect beliefs, attitudes, practices, and cross-cultural relationships (Irish, Lundquist, & Nelson, 1993). Insights concerning diversity in death and grief practices can prevent misunderstandings between individuals that occur when there is a lack of knowledge about the background and culture of those involved. Although there has been a surge in the popularity of the topic of death in recent decades, there has been minimal focus on the assessment of change in death attitudes and behaviors within the parameters of multi-culturalism (Irish, Lundquist, & Nelson, 1993). Diversity became an important topic in the 1990s and 2000s because of ethnodemographic trends. Demographic projections suggest that women and racial minorities will predominate in tomorrow's marketplace, beginning early in the 21st century. It is understandable then that the growing influence of diversity emphasizes the need for greater understanding of cultural variations in dealing with death and bereavement.

Richard Kalish and David Reynolds laid the foundation for the investigation of multicultural attitudes toward death and grief in the 1970s. In 1976, they published *Death and Ethnicity: A Psychocultural Study,* based on the results of their large-scale project focusing on death attitudes, beliefs, and customs among individuals of varying ethnocultural backgrounds. The authors stated that their purpose was to "learn much more about how a cross-section of a general population felt concerning death and bereavement" and "to understand better how and why groups differed in their views of death and bereavement" (pp. 2–3). Although Kalish and Reynolds used several sources of information, including newspaper analysis, interviews with professionals from each of many ethnic groups, observations of persons in various settings, and the comments of experts, they derived the data predominantly from a community survey of 434 respondents from Los Angeles County conducted in the fall of 1970. Participants were members of four ethnic groups, including "109 African Americans, 110 Japanese Americans, 114 Mexican Americans, and 101 White Americans" (p. 13). Their sample was almost evenly divided between adult men and women (215 and 219, respectively), the mean age of all respondents was in the middle to late 40s, and respondents came from low-income groups residing in areas of high ethnic density. Various versions of the survey were pilot tested on small groups; the final questionnaire was the eighth version of the survey and comprised 122 questions. Kalish and Reynolds's 1976 book describes the results of the study in detail.

Kalish and Reynolds's (1976) work forms the basis for thanatological research from a multicultural perspective, but how relevant are their findings for the beginning of the 21st century? Attitudes and customs concerning death have likely changed substantially with time over the quarter of a century since the study was conducted. Furthermore, customs among similar ethnic groups may vary regionally based on place of residence. Consequently, Kalish and Reynolds's results are unlikely to accurately describe the death attitudes and customs of African Americans, Asian Americans, Hispanics, and Caucasians in 1999–2000. This study uses Kalish and Reynolds's survey instrument to compare their findings with those of participants of similar demographic makeup residing in north Texas. The resulting data provides insight in addressing a number of questions, including: "Have death attitudes and experience with death changed since the 1970s? If so, how have they changed? Have changes been more dramatic among some ethnic, age, or gender groups than others? What do the data suggest about current death attitudes and death experience among ethnic, age, and gender groups?"

It is hoped that the information provided by this study will improve our understanding of the needs of persons who are dying or grieving and will assist family, friends, and involved professionals in responding with care and consideration of these needs. Furthermore, current knowledge of ethnic diversity in death attitudes and customs is important in guiding health care workers and clinicians in making appropriate decisions and in developing effective programs. Additional knowledge of diversity in attitudes concerning death can be of use in counteracting the fear that the "processes of dying and grieving will be culturally stereotyped as a result of the tendency to generalize Euro-American theories about the stages of death across diverse cultures" (Irish, Lundquist, & Nelson, 1993, p. 188).

Kalish and Reynolds (1976) organized their materials by providing an overview of the results of their study, including focus on the factors of age, sex, education, and religiousness, followed by ethnographic descriptions of death attitudes of the three ethnic groups. The researchers found that the *Anglo* or Caucasian sample presented such a diverse composite of nationalities and cultural characteristics that they decided to consider the Anglo group as a comparison group rather than as a specific ethnic community. This study will follow Kalish and Reynolds's organization in reviewing the results of their study, as well as other relevant research, and in considering the Anglo American or Caucasian American sample as a comparison group.

2

An Overview of the Death-Ethnicity Relationship: Kalish and Reynolds

ENCOUNTERING THE DEATH OF OTHERS

In their study, Kalish and Reynolds (1976) found that death and dying are very much a part of the experience of adults. Most people (82% total; B (Blacks) 90%, J (Japanese) 83%, M (Mexican American) 81%, A (Anglos) 74%) knew someone who had died in the 2 years prior to the interview, and about 17% (B 25%, J 15%, M 9%, A 8%) knew personally at least eight persons who had died. Most of the deaths were from natural causes, and very few respondents knew people who had died from suicide or homicide. More than one third of the participants had talked with or visited at least one dying person in the previous 2 years, and two thirds had attended at least one funeral during that time. Attendance at funerals correlated significantly with having visited a dying person. Fewer than half of the respondents had visited a grave in the last 2 years. When the responses were examined according to ethnic groups, some reliable trends emerged. With the exception of visits to the grave, Anglos were the least likely to have contact with the dying and the dead. The intimacy of touching the body at the funeral was considered acceptable by a majority of all groups except for the Japanese, and more than half of the Mexicans and one third of the Anglos reported that they would be likely to kiss the dead person.

Ethnicity is a fundamental demographic determinant of mortality (Rogers, Hummer, Nam, & Peters, 1996), a circumstance illustrated by the differences in each ethnic group's exposure to death in Kalish and Reynolds's (1976) study. Rogers et al. employed the linked National Health Interview Survey-National Death Index (NHSI-NDI) to examine ethnic differences in mortality in the United States from a combination of demographic, socioeconomic, and health characteristic perspectives. They found that the Asian mortality rate was the lowest, partly because of healthy behaviors and socioeconomic advantages, that the Caucasian mortality rate was higher than that of Asians, partly because of the high prevalence and quantity of cigarette smoking, and that the Mexican mortality rate was next highest, partly because of socioeconomic disadvantages. The mortality rate for African Americans is the highest of the ethnic groups, also partly because of socioeconomic disadvantages, although their life expectancy had increased the most dramatically from the turn of the century through the mid 1980s. Comparison of demographic death statistics with Kalish and Reynolds's results concerning respondent's exposure to death yields somewhat unexpected findings based on current ethnic mortality rates. In Kalish and Reynolds's study, African Americans had the greatest percentage of respondents who knew someone who had died in the previous 2 years (90%) and the greatest proportion who knew personally at least eight persons who had died (25%), which corresponds with demographic mortality statistics. However, the Japanese, who compose part of the Asian ethnic group, were second most common in knowing someone who had died within the last 2 years (83%) and in knowing personally at least eight persons who had died (15%) even though Asians currently have the lowest mortality rate among the ethnic groups in the United States. The discrepancy between Asians' low mortality rates and the prevalence of Kalish and Reynolds's Japanese American respondents in having encountered death so frequently may be due to changes in mortality rates over time (1970 vs. 1995), the specificity of the ethnic group (Japanese mortality rate vs. general Asian mortality rate), location (Los Angeles vs. the entire United States), or the existence of a wider social network or social convoy of the Japanese American versus the Mexican Americans and Anglo Americans. It is interesting to compare Kalish and Reynolds's results with those of the current study to see if the same trends currently occur in north Texas.

Kalish and Reynolds found that grave visitation (other than during funeral services) also varied among ethnic groups. Japanese American respondents reported having visited someone's grave within the previous 2 years most frequently (64%), followed by Mexicans (64%) and Anglos (41%), and Blacks (29%). Kalish (1986) also examined the frequency of visits to cemeteries in 78 undergraduate students in New York. He found that 26% of the college students had not visited a cemetery for any reason during the previous 5 years, 45% had not visited a cemetery for burial during that period, and 62% had not visited a cemetery for purposes of attending a grave. Kalish did not include ethnicity as a factor, but noted that 35% of the participants were Black and 2 were of Asian ancestry. Study results indicated that neither age, nor gender, nor death fear (based on one Likert-type item) were related to frequency of cemetery visits; however, the great majority of the respondents were in their 20s or very late teens. It is difficult to adequately compare the frequency of cemetery visits of the New York college sample with that of the older, larger, more ethnically diverse Los Angeles sample beyond noting the relative infrequency of cemetery visits in both groups.

COMMUNICATING WITH PERSONS DYING

Kalish and Reynolds's (1976) survey included questions concerning whether patients should be made aware of their impending death. More than half of the participants indicated that dying persons (described as about the same age and of the same gender as the respondent) should be told that they are dying, and more Anglo-Americans favored informing dying persons than members of other ethnic groups (B 60%, J 49%, M 37%, A 71%). The majority of respondents in each group felt that it was the physician's task to communicate to individuals that they were dying, with family members listed as the second most appropriate choice. Three fourths of the study participants indicated that they wished to be informed if they were dying. Each ethnic group had a higher proportion of persons desiring themselves to be informed than feeling that others should be told, with the Japanese Americans and the Mexican Americans showing the greatest discrepancy between their own desire to know and their willingness to let others know. Very few participants (between 4% and 7% of each group) related having ever told dying persons that they were dying, and most respondents felt incapable of serving as an informant.

A review of the literature on wishing to be informed of a fatal illness indicates that prior to 1970, the majority of physicians did not favor telling fatally ill patients about the reality of their condition (Feifel, 1965; Oken, 1961), but since then there has been a tendency among physicians to inform dying patients of their condition (Mount, Jones, & Patterson, 1974; Travis, Noyes, & Brightwell, 1974). Studies of patient populations indicated that the majority of patients want to be told of a fatal illness (Feifel, 1965; Levy, 1973; Mount et al.), as do the majority of adult individuals living in the United States, according to a 1978 Gallup poll (Blumenfield, Levy, & Kaufman, 1979). The Gallup Organization interviewed a national sample of 1,518 adults using a sampling procedure designed to produce an approximation to the adult civilian population (Blumenfield et al.). Results indicated that 90% of all adults wanted to be told if they had a fatal illness, with 87% of women as compared with 92% of men wanting to be informed. The study considered only two ethnic categories, "White and Non-White," and found that a significantly smaller percentage of Non-Whites than Whites (82% vs. 91%, respectively) wanted to be informed of a fatal diagnosis. In Kalish and Reynolds's (1976) study, 77% of both Anglos and Japanese, 71% of Blacks, and 60% of Mexicans reported that they wished to be told if they were dying. The results of the Gallop poll suggested that the desire to be informed concerning one's own fatal diagnosis may have increased since 1978, or the differences may be due to other factors such as the greater ethnic representation, low socioeconomic status, or circumscribed location of Kalish and Reynolds's study.

GRIEF AND MOURNING

Mourning rituals represent the public face of grief. The range of emotions that constitute grief—the feelings of loss, anger, sorrow, and self-destructive depression—are given different emphases in different societies (Counts & Counts, 1991). There are no emotions that are universally present at death; rather, cultural matters determine what emotions are felt, how they are expressed, and how they are understood (Rosenblatt, 1997). Accordingly, cultures vary in their consideration of the appropriate expression of emotions in displaying grief. Expression of all of the emotions of grief in public is accepted in many cultures and is often viewed as therapeutic. However, in many North European societies, death is seen as a private event, and people are either prohibited or limited from openly sharing their loss with the rest of the community (Laungani & Young, 1997).

A number of questions in Kalish and Reynolds's (1976) survey instrument addressed grief and mourning. Respondents were asked about: (a) their ability to express grief openly, (b) their willingness to carry out their spouse's last wishes, (c) whom they would turn for comfort and support, (d) the extent to which they perceive death of others to be tragic, (e) their attitude toward various mourning customs, and (f) their definition of abnormal grief. Regarding the open expression of grief, most respondents indicated reluctance to cry or publicly display their emotions. Less than half would worry if they could not cry (with the exception of Mexican Americans, 50% of whom stated that they would worry). Three fourths of the Blacks, Japanese, and Anglos indicated that they would "try very hard to control the way (they) showed (their) emotions in public," but less than two thirds of Mexicans agreed with the statement. Nevertheless, apparently participants felt that emotional expression is appropriate in private since the great majority of all groups and almost all of the Mexican Americans indicated that they would let themselves "go and cry (them)selves out."

When respondents in Kalish and Reynolds's (1976) study were asked if they would carry out their spouse's last wishes even if the wishes were felt to be senseless and inconvenient, two thirds of the African Americans and over 80% of the others indicated that they would. Inquiry concerning sources of comfort and support in bereavement revealed that most respondents would turn to a family member, although many also cited clergymen. Friends were less frequently selected, and about 8% of the participants said that they would not turn to anyone. For practical help, such as keeping the household going, most people would seek such help from relatives (B 50%, J 74%, M 65%, A 45%), with Anglo respondents least likely to have expectations of their family in times of crisis. Regarding the extent to which a particular death is perceived as tragic, responses seemed to vary as a function of the age, the sex, and the kind of death involved. Additionally, different ethnic groups varied considerably in the strength of their opinions. For example, 20% of Anglos viewed sudden death as more tragic whereas 68% of Anglos saw slow death as more tragic. However, 42% of Japanese and 41% of Mexicans considered sudden death more tragic whereas 50% of both groups viewed slow death as more tragic. Thirty four percent of Japanese estimated that a man's death was more tragic than a woman's death, 29% stated that a woman's death was more tragic, and 36% felt the deaths were equally tragic. However, only 9% of Mexicans viewed a man's death as more tragic versus 36% who saw a woman's death as more tragic, with 55% of Mexicans indicating that the deaths were equally tragic. Blacks viewed a youth's death (approximately aged 25 years) as most tragic (45%) and an elderly person's death (approximately aged 75 years) as least tragic (67%). Anglos found a child's death (approximately aged 7 years) to be the most tragic (44%) and overwhelmingly viewed an elderly person's death to be least tragic (82%).

A study by Owen, Fulton, and Markusen (1982) supports the finding that the death of elderly people is often seen as less tragic than the deaths of individuals in other age groups. Owen et al. found a common response was that elderly people "have had their life," and it is only "normal" and "natural" that they die. This attitude appears to be endorsed among many of the Anglo participants in Kalish and Reynolds's (1976) study. An important factor in determining the impact and meaning of death is the type of death that occurs. Whereas the impact of the death of an aged parent may be relatively small, the death of a child or spouse usually has a major effect (Moller, 1996). The greatest negative impact of a death appears to occur in parents who have lost a child (McIntosh, 1999). Research findings have indicated that there is greater intensity of grief and duration of bereavement associated with the death of a child than occurs with the loss of a parent or a spouse (DeVries, Lana, & Flack, 1994; Sanders, 1989). Kalish and Reynolds's findings suggest that there are ethnic differences in the extent to which a death is viewed as tragic depending on the age of the child, but the study does not consider the relationship of the deceased to the respondent (child, parent, spouse, sibling, etc.). Grief and mourning are influenced by a variety of factors beyond those of age, gender, and sudden death versus prolonged dying examined in the Kalish and Reynolds's study. Factors such as the type and quality of the relationship, religious orientation, and circumstances of the death in addition to ethnic background all combine to make bereavement a unique, personal experience for survivors (Moller).

Kalish and Reynolds (1976) investigated other mourning ritual beliefs in addition to views concerning the open expression of grief. Participants were questioned about their attitudes about the appropriate length of mourning before returning to usual activities, dating, and remarriage, and the appropriate length of time for wearing black. A majority of all ethnicities felt that a week or less was enough time to remain away from work, and half of those indicated that the bereaved should be able to return to work as soon as they wished. Responses were more conservative regarding dating; the median response for all groups was that the bereaved should wait between 6 months and 1 year. Blacks and Anglos tended to be more casual than Mexican and Japanese regarding the time bereaved persons should wait. More Anglos and Blacks than Mexicans and Japanese responded that it was unimportant to wait any specified time period before beginning dating (B 30%, J 17%, M 17%, A 25%), and Blacks and Anglos were less likely to feel that one needed to wait 2 years or more before dating (B 11%, J 34%, M 40%, A 21%). The same trends occurred in regard to appropriate time prior to remarriage. A larger percentage of Black and Anglo respondents indicated that it was unimportant to wait before remarrying (B 34%, J 14%, M 22%, A 26%), and more Japanese and Mexican respondents than Blacks and Anglos felt that the bereaved should wait 2 years or more (B 11%, J 26%, M 20%, A 11%). One year was the median time period indicated as appropriate by all groups. Participants were more lenient in stipulating how long the bereaved should wear black. More than 40% of the Japanese and more than half of all other groups indicated that wearing black clothing was unnecessary.

A study by Pratt (1981) examined the influence that business temporal norms have exerted on changing bereavement practices. Pratt suggested that business policies influence the collective meaning, norms, and ritual forms of mourning by establishing rules and time concepts to govern the bereavement situation. Contracts stipulate allowable paid absences for deaths as well as the necessary degree of relationship to the deceased for bereavement leave. The study found that nearly three fifths of companies set paid funeral leave provisions at 3 days. According to Pratt, "Bereavement is thus framed as a distinctive event in time and space. This reinforces the bereaved person's mourning responsibilities during the three days at home, and calls for decisive termination of the mourning and return to full performance of duties at the workplace when the three days are spent" (p. 324). The trend for limited bereavement leave is reflected in society's prescribed period of mourning. In 1927, Emily Post stated that the appropriate period of formal mourning for a widow was 3 years; however, by 1950 Post reported that a formal mourning period of more than 6 months was rare (as cited in Pratt, 1981). In the 70s, Amy Vanderbilt (1972) suggested that the bereaved family should try to pursue their usual social course within a week or so after the funeral. Finally, the latest edition of Emily Post's Etiquette (1997) states:

> The return of close relatives of the deceased to an active social life is up to the individual. . . . A widower or widow may start to have dates when he or she feels like it, but for a few months these should be restricted to evenings at the home of a friend, a movie or some other inconspicuous activity. After six months any social activity is permissible. One year is generally considered the appropriate "waiting period" before remarrying, but there are many valid reasons for shortening that time. . . . Those who consider themselves in mourning do not go to dances or other formal parties, nor do they take a leading part in purely social functions. However, anyone who is in public life or business or who has a professional career must, of course, continue to fulfill his or her duties." (p. 612).

Post's recent etiquette book acknowledges cultural variations by including sections on Jewish, Buddhist, Hindu, and Islamic funerals.

Kalish and Reynolds (1976) extended their investigation of cultural perceptions of grief by asking respondents how they knew when grief was abnormal. About 30% stated that they did not know, and there was considerable variability in the responses of the remainder who described abnormal grieving. Half of the Black respondents indicated that they would look for abnormal behavior. Many Mexican Americans respondents felt that abnormal grieving was evident when the bereaved underreacted or failed to show any overt signs of grief. One fourth of the Anglo respondents stated that they would look for withdrawal and extreme apathy, whereas two fifths of the Japanese gave answers that could not be coded in the available categories.

Studies of bereavement across cultures indicate that there are indigenous notions of grief pathology in many societies; hence, what is regarded as abnormal grief differs widely from culture to culture (Rosenblatt, 1997). The American perspective of *abnormal bereavement,* according to Leming and Dickinson (1994), is preoccupation with the death of the loved one and refusing to make attempts to return to normal social functioning. Another definition (Kamerman, 1988) states that the symptoms of normal grief are present in pathological grief reactions, but in wildly exaggerated form. It seems that the definition of pathological bereavement may be somewhat ambiguous within as well as between cultures.

ENCOUNTER WITH THE DEATH OF SELF

"Some people say they are afraid to die and others say they are not. How do you feel?" Kalish and Reynolds (1976) asked study participants to respond to this query and also asked what most influenced their feelings toward death. More than a quarter of all respondents indicated that they were afraid of dying (B 19%, J 31%, M 33%, A 22%), whereas half related that they were unafraid (B 50%, J 50%, M 54%, A 53%). The remainder of the responses were uncodable or indicated that participants were neither afraid nor unafraid. As to factors which influenced death attitudes, more than one third of the participants indicated that the death of someone close influenced them most (B 26%, J 41%, M 39%, A 35%), with religious background as the second most influential factor (B 40%, J 13%, M 21%, A 25%). Almost 19% stated that having been close to their own death, or believing themselves to be close to death, was most influential in determining their attitude toward death. When asked how often respondents thought about their own death, many respondents related that they rarely or never thought about it (B 41%, J 69%, M 38%, A 47%); however, one sixth of the participants indicated that they thought about it daily and one fourth thought about it weekly (B 34%, J 10%, M 37%, A 25%).

Death anxiety has been a dominant theme in empirical studies on death (Wong, Reker, Gesser, 1994). Researchers have investigated death fear from both conscious (overt) and unconscious (covert) perspectives. A common belief is that death anxiety is universal and its absence indicates denial of death (Becker, 1973; Marshall, 1980). However, Kalish and Reynolds's (1976) study addresses only conscious levels of death fear, and the authors stated that their policy of assuming face validity of statements directed their acceptance of responses as accurately reflecting the feelings of the respondents when the question was asked. In another study addressing overt death anxiety, Bengtson, Cuellar, and Ragan (1977) interviewed 1,269 Los Angeles county adults from varying social categories defined by race, age, social class, and sex. Participants were asked directly: "How afraid are you of death? Would you say you are: not at all afraid?/somewhat afraid?/or very afraid?" They found that 63% responded "not at all afraid," 33% responded "somewhat afraid," and 4% responded "very afraid." Analysis of the results indicated that there were significant contrasts only in terms of age group membership, with no meaningful differences among the three racial groups (Blacks, Mexican Americans, and Whites) or by socioeconomic status. Bengtson et al. stated that the main effect of gender "approached statistical significance," with women tending to express greater fear than did men. Regarding age, results revealed that expressed fear of death decreased with age in the sample of middle aged and elderly individuals, particularly among the two racial minority groups. Bengtson and his associates also examined the frequency of thinking about death. Responses varied among "not at all" (33%), "occasionally" (58%), and "frequently" (9%), with little systematic variation predictable by the stratum variables of ethnicity, sex, age, and socioeconomic status. Further consideration of the impact of age and gender on death anxiety will be given in subsequent sections on the roles of age, sex, education, and religiousness.

Regarding factors influencing death attitudes, Florian, Mikulincer, and Green (1994) found that middle-aged subjects who had experienced a personal loss in the previous 3 years reported greater fear of death than subjects who had not experienced any loss. Another study by Florian and Mikulincer (1997) revealed that both early and recent loss were related to higher levels of fear of personal death. This finding not withstanding, other studies have failed to discover any relationship between personal experience with loss and fear of death (Franke & Durlak, 1990; Pratt, Hare, & Wright, 1985; Tokunuga, 1985). Regarding the relationship between religion and death anxiety, simple face-valid measures of religiousness and death fear have produced equivocal results (Neimeyer, Dingemans, & Epting, 1977; Pratt et al., 1985; Wagner & Lorion, 1984). Another factor influencing death attitudes indicated by almost one fifth of the respondents in Kalish and Reynolds's (1976) study was that of having been close to one's own death or believing one was close to death. Kalish and Reynolds, however, did not inquire if the respondents experienced a "near-death experience." In a study of nearly 300 individuals who reported that they had a near-death experience, had a brush with death without a near-death experience, or had no brushes with death, Greyson (1992) found that individuals who had a near-death experience were less threatened by the prospect of their own deaths than were persons in the other two groups.

Reviews of the literature on death anxiety indicate that it is actually a multidimensional construct, which has cognitive, affective, and attitudinal components (Kastenbaum & Costa, 1977; Neimeyer & Van Brunt, 1995). Not surprisingly, numerous scales have been developed which focus on various aspects of death attitudes. Thus, the often ambiguous and contradictory findings that are reported in many studies may be due to the measurement of different dimensions of death fear. Research has also identified a number of factors relating to death anxiety, including demographic and situational factors as well as personality characteristics. Regardless of the particular structure of death anxiety, the Kalish and Reynolds (1976) study addresses only general overt fear of death.

Respondents in Kalish and Reynolds's (1976) study were asked to indicate whether they agreed or disagreed with several statements regarding death (i.e., "People can hasten or slow their own death through a will to live or a will to die," "Death may someday be eliminated," "Accidental deaths show the hand of God working among men," and "Most people who live to be 90 years old or older must have been morally good people;" Appendix p. 210). A majority of each group agreed that people can affect their own death by their will to live or die (B 88%, J 85%, M 62%, A 83%), and a majority viewed accidental deaths as reflecting the hand of God (B 63%, J 63%, M 71%, A 56%). Only a small percentage of participants in any group felt that death would ever be eliminated. Approximately 40% of Black, Japanese, and Mexican American respondents believed that people who lived until their 90s were necessarily morally good, but only 20% of Anglo Americans held that belief.

Kalish and Reynolds (1976) asked respondents to indicate the personal importance of several reasons for not wanting to die. The participants related that they were most concerned by the possibility of causing grief to their friends and relatives (B 74%, J 62%, M 78%, A 79%). Concern over not being able to care for dependents was also important to more than half of the Black respondents and to 75% of each of the other groups. Fear of pain was another major consideration (B 54%, J 56%, M 57%, A 54%). Respondents stated that less important reasons for not wanting to die were being uncertain as to what might happen to them, not being able to have any more experiences, having plans and projects come to an end, and fear of what might happen to their bodies.

Death is feared for different reasons, including loss of self, anxiety about the unknown, pain and suffering, concern for the welfare of surviving family members, and lost opportunities for salvation and atonement (Feifel & Nagy, 1981; Fry, 1990). Florian and Kravitz (1983) developed a multidimensional model of the fear of death that identifies three general components of death fear: (a) intrapersonal, (b) interpersonal, and (c) transpersonal. The *intrapersonal* component consists of fear of annihilation of the body and fear of not fulfilling one's goals. The *interpersonal* component consists of fear of loss of social identity and fear for the welfare of loved ones, whereas the *transpersonal* component consists of fear of the unknown nature of death and fear of punishment in the afterlife. In their investigation of the impact of early and recent losses on the fear of personal death in adulthood, Florian and Mikulincer (1997) found differential patterns of association between each kind of loss and each of their theoretical components of death fear. Their results indicated that:

> On the one hand, persons who had experienced early losses were more likely to attribute their fear of death to the loss of social identity, the consequences of death for family and friends and the loss of self-fulfillment. On the other hand, persons who reported a recent loss were more likely to attribute their fear to the annihilation of the body, the unknown nature of death, and the loss of fulfillment. . . . Whereas in most of the factors early and recent losses had separate effects, with regard to the loss of self-fulfillment factor they had an additive effect. (p. 17).

Cicirelli (1998), who examined personal meanings of death in relation to fear of death, also identified three dimensions of death meanings: (a) *extinction* (which includes personal extinction, pain and suffering, end of one's dreams, separation from loved ones, and loss), (b) *afterlife* (which includes reunion with loved ones, death as the beginning of something beyond, and death as the beginning of a new adventure), and (c) *legacy* (which includes death as an opportunity for one's accomplishments to be evaluated for posterity, to attain symbolic immortality, to die nobly for a cause, and to be eulogized for great accomplishments). In his study of 265 college students, Cicirelli found that extinction was the only death meaning that differed significantly by age and gender. Younger participants and women endorsed extinction as a personal death meaning more strongly than did older participants and men. Kalish and Reynolds's (1976) findings concerning reasons for not wanting to die are comparable only in a general way to the above studies; however, it appears that concern over loss of relationships is prevalent in each. As Parkes (1997) stated in the summary of his book, *Death and Bereavement Across Cultures*, "For many people it is not so much the loss of individuality that we fear but the loss of others to whom we are attached" (p. 242).

Kalish and Reynolds (1976) included questions about supernatural and mystical feelings in their inquiry of death encounters. Participants were asked if they had ever experienced or felt the presence of some-one after that person had died. Nearly half of the individuals in the study responded affirmatively (B 55%, J 29%, M 54%, A 38%), and one fourth of these stated they were awake when they experienced the pres-ence. As to mystical feelings, more than one third of the Mexican Americans and between 12% and 15% of the other groups stated that they had experienced the "unexplainable feeling that (they) were about to die." Even more participants indicated that they had had such a feel-ing about someone else (B 37%, J 17%, M 38%, A 30%), and more than 70% of those stated that the premonition was validated by actual death.

Paranormal experiences among the bereaved have frequently been reported in the literature (Berger, 1988; Fox, 1992; Marris, 1958; Palmer, 1979; Parkes, 1972; Rees, 1975; Yamamoto, Okonogi, Iwasaki, & Yoshimura, 1969). Rees interviewed 227 widows and 66 widowers and found that 46.7% (50% of the men and 45.8% of the women) had had paranormal experiences related to their deceased spouses. Experiences included a sense of presence of the dead spouse (felt by 39.2%), visual experiences (13.3%), auditory experiences (13.3%), and speech with the deceased spouse (11.6%). When Parkes studied 22 widows, he learned that almost one half of them saw or heard their dead husbands. Similarly, Marris found that about 50% of the 72 wid-ows he interviewed had such experiences. Paranormal reports related to bereavement also occur in other countries. Japanese researchers (Yamamoto et al.) interviewed 20 widows in Tokyo and found that 90% had supernatural experiences. Palmer conducted a community mail survey of psychic experiences in Charlottesville, Virginia, and found that paranormal experiences were not limited to the bereaved. Nearly 40% of the respondents claimed to have had waking extrasensory per-ception (ESP) experiences, 36% claimed to have had ESP dreams, and 14% claimed to have had out-of-body experiences. The percentages of supernatural and mystical feelings reported in the above studies are similar to the percentages found by Kalish and Reynolds (1976) in the Los Angeles multicultural study of death attitudes.

PREDICTING THE FUTURE

The Kalish and Reynolds's (1976) survey requested participants to think about the future and predict how and when they would die. Many did not respond (B 37%, J 9%, M 34%, A 21%). Of those responding, almost all predicted a natural death for themselves (about

90%), and a median age of death at 75 years. African Americans as a group expected to live significantly longer than any of the other groups. Bengtson, Cuellar, and Ragan (1977) also found that Blacks expressed greater longevity expectancy than Mexican American or Whites in their study of the influence of race, age, sex, and socioeconomic status on death attitudes.

When Kalish and Reynolds (1976) asked participants how they wanted to die, relatively few refused to respond (fewer than 7%). Most respondents stated that they wanted to die a natural death; however, 25% of the Japanese and 7% of the Mexicans wanted to die in an accident, whereas 2% of the Blacks and 3% of the Anglos wanted to die by suicide. As to when they wished to die, the median age was 80 years, with the 25th percentile at age 70 and the 75th percentile at age 90. In responding to where they wished to die, most individuals indicated that they preferred to die at home. The Japanese and Anglo respondents preferred a home death by more than a 4:1 ratio, Blacks preferred a home death by a 2:1 ratio, and Mexicans preferred home death by a little less than 2:1.

In another study of death preference, Zusman and Tschetter (1984) interviewed 500 individuals from rural North Carolina as to whether they preferred to die at home versus a hospital setting and the reasons for their choice. Results indicated that the majority of respondents (68%) would prefer to die at home if given the chance. Statistically significant differences revealed that those who wished to die at home tended to be White, younger, more educated, not satisfied with the quality of the medical services, in excellent health, and afraid of hospitals. Financial reasons were most likely to be given as the reason for preferring to die at home, followed by individual reasons, and then by family and health considerations.

Kalish and Reynolds (1976) also inquired about how respondents would like to spend their last 6 months if they learned that they had a terminal illness. Approximately one fourth of the participants said that they would make no change in their lifestyle (B 31%, J 25%, M 12%, A 36%), whereas one fifth related that they would focus attention on their inner life. About one sixth of the respondents (B 16%, J 24%, M 11%, A 17%) stated that they would undergo a marked change in lifestyle (e.g., traveling, satisfying hedonistic demands, trying to soak up as many experiences as possible). Nearly 40% of the Mexicans and about 20% of the other groups responded that they would devote their remaining time to those they loved.

Regarding acceptance of death, more than one third of the participants indicated that they would fight rather than accept death, and there were no differences by ethnicity. There were some ethnic differences in how respondents predicted that they would handle pain. Well over half of the Blacks and Japanese would tell someone of their pain rather than enduring it in silence; however, less than half of the Mexicans or Anglos reported that they would do so. Similar proportions of the groups would refrain from encouraging their families to be with them, if it were inconvenient. Results suggest that the highly familistic Mexican Americans would encourage their family to be with them although the Japanese, also considered familistic, would not. In addition, nearly 90% of all Mexican Americans, and more than half of the respondents in each of the other groups, stated that they would call for a clergyman if they were dying.

PREPARING FOR DEATH

Kalish and Reynolds polled study participants about arrangements they had made in preparation for death. Nearly 70% of the respondents reported that they had some life insurance (B 84%, J 70%, M 52%, A 65%), and about one fifth had completed wills (with more Anglo and fewer Mexican Americans). Approximately one fourth of the Black, Japanese, and Anglo Americans stated that they had invested in a cemetery plot, but only about one eighth of the Mexican Americans reported having done so. About one eighth of the respondents indicated that they had made funeral arrangements. When asked if they had seriously talked with others about their eventual deaths and arranged for the handling of their affairs, about one fourth of the entire sample responded affirmatively, with fewer Japanese and more Anglo Americans responding that they had.

On the basis of a 1983 national survey conducted by the National Research and Information Center (Leming & Dickinson, 1994), 9.2% of Americans have made prearrangements for funerals, and another 62% feel that they should make funeral arrangements. Leming and Dickinson estimated that about one million people a year prearrange their funerals, as compared with 22,000 in 1960. Furthermore, AARP projected that the annual number of Americans prearranging their funerals will have increased to 5 million by the year 2000.

FUNERALS

Kalish and Reynolds (1976) asked respondents a number of questions concerning funerals and burial arrangements. Respondents estimated that the modal cost for an adequate funeral was $1,000, with means varying among the ethnic groups (B $1,075; J $1,948; M $1,209; A $1,179). More Japanese Americans indicated that they anticipated that family and friends would share in the expenses (B 27%, J 43%, M 30%, A 27%), but more Japanese also rejected the wish for a big, elaborate funeral (B 79%, J 92%, M 89%, A 89%). Most of the participants stated that they wanted a clergyman selected by their family to preside at their funerals, and most preferred that the clergyman be of their own ethnic group (with the exception of Blacks, more than half of whom were indifferent to the race of the clergyman). Similar figures were found for the selection of a funeral director of the ethnic group of the participant. The desire for a wake varied, with percentages of pro and con as follows: for Blacks, 25% versus 53%; for Japanese, 41% versus 46%; for Mexicans, 68% versus 15%; and for Anglos, 22% versus 72%. Japanese preferred that the wake be held in the church, but the majority of respondents from other groups preferred the funeral home. Regarding location of the funeral, two thirds of the African Americans and three fourths of the Japanese Americans reported that they wanted the funeral in a church, whereas half of the Mexican and Anglo Americans wanted the services in a funeral home. In addition, about half of each ethnic group felt that children under the age of 10 should not be permitted to attend the funeral.

In recent decades, a number of criticisms have been directed toward funerals and the funeral industry. According to Moller (1996), three primary criticisms of the American funeral have emerged, which concern funeral costs, superficiality, and the increased control by the funeral director. The cost of funerals has risen to the extent that the funeral of a loved one can be the third largest expenditure that individuals or families make during the course of their lives. In 1935, the expense of an average adult funeral was about $350, by 1960 it had increased to about $1,100, and by 1980 it had reached $2,200 (Moller). In 1991, according to a survey by the Federated Funeral Directors of America, the average cost for an adult funeral was $3,507 (Leming & Dickinson, 1994). Those figures do not include the additional expenses of cemetery property, grave openings, outer vaults, purchase and engraving of a headstone, fees for clergy, musicians or singers, flowers, special transportation needs, obituary notices, memorial cards and copies of death certificates, or police escorts (Leming & Dickinson; Moller). The second criticism, that funerals have become superficial rituals, is based on the assertion that funerals have lost their viability as supportive mechanisms because American communities have been so dissipated by urbanization and individualism that the funeral can no longer realistically provide social support (Moller). The growing dominance of the funeral director is criticized because it is perceived to increase focus on the body of the deceased, thus exaggerating the importance of the physical remains in comparison with the spiritual aspects of the funeral (Moller). Furthermore, Moller suggests that the professional dominance of the funeral director has led to increased secularization of the funeral and reduction in the role of the clergy in shaping the funeral and assisting the family.

Kalish and Reynolds (1976) also inquired about customs and rituals pertaining to the disposal of the body. One fourth of the Anglo and Black respondents as well as one third of the Japanese and Mexicans stated that they would object to an autopsy. Regarding burial versus cremation, Mexican and African Americans preferred burial by nearly 20:1, and Anglo Americans preferred burial by about 3.5:1. However, more than half of the Japanese Americans preferred cremation, one third desired burial, and the remainder were mostly undecided. In addition, participants were asked where they wanted their bodies or ashes deposited. More than half of each group selected Los Angeles, with 17% preferring a location other than Los Angeles, but within the United States, and 9% selecting another country.

There is a move toward cremation rather than burial in the United States. In 1976, about 7% of deaths resulted in cremation (Kamerman, 1988), by 1979, about 9% of deaths ended in cremation (Kalish, 1981), and by 1985, the proportion of cremations had risen to approximately 12.5%. In 1991, 17% of bodies in the United States were cremated, 78% were buried, and 5% were entombed (Leming & Dickinson, 1994). Cremation is more common in other countries, including Japan. In 1980, 91% of those who died in Japan were cremated, and the percentage in the major cities was almost 100% (Kamerman). The prevalence of cremation for disposal of the body in Japan was reflected in the preference for cremation among the Japanese American respondents in the Kalish and Reynolds study.

VARIABLES YIELDING NO SIGNIFICANT EFFECTS: KALISH AND REYNOLDS

Kalish and Reynolds (1976) also investigated variables that revealed no significant differences, either for the entire sample or between pairs of ethnicities. They found that the subcultures essentially agreed on several categories of death-related attitudes and behavior. One category concerned the familiarity of contact with the dead. Respondents from all four groups were fairly similar in regard to knowing persons who had died from accidents, natural causes, war-related incidents, and suicide. There were also no significant differences in the frequency of visiting a dying person or in having known someone who died under circumstances in which the decision was made to inform or not inform the dying individual.

Another category that yielded similar responses among the groups concerned acceptance of death. Approximately 60% of all participants related that they would accept their own deaths peacefully. Over three fourths felt that death would never be eliminated, and 60% believed that accidental deaths showed God working among men. The groups also agreed that the deaths of elderly people are less tragic than those of other ages.

In addition, there was a consensus among respondents in the tendency to ignore (avoid? deny? transcend?) death. Fewer than 15% of participants had made funeral arrangements, only 25% were paying on a funeral plot, and more than 80% indicated that they did not particularly care what happened to their body after they died. Furthermore, less than half recalled having dreamed about dying or their own death.

A fourth category of agreement among individuals of the various ethnic groups was in some of the role behavior related to death. The majority of respondents from each group agreed that it was the physicians' role to inform patients of a terminal illness, and 50% of each group viewed a relative as the appropriate person to turn to if a spouse died. There were also fairly uniform views toward persons threatening suicide; similar percentages in all groups felt that those who threatened suicide wanted attention, were emotionally sick, needed sympathy, and needed professional help. Respondents across ethnic groups also had similar attitudes about proper periods of bereavement in roughly equal proportions. About one third of each group felt that 2 weeks or less was the correct period of grieving for the bereaved, one third of each group believed 1 to 3 months proper, and one third chose 6 months or more as appropriate.

There were also some other items for which there were no significant differences among ethnic groups. Around 80% of respondents in all groups felt that a person dying of cancer sensed it without being told. Forty five percent of each of the groups felt that an unimportant factor in not wanting to die was that the process of dying might be painful. Finally, about 25–30% of the respondents in each ethnic group indicated that they would object to having an autopsy performed on their body. Overall, each ethnic group was well acquainted with death, in some ways accepting it, but in other ways ignoring it, and they showed agreement on some death-related role behaviors and role expectations.

3

Factors Influencing Death Attitudes: Kalish and Reynolds

THE ROLE OF AGE

"Different age groups perceive death differentially and react to it in terms of these perceptions" (Kalish & Reynolds, 1976, p. 50). Although their study confirmed the differential impact of age on death attitudes, Kalish and Reynolds (1976) acknowledged that cohort effects may have distorted or influenced the findings. The researchers noted the difficulty of determining the degree to which differences between age groups were due to the process of aging versus those attributed to the exposure of cohorts to unique life events. Having noted the cohort confound and the necessity of its consideration, Kalish and Reynolds (1976) nonetheless analyzed participants' responses to survey questions based on categorization by three age groups: 25–39 years old (Young or "Y"), 40–59 years old (Middle-aged or "M"), and 60 years and older (Old or "O"). Each age group contained approximately equal numbers of men and women.

Analysis of data revealed that the older the respondents were, the more likely they were to feel themselves religiously devout in comparison with others in their ethnic group (Y 9%, M 17%, O 27%). Results were consistent for both men and women. Furthermore, older individuals were more likely to consider their religious background as most important in influencing their attitudes toward death. The findings indicated that no other influence was more important to older people than religion, although participants in the younger groups indicated that the death of someone they knew had been more influential than their religious background. Men and women responded quite similarly to the question, but there were major ethnic differences. A greater proportion of older Blacks (70%) credited religion as the dominant force in influencing their death attitudes than did the older members of the other groups (J 15%, M 33%, A 35%). Furthermore, the generation gaps were most evident in the Black community.

Kalish and Reynolds (1976) found that older respondents were also significantly more likely to believe in life after death (Y 48%, M 48%, O 64%), although fewer older than younger participants said that they believed in hell. In addition, older respondents were more likely to turn to their clergymen for comfort following his loss of a loved one (Y 19%, M 24%, O 48%).

A more recent study by Harley and Firebaugh (1993) examined trends over the past 2 decades in Americans' beliefs in an afterlife. According to General Social Survey Data, there has been little change among adults in the United States between 1973 and 1991 in the belief in the existence of an afterlife. Harley and Firebaugh used annual General Social Surveys from 1973 through 1991 and examined change within birth cohorts as well as across cohorts to determine the proximate sources of stability. Although they expected to find age-related trends, they found no evidence that belief in an afterlife increased notably with age. Furthermore, they failed to find evidence that this belief has declined with successive birth cohorts. In fact, they discovered that the aggregate trend was nearly flat. It will be interesting to compare Harley and Firebaugh's findings with trends that emerge from the present replication of Kalish and Reynolds' (1976) study.

Relating to Others

Interactions with the dying. Kalish and Reynolds (1976) found age-related differences in respondents' attitudes toward informing terminally ill persons of their condition. Nearly 60% of the nonelderly sample approved of telling the dying of their status, but only 40% of the oldest group approved. However, examination of the individual ethnic groups revealed that almost all of the age-related differences were found among the Japanese. When Kalish and Reynolds (1976) asked the respondents if they would want to be told of their own impending death, nearly 75% responded affirmatively, and the age differences disappeared, except among the older Japanese. In addition, 82% of the participants indicated that a person dying of cancer senses that death is coming, with no differences among the age groups. There was an age-related difference in the perception of whether a sudden or slow death is more tragic. Older people were relatively more likely to consider a sudden death as more tragic than a slow death (Y 31%, M 36%, O 45%). The researchers suggested that elderly people tend to view a slow death as providing time for getting in touch with loved ones and bringing affairs to a close. The death of elderly persons was perceived to be the least tragic by over 70% of the participants, with no particular differences between the age groups. The 25- to 39-year-old group indicated that they viewed the death of children as the most tragic, whereas the other two age groups found the death of a young person as most tragic.

Contact with death. Death is considered to be more salient and less frightening for elderly people, possibly because they tend to have had the most contact with death. Kalish and Reynolds (1976) found that respondents in the oldest group were the most likely to know someone who had died within the previous 2 years. This trend was true for both men and women as well as for the four ethnic groups. Results showed that African American respondents were the most familiar with death across the age groups, with many more African Americans reporting to have known five or more people who had died and the fewest reporting to have known none. Furthermore, older people were the most likely to have attended funerals and visited cemeteries. Nonetheless, it was participants from the young age group who reported that they would be the most likely to touch or kiss the body, whereas the middle-aged group were the least willing to initiate physical contact with the body.

Grief and bereavement. Kalish and Reynolds (1976) also found age-related differences among study participants in their attitudes toward grief and bereavement. When respondents were asked when they would begin to worry that grieving behavior, such as crying or depression, had been going on too long, results revealed that the older the respondent, the longer the permissible time. Kalish and Reynolds (1976) also inquired about the proper length of mourning time prior to remarriage, the appropriate period for bereaved to wear black or other mourning symbols, and the proper length of time before bereaved should return to work or begin dating. The responses were quite similar among the age groups, and for three of the four questions, the youngest group had the smallest proportion stating that it was really unimportant.

In their study, age was not a predictor of the probability of the participants' feeling constrained about expressing grief in public. Although no age-related trend emerged concerning age and public expressions of emotion, the researchers found that younger respondents indicated more willingness to express grief privately through tears than did the elderly respondents. The trend was significant for both men and women, and for both Japanese and Mexican Americans. It was consistent, but not significant for Anglo Americans as well. Yet, among African Americans, the middle-aged group related the greatest willingness to cry in private.

The Death of Self

Preparing for one's own death. As they anticipated, Kalish and Reynolds (1976) found that older people were more likely to have made preparations for their death than were younger people. Study results showed that funeral arrangements had been made with significantly greater frequency by older persons of both sexes and all ethnicities. Older respondents were also more likely to have paid for a cemetery plot and to have arranged for someone else to handle their affairs. In only one area, the purchase of life insurance, were middle-aged participants more prepared than those in the older age group. Nonetheless, nearly two thirds of the elderly respondents did carry some life insurance.

There were no age trends among participants in the desire for an elaborate funeral, with the exception of a significant relationship among African Americans, with more of the younger respondents desiring an expensive funeral than other age groups. Nor were there age-related trends in the desire for a wake. Yet, older participants in the study were significantly more likely to object to autopsies and were more fearful about what happens to the body after death.

To cease to be. The study results revealed that elderly respondents admitted to thinking about death more often than other age groups. Kalish and Reynolds (1976) found that twice as many elderly participants indicated that they thought about their death every day than did participants in other age groups. The middle-aged group reported thinking about death the least often. The researchers found that elderly respondents were also the least likely to state that they were afraid of death (Y 40%, M 26%, O 10%) and the most likely to claim that they were able to face dying (Y 36%, M 52%, O 71%). The trend occurred for both men and women. In addition, elderly participants were the most likely to indicate that they would accept death peacefully rather than fight death actively (Y 53%, M 65%, O 74%).

Examination of the research literature on death anxiety reveals that although a few studies (Lester, 1972; Pollak, 1977; Templer, Ruff, & Franks, 1971) reported no relationship between age and death anxiety, most found less death anxiety among older adults. Feifel and Branscomb (1973) indicated that subjects older than the age of 50 answered "no" to the question, "Are you afraid of your own death?" more often than younger subjects. In a study of 699 Virginian residents, Nelson (1979) found that age was negatively correlated with death avoidance, fear, and reluctance to interact with dying as measured by a multidimensional inventory. Gesser, Wong, and Reker (1987) examined three age groups (young: 18–25; middle-aged: 35–50; elderly: 60+) and discovered that general fear of death and dying displayed a curvilinear relationship with age, such that death anxiety was relatively high in the young, peaked in the middle-aged, and was minimal in old age. In addition, Gesser et al. found an increase in death acceptance in old age. In some respects, the focus on consciously expressed death fears must be seen as a limitation of the studies just described.

In their study, Kalish and Reynolds (1976) also asked respondents about the age at which they expected to die and how long they hoped to live. The results revealed age-related trends, wherein the age at which the younger participants expected to die (median age of 70 years) was significantly lower than the age at which the middle-aged participants expected to die (age 75 years), which was lower than the age at which elderly participants expected to die (age 80 years). Furthermore, there was no differentiation between the sexes—men and women anticipated living the same number of years. As for the age to which the respondents hoped to live, the younger and middle-aged participants suggested 80 years as a median preferred age, but the older participants selected a median age of 88 years. Although actuarial tables indicate that women tend to outlive men, Kalish and Reynolds (1976) found that men desired to live longer than did women when the data were examined according to gender. Young and middle-aged men said that they wished to live to a median age of 80 years, and elderly men wished to live to 90 years; however, young and middle-aged women wished to live to a median age of 75 years, and elderly women to a median age of 85 years.

Kalish and Reynolds (1976) found marked age-related differences in how respondents from each group indicated that they would spend the last 6 months of their lives. For the young participants, the modal response was to focus concern on others and be with loved ones; for the middle-aged participants, the modal response was that they would not change their lifestyle; for the elderly participants, the modal response was that they would withdraw into prayer, contemplation, or other inner-life involvement. There were also some significant differences among the age groups in their reasons for not wanting to die. Respondents in the young group indicated greatest concern and persons in the old group expressed the least concern for the impact that their death would have on survivors and for the loss of the ability to have experiences. Participants in the older group were the most likely to fear what happened to the body following death, whereas members of the young group were least likely to indicate such concern. Finally, Kalish and Reynolds (1976) found no age-related differences regarding the desire to be informed when one was dying; rather, between 69% and 73% of each age group stated that they would wish to be told.

THE ROLE OF GENDER, EDUCATION, AND RELIGIOUSNESS

Gender

Kalish and Reynolds (1976) reported that analysis of the demographics of the participants in their sample revealed that neither education, age, nor religiousness differentiated men from women in their study and indicated surprise at the relatively few gender differences that emerged from the data. Kalish and Reynolds (1976) found that traditional sex roles did emerge in feelings about the mourning process. More female respondents than males indicated that they did not feel that they must control their emotions and stated that they would be willing to cry. Women viewed the grieving process as requiring more time than did men. In addition, women were more willing for the bereaved to wear black longer, to remain away from work longer, and to grieve longer without being concerned that the process was going on for too long a period.

Kalish and Reynolds (1976) found that male participants in the study had made more practical preparations for death than had women, such as having life insurance and making wills. A substantial number of men indicated that they were either indifferent or undecided about several funeral-related matters. For example, more male than female respondents indicated that they were undecided as to whether they wanted many or few people attending their funeral, whether they wanted an open or closed casket, whether they wanted burial or cremation, whether they wanted a wake, and whether young children should attend the funeral.

Regarding fear of death, Kalish and Reynolds (1976) found no gender differences for either the entire group or within any of the individual ethnic groups in participants' responses to the question, "Some people say they are afraid to die and others say they are not. How do you feel?" However, there were gender differences in the frequency of thinking about death and in anticipated acceptance of death. Female respondents reported that they thought about death more than males reported having such thoughts. Also, more women stated that they would accept death passively rather than fight it actively.

Kalish and Reynolds (1976) interpreted women's responses to how they would spend the last 6 months of their life if told they had a terminal illness as "social and nurturant" in nature, and men's responses as oriented to "action and work responses." Overall, the researchers felt that the data provided some substantiation for traditional sex roles and suggested that the men appeared "more pragmatic, controlled, aggressive, and individualistic" and that the women were "more sentimental, emotional, passive, and familistic" (p. 80) in their attitudes and behaviors about death.

Education

Kalish and Reynolds (1976) investigated the influence of education on respondents' death attitudes, but added that level of education was related to age and ethnicity in the study sample. They found that for their sample, Mexican American respondents, as a group, and elderly respondents, as a group, had less education than other ethnic and age groups. The mean educational level, in number of years, for the other three ethnic groups was quite similar (B 10.6 years, J 12.4 years, M 6.5 years, A 11.1 years).

In considering participants' interactions with dying people and death, Kalish and Reynolds (1976) found that physical contact with the dead (touching and kissing the body) was more acceptable to those with less education. The respondents with fewer years of formal education were also more likely to express their emotions openly, anticipate longer periods of mourning as necessary, postpone remarriage and dating for longer periods, and suggest that the bereaved wear black for a longer time than were those with more formal schooling. The less educated respondents also were less likely to believe that dying persons should be informed of their status.

Regarding issues related to their own death, college-educated participants were (a) less likely to call a clergyman when death was imminent, (b) would not expect family members to attend them if it was inconvenient, and (c) were much more likely to want to be informed if they were dying. There was also variation among participants with different levels of education in how they would want to spend their last 6 months of their lives if they were terminally ill. The respondents with less education were more likely to choose to spend their remaining time in contemplation, or other inner-centered activity, and indicated more concern for others than did those with more education. The more educated participants tended to indicate that they would choose to live as before or to fill their remaining months with as much living as possible. In addition, those who attended college indicated the greatest fear of death, whereas those who attended only grade school indicated the least fear of death.

Kalish and Reynolds (1976) also found differences among education groups in the extent of preparation for death. Respondents who had attended only grade school were the least likely to have life insurance whereas those who graduated from high school were most likely to have insurance; however, the researchers stated that the findings may be due to income level as well as education. Yet, results revealed that the better educated were the least likely to have made funeral arrangements.

There were also ideological differences expressed by respondents with different levels of education. In response to whether participants agreed or disagreed with the statement, "Accidental deaths show the hand of God working among men," the better educated tended to disagree. Similarly, the better educated were more likely to disagree with the statement, "Most people who live to be 90 years old or older must have been morally good people." After examining the analysis of data on educational level and death attitudes, Kalish and Reynolds (1976) noted that more education appeared to be related to a "more pragmatic, secular, rationalistic, and individualistic approach to death and grieving" (p. 84). Nevertheless, the researchers asserted that education, age, religiousness, and ethnicity were interrelated in such a way that the factors could not be accurately extracted for separate examination and were better considered in interaction.

Religion

Kalish and Reynolds (1976) found that religious affiliation was strongly tied to ethnicity in their sample. They reported that more than half of the African Americans were Baptist, one third belonged to other Protestant denominations, and 6% were Catholics. Among the Mexican Americans, 90% were Roman Catholic, and 8% were Protestant. As for the Japanese Americans, more than half were Buddhist, and 15% were Methodist. The religious composition of the Anglo Americans in the sample was 17% Roman Catholic, 20% Baptists, and 45% other Protestant. To assess the degree of religiousness, participants were asked to compare themselves with other members of their religious group and state whether they felt they were more, about the same, or less devout than most. Nearly half of the Anglo Americans and more than half of the other groups rated themselves as "about the same" (B 64%, J 52%, M 50%, A 46%). One out of six African Americans perceived him- or herself as less devout than his or her denominational peers, whereas slightly more than twice the proportion of other ethnicities made the same claim (B 16%, J 36%, M 33%, A 36%).

About half of the entire sample indicated that they definitely believed in some form of life after death (B 59%, J 47%, M 40%, A 66%). The remainder either did not believe in an afterlife or were uncertain about it. Regarding their conception of an afterlife, about two thirds of the Black, Mexican, and Anglo participants who indicated they believed in life after death described some form of heavenly paradise, but over 40% of the comparable group of Japanese spoke of return to earth in some fashion of spirit form.

Kalish and Reynolds (1976) found that religiousness was closely related to age and to marital status. Fewer of the devout had never been married and more were widowed. Those who rated themselves as more devout than average also appeared to have had more contact with dying and dead people. The more devout indicated that they (a) had attended more funerals in general and more funerals recently, (b) had visited gravesites of family and friends more frequently, and (c) had called upon dying relatives and friends more often. However, because the more religious also tended to be older, the researchers noted that it was difficult to determine whether the greater frequency of contact with dead and dying people was due to the dying off of certain age cohorts or to religious feelings affecting attitudes toward death.

When Kalish and Reynolds (1976) investigated fear of death and religiosity, they found that the more devout respondents claimed to be more accepting of death and dying and less fearful. Again, the devout were disproportionately elderly, so the results may have been due to age rather than the depth of the respondent's religiousness. The researchers reported that they found a low correlation between belief in afterlife and fear of death.

Kalish and Reynolds (1976) interpreted their overall results concerning religiousness and attitudes toward death as indicating a strong religious overtone running through all of the ethnic groups. The researchers suggested that the Japanese Americans appeared the most pragmatic, and the Mexican Americans the most traditional and emotive. Kalish and Reynolds (1976) concluded that the role of the church and clergy ranged from moderate to very important among the respondents in the study's sample.

RACE AND ETHNICITY

African Americans

"To be Black in America is to be part of a history told in terms of contact with death and coping with death" (Kalish & Reynolds, 1976, p. 103). According to Kalish and Reynolds (1976), the attitudes and behaviors of African Americans toward death need to be understood with reference to the struggle, violence, suppressed anger, and exploded aggression that have followed African Americans since the earliest days of slavery. Preoccupation with violence and death is found in Black folklore, music, literature, art, and poetry. Against this background, it is not surprising that Kalish and Reynolds (1976) found that the African American perspective on death differed in a variety of ways from the views of other cultural groups.

Demographic Background

Analysis of data showed there was a relatively high percentage of widowed, divorced, and separated African Americans in the study's sample (B 38%, J 13%, M 17%, A 24%), with women significantly more likely than men to report that they were widowed or separated. Black women were also less likely than women of other groups to indicate that they were housewives and more likely to be categorized as unskilled workers. Furthermore, African Americans had the shortest average residence in California, with only 10% of the Black participants born in California and only 5% in Los Angeles. They resided in areas of high ethnic density; in fact, more African Americans than others estimated that at least 75% of the people on their block were of similar ethnicity (B 87%, J 11%, M 64%, A 51%).

Kalish and Reynolds (1976) found that religion tended to be very important among African Americans. Blacks perceived themselves as more religious than others of their own ethnicity rather than less religious (B 20% vs. 16%, J 12% vs. 35%, M 18% vs. 33%, A 18% vs. 36%). Older respondents, especially older women, viewed themselves as relatively more devout than the young.

Expectations Regarding Death

Study results revealed that, compared with other groups, African Americans as a whole expected to live the longest and indicated that they would like to live the longest. However, such expectations are not in keeping with life expectancy statistics, wherein actuarial life expectancy tables at the time of the study predicted that Black respondents could expect to live an average of 77 years as compared with 80 years for Anglo Americans. Kalish and Reynolds (1976) noted that neither the Black respondents' wishes nor their overtly expressed expectations of longevity seemed to reflect awareness of the mortality statistics. The researchers interpreted the data as indicating that, among the groups studied, the African Americans were the most optimistic and eager to live a long life in spite of the discrimination and stresses that the Black participants faced. Kalish and Reynolds (1976) noted that more Black men and women expected to be alive close to or beyond 100 years of age than any other group (men vs. women = B 22% vs. 33%, J 6% vs. 0%, M 4% vs. 8%, A 9% vs. 14%, respectively). Furthermore, more Black male and female respondents indicated the desire to live beyond their 98th birthday than did male or female participants of other ethnic groups (men vs. women = B 52% vs. 39%, J 25% vs. 0%, M 9% vs. 7%, A 16% vs. 16%, respectively). The researchers also noted the low suicide rate of African Americans, especially older Blacks, in Los Angeles and nationally. Kalish and Reynolds (1976) concluded that whether it was due to the religiousness or their survival of ordeal, the Black respondents in the study expressed resiliency and a high acceptance of life.

Encounters With Death

Study results revealed that the African American respondents had more contact with death during the previous 2 years than had respondents in other groups. More Black participants indicated that they had known at least eight individuals who had died in the previous 2 years, whereas fewer indicated that they had known none at all (knew eight vs. knew none = B 25% vs. 10%, J 15% vs. 17%, M 9% vs. 19%, A 8% vs. 25%). Furthermore, African Americans in the study reported significantly more contact with victims of homicides, accidents, and wartime deaths than did other groups. Yet, in spite of their exposure to death, Black participants did not relate that they thought or dreamed about their own death more than did respondents in the other groups. In addition, African Americans did not indicate greater frequency than did other groups in reporting that (a) they had had the unexplainable feeling that they or someone else was about to die, (b) they had experienced or felt the presence of someone after he or she died, or (c) they had felt close to death themselves. Only 19% of the Black respondents acknowledged that they were afraid of death. Kalish and Reynolds (1976) stated that the results, taken at face value, suggested that African Americans, especially the elderly men, have lower overt fear of death than do participants of the other groups. Furthermore, the influence of the Black participants' frequent encounters with the deaths of others, particularly sudden and unexpected death, does not appear to have differentiated them from other groups.

Kalish and Reynolds (1976) found that a pattern of differences did emerge in another area. Respondents were asked to evaluate the importance of seven losses listed in the survey that their own deaths would produce: (a) concern regarding their body after death, (b) inability to care for dependents, (c) uncertainty as to what would happen after death, (d) inability to continue having experiences, (e) grief caused to survivors, (f) cessation of plans and projects, and (g) pain during the dying process. On six of the seven items, Black participants were more likely than were any of the other three groups to indicate that the reason was *Not Important.*

Support Systems in Facing Death and Loss

Kalish and Reynolds (1976) characterized the Japanese American and Mexican American subcultures as familistic and noted that the strong bonds of responsibility and expectations within the families encouraged members to rely on each other in handling death-related crises. However, the authors found that, in general, African Americans and Anglo Americans do not exhibit the same pattern of exclusive dependence upon supportive family interrelationships. The authors suggested that family support is found, but the boundaries are narrower and the scope is more situationally determined. They reasoned that subcultural groups defined for themselves areas and times in which family support could be expected and those in which it could not.

In accordance with this hypothesis, study results revealed that African Americans were the least likely to indicate that they would encourage family members to spend time with them while they were dying if it were inconvenient and that Blacks were least likely to be willing to carry out inconvenient last wishes of a dying spouse. When respondents were asked who would provide practical assistance during bereavement, a high proportion of African Americans (42%) and Anglo Americans (45%) stated that they would rely on friends, church members, neighbors, and other nonrelatives (vs. 9% and 14% for Japanese and Mexican Americans, respectively). Nevertheless, about half of the Black respondents related that they would turn to some relative for comfort in time of grief.

The study results suggested that many African Americans find support during the crisis of death and dying in religion and the church. The researchers found that more Black respondents than Japanese or Anglo respondents said that they would call for a clergyman if they were dying, and many more cited their religious background as being most influential in their attitudes toward death (B 40%, J 13%, M 21%, A 25%). Regarding belief in life after death, well over half of African Americans indicated that they believed that they would live on in some form after death, and virtually all who did also believed in a hell (B 96%, J 55%, M 88%, A 75%). However, relatively few of those believers felt that "those in heaven watch over earth" (B 39%, J 100%, M 82%, A 83%). Kalish and Reynolds (1976) regarded this finding as an important and unique element in the Black respondents' conceptualization of death because they felt that such a belief served to (a) cut off relationships abruptly at death, (b) make understandable existing misery, and (c) influence postdeath behaviors such as grave visiting. Kalish and Reynolds surmised that the family provided less support through interactions in this life and less caring and guidance when family members had gone on to their next life. Thus, the gap was filled for African Americans by friends and by the church.

Regarding African Americans' attitudes toward mourning, Kalish and Reynolds (1976) found that Black participants compared with members of the other groups were more likely to indicate that it was "unimportant to wait" before remarrying, resuming dating, or ceasing to wear signs of mourning. When asked about expression of grief, 79% of Black respondents reported that they would try very hard to control the way they express emotion in public, although the researchers found that all professional sources (chaplains, funeral directors, deputy coroners, ambulance drivers, nurses, physicians, etc.) regarded African Americans as freely expressive when grieving. Kalish and Reynolds (1976) broadly characterized their findings concerning emotional expressiveness of the four subcultures as follows:

> Mexican Americans are publicly expressive and incorporate this into their ideology; Japanese Americans are publicly inexpressive and find this consistent with their ideology; African Americans and Anglo Americans, who respond to these questions about expression control almost identically, behave quite differently from one another, with the greatest discrepancy among the African Americans whose expressive style allows for the acting out of feelings despite effort to exert self-restraint. (p. 108)

Arrangements for Death

Study results indicated that a significantly higher proportion of African Americans had taken out life insurance than had other groups (B 84%, J 70%, M 54%, A 65%), and a proportion of these were likely burial policies. Yet, Black respondents were no more likely than were respondents of other ethnic groups to have a will, to have made funeral arrangements, or to have arranged for someone else to handle their affairs. Furthermore, only one in four of the Black participants indicated that they had discussed death seriously with anyone (B 26%, J 16%, M 33%, A 37%).

Funerals

Kalish and Reynolds (1976) found that although interviews with professionals, pertinent literature, and personal observations all indicated that funerals were important in the African American community, African American respondents showed a much higher rate of indifference when discussing their funerals than the other groups. Fewer than

10% related that they wanted a big, elaborate funeral, and only 20% stated that they wanted many friends and acquaintances at their funeral (14% and 24%, respectively, were indifferent or did not know). Furthermore, this trend increased with age.

Indifference was also evident in the large proportions of Black participants who indicated that they were undecided or indifferent as to (a) whether the family should select the clergyman (25%), (b) whether the clergyman should be Black (52%), (c) whether the funeral director should be Black (54%), (d) whether the casket should be open (40%), (e) whether there should be a wake (22%), (f) whether children ought to be allowed to attend (30%), and (g) where the funeral should be held (13%). Kalish and Reynolds (1976) noted that in each of these instances, more African American participants than any other group stated indifference or uncertainty.

Kalish and Reynolds (1976) found that the great majority of African American respondents who were not indifferent about the funeral arrangements had the following opinions: (a) were opposed to elaborate funerals, (b) did not expect friends to assist in covering funeral costs, (c) preferred a funeral attended by only relatives and close friends, (d) desired Black clergymen and Black funeral directors, (e) did not want a wake, (f) desired the funeral service in the church, (g) were not opposed to an autopsy, and (h) wanted to be buried. Generally, these responses were fairly similar to those of other ethnic groups.

Kalish and Reynolds (1976) also discovered that Black participants were equally likely to touch or not touch the body at the funeral service (48% vs. 47%, respectively), and that participants were strongly opposed to kissing the body (12% vs. 82%, would kiss as opposed to would not, respectively). Black respondents indicated that they had visited gravesites the least often during the previous 2 years as compared with the other groups (No visit: B 71%, J 36%, M 55%, A 59%).

To explain the study findings, Kalish and Reynolds (1976) supported an explanation based upon differing methodologies for reconciling the opposing trends that they found in African Americans' responses toward death. In attempting to reconcile the attitude of practical unsentimentality (manifested in the voiced preference for emotional self-restraint in grief and responses of indifference to funeral arrangements) with the depth of feeling (shown by the observed acting out of emotions in bereavement and the elaborate funerals characteristic of the subculture), the authors suggested that there was a preferred self-image among the Black respondents of being "cool," of not caring, or of not being susceptible to emotional pain. Nevertheless, Kalish and Reynolds proposed that, when the actual encounter with death occurred, this self-image of not caring was overwhelmed by depth of feelings, and one's emotions were displayed. The authors also pointed out that the Black participants in the sample were urban dwellers who were likely to be more sophisticated and farther removed from the rural South where there might be less of a tendency to present a cool self-image. Kalish and Reynolds (1976) stated that the inconsistencies between voiced unsentimentality versus expressed emotion did not imply an attempt at posturing or deceiving; rather, the authors noted that an apparent contradiction often exists between what people say they wish to do and what they actually do. The authors speculated that the conflict for survival by African Americans might have been so intense that an overt admission of vulnerability had to be denied. However, Kalish and Reynolds (1976) emphasized that this was only one possible interpretation of the data.

Other Work With African Americans

Kalish and Reynolds's (1976) study is the earliest, most authoritative work on African American attitudes toward death and dying (Barrett, 1993). There have been few actual studies that have examined the character of Blacks' experiences with death and dying, so writings on the topic have tended to draw from anecdotal accounts, the literature of African Americans, including spirituals and poetry, and from art to understand death attitudes. There has also been research focusing on the African perspective on death and funeral rites to compare African practices with those of African Americans (Fenn, 1989; Frazier, 1966; King, 1980; Nichols, 1989). The results of such studies provide varying conclusions.

Research on contemporary African American death attitudes and practices is sparse. For example, Brown (1990) reported that African Americans have a stronger sense of family involvement in providing care for the terminally ill than would be predicted by Kalish and Reynolds's study. However, Brown stated that he based his knowledge on his experiences, insights from literature, and discussions with Black ministers, professionals, and other Black individuals rather than on more formal studies. Perry (1993) used a similar knowledge base in his writings concerning African American customs in death and dying. Perry attributed his understanding of how African Americans confront dying, death, and grief to a review of the scholarly literature; an analysis of newspaper articles, novels, and plays; numerous unstructured interviews with African Americans; and attendance at hundreds of Black funerals. Perry stated that he had interviewed 120 African American persons from the middle- and upper-lower classes across 10 states, and he concluded that:

In sum, historical Black funerals in America have numerous vestigial elements based on traditions from West Africa. Such rituals are more common among those in the rural South, among more evangelical religious
groups . . . , and within population segments having less educational and
fewer economic resources. Modern nontraditional Black funerals are
more prevalent in urban areas, in the North, within the upper economic
and social classes with more education, and among Roman Catholic and
mainline Protestant congregations. Thus, the funeral customs of many
African Americans have come to be similar to those of the dominant
majority, although they may remain distinctive in some particulars. The
customs of others have remained both culturally and ethnically distinct
from those of the dominant white society. (p. 65)

Yet, a few studies have been conducted that have examined ethnic
differences in the area of death anxiety. Sanders, Poole, and Rivero
(1980) administered the Templer Death Anxiety Scale to 31 African
Americans and 31 Caucasian Americans between the ages of 60 and 87
in rural Mississippi. They found that African Americans scored higher
than Caucasians on death anxiety. Myers, Wass, and Murphy (1980) also
found higher death concern scores among elderly African American
men as compared with elderly male Caucasians, but only 22 individuals
were tested. Larger studies have tended to find fewer overall differences in death anxiety. Two studies using college students (Davis,
Martin, Wilee, & Voorhees, 1978; Pandey & Templer, 1972) found no
significant differences in death fear between Black and Caucasian participants. Davis et al.'s study included 92 African Americans and 291
Euro-Americans, while Pandey and Templer's study tested 134 African
American students and 124 Euro-American students. In another large
study, Thorson, Powell, and Samuels (1998) administered the Revised
Death Anxiety Scale to 293 students of European heritage and 102 students of African heritage. Their results similarly found no significant
mean difference in the total scores for the groups, but findings did
indicate that Euro-Americans expressed greater anxiety over the uncertainty associated with death and with the loss of being, whereas African
Americans were more concerned with the pain associated with dying.
The question of the existence of ethnic differences in death anxiety
remains unanswered, however, because of the age differences of the
participants in the studies. The results of the larger studies were based
on responses from younger individuals, whereas the smaller studies,
which yielded different findings, were based on the responses of elderly
individuals. It is significant that age has been shown to be an important
factor in death anxiety.

Overall, examination of the literature on African American death
attitudes emphasizes the need for additional scientific studies on the

subject. Thusfar, Kalish and Reynolds's (1976) work has remained the most comprehensive research-based study on African American attitudes and beliefs about death and dying.

Japanese Americans

When Kalish and Reynolds's (1976) conducted their study, they noted the large size of the Japanese American population in Los Angeles (104,078 persons, according to the 1970 census), second only to the 217,000 Japanese American residents in Hawaii. The researchers reported that the Japanese Americans could be differentiated into age and/or generation categories. The Issei, or first generation Japanese American, were born in Japan and immigrated to the United States. Kalish and Reynolds (1976) stated that Issei tended to be steeped in the Japanese culture, often spoke English poorly, if at all, and frequently led much of their lives in Japanese enclaves. They found that the Nisei (second generation) often had achieved considerable success in spite of hardships they faced during World War II with Relocation camps and that Nisei tended to be proud of the educational success of their children. The authors characterized the Sansei (third generation) as more like their non-Japanese age peers and reported that Sansei frequently married out of their ethnic group. The Yonsei (fourth generation) were mostly too young at the time of the study to have made much impact on the community. Kalish and Reynolds (1976) found that awareness of generational grouping was useful because the Japanese American respondents from the different generation and/or age groups often had divergent attitudes and behaviors related to death. In addition, the authors cautioned to use careful generalization of the study findings to Japanese Americans outside of the Los Angeles area because they felt that geographic distinctions made by Japanese Americans were important variables affecting attitudes and behaviors.

Demographic Background

Results of Kalish and Reynolds's (1976) data indicated that the Japanese Americans had the highest median level of education of the four groups studied (B 11.6 years, J 12.0 years, M 6.0 years, A 11.8 years). The Japanese American respondents also had the lowest percentage of unskilled workers (B 38%, J 14%, M 25%, A 15%) and the highest percentage of skilled workers (B 34%, J 46%, M 34%, A 41%). Nearly one half of the Japanese American participants were born outside of the United States, and the mean number of years these first-generation immigrants had lived in the United States was 35.6 years.

There was also a high mean number of years of residence in California, which indicated a relatively stable population in terms of geographic mobility.

Kalish and Reynolds (1976) stated that it was important to note three social structural elements and some related value orientations to understand many of the Japanese American attitudes and behaviors related to death. The relevant social structural features indicated were (a) family organization, (b) generational characteristics, and (c) community ties. The authors reported that the values and orientations important in understanding Japanese American social relations included social sensitivity, controlled communications (notably controlled expression of emotions), shame, work ethic, some formal religious concerns, contact with death, and funerary and mourning customs.

Family Organization

According to Kalish and Reynolds (1976), the Japanese American family is characterized by an emphasis on reciprocal obligations and cohesiveness. In fact, none of the Japanese American respondents in the study reported that they were divorced or separated. Data indicated that 71% of the Japanese American participants were married, 16% had never married, and 13% were widowed. In addition, the Japanese Americans were more likely to live with elderly individuals than were respondents in other ethnic groups. Examples of the family obligation theme were found in Japanese American responses to some survey questions. The Japanese Americans were the most likely to state that they would agree to carry out their husbands' or wives' last wishes even if the wishes seemed senseless or were inconvenient (B 65%, J 85%, M 78%, A 80%). The Japanese Americans were also the most likely to rely on their relatives for help with practical problems if their spouse died. Kalish and Reynolds (1976) found that Japanese families tended to participate more extensively in funeral activities in that family members attended the cremation or graveside service the day after the funeral in addition to participating in the formal funeral service attended by the community.

Another example of the influence of the family organization is that decisions about the funeral service and burial of an Issei might be dominated by the deceased's surviving siblings over the wishes of adult Nisei offspring. The authors also noted that during the funeral service there was often a prescribed order in which the immediate family survivors entered the funeral hall: "wife, eldest son, other sons according to age, married daughters' husbands and married daughters by age, then unmarried daughters by age, followed by parents and siblings of the deceased" (p. 128).

Intergenerational Factors

Despite the familistic solidarity exhibited by the Japanese Americans, study participants also showed considerable intragroup variation by age. There were major differences in the responses of the Japanese American age and/or generation categories. Kalish and Reynolds (1976) found that one of the major barriers to intergenerational understanding and communication was language. The authors reported that 40% of the interviews with the Japanese American respondents were conducted primarily or completely in Japanese. They learned that although many of the Niseis were bilingual to some extent, the language barrier between Issei and Sansei generations was great.

Kalish and Reynolds (1976) found that the Isseis' reactions to death tended to be similar as a group and somewhat distinctive from the reactions of other Japanese American generational groups, especially the Sansei's. The Issei respondents exhibited a controlled acceptance in their grieving. The authors stated that the Issei's orientation of acceptance was not passive but was an active one of adjustment to what is perceived as inevitable reality rather than trying to adjust external reality to meet one's own needs. In contrast, the authors found that Sansei respondents sought to understand and control the external world, exhibiting a more Western mode.

The intergenerational conflict over orientation reportedly caused some "in-family" problems. Because funeral services were either Buddhist or Christian but never both, families sometimes argued over which was appropriate. Furthermore, Kalish and Reynolds (1976) noted that funerals, Memorial Day ceremonies, and other death-related ceremonial practices required representatives of Japanese American groups to make public speeches, bestowals, or appearances. The Isseis appeared comfortable in these ritual representations, but the authors found many Niseis and most Sanseis to be uncomfortable and self-conscious in these public roles. In addition, Issei indicated that they were the most superstitious of the three generations. Issei respondents tended to observe the general taboo on discussion of death and to know and practice superstitious avoidances and positive acts to keep harm and death away from their family.

Kalish and Reynolds (1976) found that Sanseis tended to avoid funerals, because of the unintelligibility of much of the funeral service itself, especially Buddhist services, as well as to a general avoidance of death-related activities. Sansei respondents generally reported little religious contact, and what contact there was tended to be superficial. The authors found that the Sansei participants appeared to be fairly successful in avoiding thoughts about death.

Community Ties

According to Kalish and Reynolds (1976):

> The Japanese American funeral is a community event attended by representatives of groups, in broad contrast to Anglo funerals, which are attended by individuals, and Mexican Americans' funerals which are attended by relatives and intimates. A Japanese American who dies leaves behind a relatively large pool of potential funeral participants, because any group with which he was affiliated (even by knowing well one member of the group) or any group that was affiliated with a group (e.g., the deceased's family) of which the deceased was a member, would feel some obligation to send at least one representative to the funeral; the closer the relationship, the greater the number of representatives that should be sent. (p. 132)

Representatives of groups such as Buddhist churches, Veterans of Foreign War posts, or business organizations were also sent to various Memorial Day services for Japanese Americans in the Los Angeles area. Kalish and Reynolds (1976) suggested that the community involvement in funerals was probably the basis for the finding that Japanese American respondents were the most likely to desire their funeral minister (B 62%, J 79%, M 74%, A 68%) and funeral director (B 39%, J 65%, M 47%, A 40%) to be of their own ethnicity. The tendency was especially strong among older Japanese American participants.

Another aspect of the group orientation of the Japanese Americans was their custom of gift giving, even in death-related situations (e.g., *koden* or gifts given to survivors of the deceased). The researchers discovered that there was a complex flow of carefully selected gifts of appreciation in exchange for desired esteem and good wishes that tended to bind the community together. Furthermore, the Sansei indicated that they actively participated in the gift giving (especially in the koden tribute), even though they did not participate in many of the other Issei and Nisei attitudes and behaviors relating to death.

Social-Sensitivity and Controlled Communication

Kalish and Reynolds (1976) felt that it was important to note the influence of the societal values of social-sensitivity and controlled communication on Japanese Americans to understand the Japanese American participants' attitudes toward death and dying. The authors described social-sensitivity as being extremely concerned with the evaluations and feelings of others, leading Japanese Americans "to be quick in picking up subtle cues, to spend much time and thought considering others' evaluation of themselves, and to avoid direct interactions that would upset others" (p. 123). The authors suggested that this careful internal censoring of communications also placed limits on emotional expressiveness among the bereaved so as to avoid disturbing others and preserve a nonburdensome image. Kalish and Reynolds (1976) felt that social-sensitivity also functioned to reinforce commitment to in-group custom, rules, and propriety so that no one was slighted or ignored. The structure of the funeral ceremony provided an example because Japanese Americans related that they were most comfortable within the framework of a proscribed ritual.

The Japanese American participants also tended to be quite controlled in their expression of grief. When asked if they would worry if they couldn't cry after the death of their spouse, less than half of the Japanese Americans indicated that it would worry them. More than 80% stated that they would try very hard to control their emotions in public; 71% said they would let themselves go and cry themselves out in private or public, or both. However, responses to the last question varied significantly by sex and age: Japanese American women and younger participants of both sexes were more likely to indicate that they would cry themselves out. In addition, each group had its own frame of reference for how it defined *emotional control* and *letting go*.

In response to the query as to whether dying persons should be informed that they were dying, almost half of the Japanese Americans thought that they should be told (B 60%, J 48%, M 37%, A 71%). And, like other ethnicities, Japanese American respondents would themselves wish to be informed if they were dying (B 71%, J 77%, M 60%, A 77%). Most of the Japanese Americans also felt that persons dying of cancer sensed their imminent death without being told (B 81%, J 80%, M 78%, A 89%). Very few Japanese Americans reported that they thought about their own death at least weekly (B 34%, J 10%, M 37%, A 25%), and one third stated that they never thought of their own death (B 14%, J 33%, M 10%, A 22%). Furthermore, fewer Japanese Americans admitted to ever dreaming about their own death or dying than respondents of other ethnic groups (B 22%, J 20%, M 36%, A 38%). Kalish and Reynolds (1976) noted that the Japanese participants' infrequency of thinking about death contrasted with their high funeral attendance and grave visitation, and the authors suggested that denial or suppression might be operant in some of the responses.

Shame and the Work Ethic

Kalish and Reynolds (1976) found personal embarrassment and the associated embarrassment to one's family to be an influential factor in the Japanese American culture. They suggested that an example of such feelings occurred when graves of Issei and veterans were tended with relative haste just prior to Memorial Day and subsequently left untended, thus reflecting an emphasis on obligation and shame avoidance. The authors also observed that gossip served as an effective sanctioning force in the Japanese American community. The authors noted that families tried to prevent any hints of narcotics, unwanted pregnancies, family feuds, mental illness, or suicide from becoming known. Kalish and Reynolds (1976) found that suicides were often concealed, and in such cases, there was often no obituary notice and only a private ceremony was held. Japanese American respondents indicated that they were no more likely than were other ethnic groups to have known someone who had killed him- or herself (B 25%, J 22%, M 31%, A 29%), but they were significantly more likely to have known a suicide that had been subsequently concealed and reported as a natural or accidental death (B 5%, J 20%, M 7%, A 5%).

Kalish and Reynolds (1976) also considered the Japanese work ethic as an important value affecting Japanese American attitudes and behaviors. Although a strong work ethic is associated with the Japanese, the Japanese American participants in the study did not indicate this characteristic in response to questions about why they would not want to die. Nearly half of the Japanese American respondents indicated that the fact that dying would mean the end of all their plans and projects was unimportant (B 66%, J 44%, M 51%, A 64%), and only a small number (B 6%, J 8%, M 13%, A 6%) stated that they would first attempt to complete projects and tie up loose ends if they learned they had only 6 months to live. In addition, Japanese Americans did not indicate that they would return to work any sooner than other ethnicities after the death of a spouse. The work orientation was reflected, however, in the scheduling of funerals. Japanese American funerals are traditionally held in the evenings so that people need not miss work to attend.

Religion

Kalish and Reynolds (1976) stated that it was difficult to assess the influence of religion on Japanese attitudes toward death because what influence there was appeared to be expressed through ritual rather than through personal commitment. Data from the study revealed that about half (51%) of the Japanese Americans indicated that they were Buddhist, 15% stated that they were Methodist, and 12% indicated that they had no religious preference. When asked about their belief in the existence of life after death, nearly half of the Japanese American participants said they believed that they would live on in some form after death (B 59%, J 47%, M 40%, A 66%). Forty-three percent of those who stated that they believed in an afterlife described it as returning in spirit form rather than living in paradise (24%), and all of those that believed in heaven felt that those in heaven watched over the earth. Kalish and Reynolds (1976) stated that such beliefs permitted family ties to extend beyond death. Nonetheless, only half (B 80%, J 51%, M 69%, A 83%) of the Japanese American respondents indicated that they wished that there were life after death. Kalish and Reynolds (1976) speculated that the reason that comparatively few Japanese Americans indicated a desire for life after death might be a sense of "world weariness" because of feelings of responsibility and preservation of "face" found among Japanese Americans. The authors also reflected that Japanese Americans may desire nirvana rather than life after death because nirvana is not properly classified as life after death, but rather as withdrawal from the repetition of reincarnations.

Contact With Death

Eighty-three percent of the Japanese American respondents indicated that they knew someone personally who died in the previous 2 years, and respondents related that the great majority of the deaths were due to natural causes. Relatively few Japanese Americans reported that they had ever felt that they were close to dying themselves (B 48%, J 31%, M 49%, A 37%), and fewer still related that they had experienced paranormal or mystical feelings of contact with persons already dead (B 55%, J 29%, M 54%, A 38%). One third of the participants who indicated that they had had a paranormal experience said that they psychologically felt the presence of the deceased rather than seeing, hearing, or touching the dead person. However, Kalish and Reynolds (1976) reported that several psychic experiences were related in detail.

In regard to overt death anxiety, 31% of the Japanese Americans stated that they were afraid to die (B 19%, M 33%, A 22%), and fewer participants indicated fear of dying in each increasing age category. Japanese American respondents indicated that they were most influenced in their attitudes toward death by (a) the death of someone close (41%), (b) being close to death themselves (18%), and (c) their religious background (13%). Other results about fear of death were similar to those found in other ethnic groups.

Death Attitudes, Customs, and Rituals

Kalish and Reynolds (1976) asked study participants about what death they considered most tragic. Half of the Japanese Americans stated that they believed slow death to be more tragic than sudden death (B 58%,

J 50%, M 50%, A 68%). As to age of the deceased, all groups tended to view the deaths of youths or children as more tragic, but the Japanese American respondents were significantly more likely than were others to feel that middle-aged deaths were most tragic (B 8%, J 22%, M 6%, A 5%). Furthermore, considerably more Japanese Americans than other participants indicated that the death of a man was more tragic than the death of a woman (B 10%, J 34%, M 9%, A 16%). Examination of the findings revealed that a somewhat greater percentage of Japanese American women than men believed a male's death to be more tragic than a female's.

Kalish and Reynolds (1976) found that Japanese American respondents answered similarly to other ethnic groups in selection of the most tragic way to die, indicating accidents (32%), homicides (32%), suicides (10%), and natural death (1%) as most tragic. Yet, when asked to indicate which types of death were least tragic, fewer Japanese Americans chose natural causes (B 76%, J 64%, M 83%, A 87%), and many more Japanese selected suicide (B 14%, J 26%, M 14%, A 7%) than did respondents of the other ethnic groups.

Morning customs. Of the four groups, Kalish and Reynolds (1976) found that Japanese Americans and Mexican Americans responded with the most conservative and restrictive norms. Few Japanese American participants (B 30%, J 17%, M 17%, A 25%) believed that it was acceptable to start dating any time after a spouse's death, and 34% of the Japanese (B 11%, M 40%, A 21%) felt that the surviving spouse should wait 2 years or longer. The Japanese Americans also had more conservative attitudes toward remarriage in that 26% stated that the surviving spouse should wait at least 2 years (B 11%, M 20%, A 11%), and only a small percentage of the Japanese American respondents felt that it was unimportant to wait any minimum time (B 34%, J 14%, M 22%, A 26%).

The wearing of black as a symbol of mourning has decreased in American society, and the decrease was reflected in the Japanese American responses. Nonetheless, the answers of the Japanese American participants continued to be on the conservative side as compared with responses of participants from the other ethnic groups. Forty-two percent of the Japanese Americans (B 62%, M 52%, A 53%) stated that it was unimportant to wear black to indicate mourning, and few (B 5%, J 14%, M 28%, A 1%) saw the need to wear black for a year or more. When asked about the appropriate length of time to be away from work after the death of a spouse, about half of the Japanese Americans (B 78%, J 53%, M 64%, A 82%) indicated that a week or less was sufficient, and one third (B 17%, J 39%, M 27%, A 9%) felt that a month or longer was necessary.

Kalish and Reynolds (1976) also found that Japanese and Mexican Americans tended to view grave visitation as more important than did Black or Anglo Americans. In response to a question concerning the fewest number of times one should visit a spouse's grave in the first year after death, 58% of the Japanese American participants and 59% of the Mexican American participants (B 13%, A 35%) stated that a minimum number of six or more visits was appropriate. Only 7% of Japanese American respondents (B 39%, M 11%, A 35%) felt that it was unimportant to visit the grave at all. In the fifth year after the death, 30% of the Japanese Americans (B 10%, M 18%, A 6%) still believed it necessary to visit the grave six or more times per year, and only 8% (B 52%, M 29%, A 43%) felt that grave visitation was unimportant. Furthermore, the authors found that Japanese Americans did, in fact, visit graves more frequently than other ethnic groups. Kalish and Reynolds (1976) attributed part of the high frequency of grave visitation among Japanese Americans to the Buddhist requirements for post funeral services on the 1st, 7th, 49th, and 100th day following the burial and then on annual anniversaries.

Funeral customs. Participants were asked a number of questions about their wishes for their own funerals. Kalish and Reynolds (1976) found that few respondents in any group indicated the desire for a large, elaborate funeral. Japanese Americans stated that they preferred a funeral with only relatives and close acquaintances significantly more often than did participants of other ethnic groups (B 58%, J 83%, M 58%, A 63%). However, in actuality, the Japanese American funerals tended to be the largest among the groups because of the wide range of group representatives obliged to attend and because the koden gift offering brought by those attending made larger funerals more economically feasible. Significantly more Japanese Americans indicated that others would share in the funeral expenses (B 27%, J 43%, M 30%, A 27%).

Regarding other funeral customs, 59% of the Japanese American participants said that they preferred the casket to be open if there was no disfigurement (B 51%, J 59%, M 51%, A 39%). Japanese Americans indicated that they would be the least likely of the groups to touch the body of their spouse at the funeral, and the least likely to kiss the body. Forty-one percent of the Japanese Americans stated that they desired a wake (B 25%, M 68%, A 22%), and about half wanted the wake to take place in a church. The authors found that a much larger percentage of the Japanese American respondents preferred cremation of the body than did members of other ethnic groups (B 4%, J 53%, M 5%, A 18%), whereas 33% of the Japanese preferred burial, and 11% indicated that they were indifferent.

Another topic addressed by Kalish and Reynolds' (1976) survey was preparations made for one's own death. The authors found that 70% of the Japanese American sample (B 84%, M 52%, A 65%) had taken out life insurance. Nevertheless, few Japanese American participants had made a will (B 22%, J 21%, M 12%, A 36%), and fewer still had made funeral arrangements (B 13%, J 11%, M 8%, A 14%). Those respondents who had done any funeral planning were generally among the elderly population.

Kalish and Reynolds (1976) concluded that the study's findings concerning the death-related attitudes and behaviors of Japanese Americans made sense within the framework of the related themes of social sensitivity and community cohesion. Kalish and Reynolds (1976) suggested that protection of others, avoidance of disturbing communications, and mutually supportive pursuits were prominent characteristics of the Japanese American participants in the sample, and these characteristics were evident in their death-related attitudes and behaviors.

Other Work With Japanese Americans

Immigration to the United States from Japan averages about 5,000 Japanese persons annually (Braun & Nichols, 1997). Currently, about two thirds of all Japanese Americans are born in the United States, as compared with about 37% of all Asian Pacific Islander Americans, and about half of the Japanese Americans marry non-Japanese (Braun & Nichols, 1997). According to population statistics, approximately 847,562 Americans of Japanese descent lived in the United States in 1990; 52% of these resided in California, and 41% resided in Hawaii (Nishi, 1995). Thus, simple arithmetic suggests that the number of Japanese Americans living elsewhere (e.g., in North Texas) is much smaller than the number residing in Los Angeles.

In addition, the composition of the Japanese culture has altered extensively since Kalish and Reynolds's (1976) work. Hirayama (1990) asserted that the characteristics of Japanese Americans are diverse. He explained that there are now five to six generational groups of Japanese Americans. In addition to the Issei, Nisei, Sansei, and Yonsei mentioned in Kalish and Reynolds's (1976) study, there are also the New Issei, or new first-generation immigrants who have arrived in the United States from Japan since the 1950s, and the New Nisei, or new second generation. The original Issei initially came to the United States as laborers, had about an eighth grade education, and were mostly from rural areas of southwestern Japan. However, the new Issei are naturalized citizens or permanent residents who came to the United States after World War II as students, war brides, businessmen, or immigrants. The new Issei tend to be better educated and more proficient in English than were the original Issei immigrants, and most of the new Issei come from urban areas of modernized Japan (Hirayama). There is also variation in the degree to which the new Issei are integrated into American society. The new Issei are heterogeneous in age, education, occupation, and place of residence, as well as in length of stay in the United States. Some tend to associate with Japanese from Japan, but many have close American friends and belong to American organizations. According to Hirayama, the new Nisei are generally born and educated in the United States and are very acculturated in American ways. Additionally, the original Issei have mostly disappeared since the few remaining ones are in their 90s or past the century mark in age.

There have been very few empirical studies examining attitudes toward death and dying in the Japanese American culture. Kalish and Reynolds's (1976) study was the most extensive. Braun and Nichols (1997) explored cultural variations in response to dying and grief among four Asian American populations in Hawaii, including the Japanese, Chinese, Vietnamese, and Filipinos. However, the sample size was small (36 total with 8 Japanese American participants), and the study was based in Hawaii, so the authors admitted that study limitations precluded generalization of findings to the United States as a whole. Braun and Nichols interviewed Asian American participants and found that many Japanese Americans are moving away from the Buddhist rituals. For example, instead of attending memorial services every 7 days for 49 days, Japanese Americans indicated that they often attended only the service on the 7th day. Braun and Nichols summarized changes that have occurred in Japanese American death attitudes as follows:

> Given their many generations in the United States, the low influx of new Japanese immigrants, their experience during World War II, and the high level of out-of-group marriage, informants said that the majority of Japanese Americans are likely to practice customs of mainstream America rather than those reflecting their Buddhist ancestry. (p. 349)

Hirayama (1990) based his writings about death and dying in the Japanese culture on personal experience and an examination of the literature. According to Hirayama, studies of three generations of Japanese Americans revealed a general linear trend of assimilation into American mainstream culture and gradual erosion of traditional Japanese behaviors and attitudes generation by generation. Nonetheless, Hirayama suggested that ethnic influences have remained and are seen in Japanese American recognition of family kinships, pride in Japanese ancestry, and in some remaining customs, rituals, and religious affiliation. He concluded that variables such as age, educational attainment, economics, years in the United States, religion, and place of residence all affect the degree of acculturation of Japanese Americans.

Mexican Americans

Kalish and Reynolds (1976) stated that the Mexican Americans living in the sections of Los Angeles where they did their interviewing shared values with those living in rural Texas or Albuquerque, but also differed from them in some respects. Half of the Mexican American participants in their study had some difficulty with English, and 65% of the interviews were conducted mostly in Spanish. Furthermore, the Mexican American respondents in the study averaged fewer years lived in the United States (21.5 years) than did the other ethnic groups surveyed. Kalish and Reynolds (1976) acknowledged that there were sampling biases in their study. The authors found that 61% of the Mexican American participants were born in Mexico, whereas 13% were born in Los Angeles, 11% elsewhere in California, and 14% in other U.S. states. They attributed the high percentage of foreign-born participants to their sampling method that purposefully oversampled the elderly population and eliminated anyone younger than 20 years of age. Furthermore, they limited their interviewing to neighborhoods with high ethnic density, which increased the proportion of respondents with traditional values and the proportion who spoke Spanish. The researchers stated that their sampling approach resulted in a group of Mexican American participants with low formal education, recent immigrant status, and limited job skills. Therefore, Kalish and Reynolds (1976) suggested caution in generalizing from these data to other communities. However, the authors observed that:

> Regardless of the diversity of Mexican Americans in the nation, or even in Los Angeles, those participating in our study showed the greatest intra-group consistency in their ideology of death. They displayed relatively few internal differences in ideology when analyzed by age, sex, education, and degree of relative religiousness. They seemed more certain of their own preferences for funeral ritual and mourning restrictions, for example, and they had apparently considered these matters and were both familiar and comfortable with the boundaries of what they felt was acceptable behavior. (p. 157)

Demographic Background

The Mexican American participants in Kalish and Reynolds's (1976) study were concentrated in the East Los Angeles area and many lived in urban "barrios." The authors found that the Mexican Americans in their sample had significantly less education than did participants of the other ethnic groups studied, with an average of 6 years of formal schooling. Forty percent of the Mexican American respondents were housewives, 25% worked at unskilled jobs, and 34% worked at skilled jobs. Nearly 90% indicated that they were Roman Catholics. When Mexican American respondents were asked to compare themselves with most members of their faith, 17% stated that they felt that they were more religious than most, 50% felt that they were as religious, and 32% felt that they were less religious than others.

Kalish and Reynolds (1976) found a relatively low divorce rate and high valuing of family ties among Mexican Americans in their sample. Seventy-three percent of the participants said they were married, 10% had never been married, 8% indicated that they were widowed, and 10% stated that they were separated or divorced. The mean age for the oldest person living in the participants' households was 52 years old, which was not significantly different than the means for the Black and Anglo American groups.

Contact With Death and Dying

The extent to which Mexican American participants had experienced the loss of others through death was similar to that of the other ethnic groups studied. Mexican Americans were about average in not having known anyone who had died during the previous 2 years (B 10%, J 17%, M 19%, A 26%) and similar to Anglo respondents in their frequency of having known eight or more persons who had died (B 25%, J 15%, M 9%, A 8%). Survey responses indicated that Mexican Americans in the study were not more likely to have attended at least one funeral in the prior 2 years (B 67%, J 84%, M 60%, A 55%) nor to have visited a dying person during that space of time (B 38%, J 42%, M 39%, A 32%). The Mexican American participants related that the deaths of acquaintances were primarily due to natural causes, and the proportions of Mexican participants who indicated that they had lost acquaintances by accidents, war, suicide, and homicide were near the average for the four ethnic groups. Kalish and Reynolds (1976) stated that "the rate of reported suicide is relatively low among Los Angeles Mexican Americans (about 5 per 100,000 persons, compared to [sic] 12 for African Americans and Japanese Americans, and 20 for Anglo Americans," p. 164). According to the authors, the homicide rate of Mexican Americans was about the same as the Anglo American rate and much lower than the African American homicide rate.

Results of the study indicated that Mexican American participants were the least likely to feel that dying persons should be informed of their condition (B 60%, J 48%, M 37%, A 71%) and the least likely to want to be told themselves if they were dying (B 71%, J 77%, M 60%, A 77%). When asked the reason for their position, many Mexican American respondents indicated that they felt that the knowledge of one's imminent death made it harder upon the patient and harder upon others.

The Family

Kalish and Reynolds (1976) observed that the Mexican American approach to death is best understood when considered in the context of an awareness of three important dimensions of traditional culture: (a) family (especially women), (b) religion, and (c) feelings. The authors asserted that women typically hold the family together with bonds of service and affection and function to maintain ties between the family and the church.

The Mexican American respondents revealed the existence of a protective network within the family for helping the dying and their survivors deal with the emotional problems associated with death. Mexican Americans were the most likely of the groups to state that they would not want children under 10 years of age to attend their funeral. Based on interviews with Mexican American funeral directors, Kalish and Reynolds (1976) interpreted this finding as a desire to shield children from the tragedy of personal contact with emotional death-related scenes. The authors felt that protectiveness was also the source of the relatively high proportion of Mexican American participants who indicated that they would like to die in a hospital (B 21%, J 16%, M 54%, A 14%) in contrast to dying at home (B 44%, J 72%, M 34%, A 61%). Mexican Americans were the most likely to state that if they were dying they would encourage their family to spend time with them even if it caused inconvenience.

When asked about the personal importance of various reasons for not wanting to die, more Mexican Americans than respondents from other ethnic groups stated that no longer being able to care for dependents was very important (B 26%, J 42%, M 47%, A 44%). Mexican Americans also indicated the importance of causing grief to relatives and friends as a concern in dying.

Kalish and Reynolds (1976) learned that Mexican Americans consider funerals to be very significant family ceremonies that often involve the gathering of friends and relatives from remote points. The importance of the funeral to the family network is reflected in the finding that more Mexican Americans stated that they would like a large funeral than did participants of other groups (B 21%, J 9%, M 33%, A

8%). Mexican Americans, along with Japanese Americans, indicated that they visited graves relatively frequently and advocated the wearing of mourning over the longest period of time. The authors discovered through interviews that there were fairly strict proscriptions in the Mexican American culture concerning public mention of anything negative about the deceased.

Mexican Americans, like Japanese Americans, indicated that should their spouse die, they would turn to family members for assistance with practical problems (B 50%, J 74%, M 65%, A 45%). However, there was a significant gender difference among the Mexican Americans in their responses. Mexican American women were more likely than men were to seek practical help from relatives in time of grief (women 75%, men 53%), and men were more likely than were women to indicate that they would depend upon no one (women 13%, men 29%).

Kalish and Reynolds (1976) described the Mexican American and Japanese American subcultures as the most familistic and found that they were also the most conservative in terms of attitudes toward the appropriate duration for mourning. Study results indicated that the Japanese and Mexican American respondents were consistently more likely to suggest longer formal mourning periods prior to remarriage, dating, and returning to work, and they were the least likely to feel that waiting was unimportant. Mexican Americans were also likely to wait longer before worrying that grieving had been going on for too long.

Kalish and Reynolds (1976) summarized their findings concerning the influence of the Mexican American family as follows:

> Throughout our work with the Mexican Americans, we have been impressed by the importance of the family—not in the sense that the family is important among Japanese and Japanese Americans, i.e., as the locus of control, of shame and pride, and of self-identity, but rather as the locus of emotional support, of control through warmth, and of shared activity. Since the family is important, the death of a family member is important, requiring attendance at the funeral, due respect through mourning, and fulfillment of reciprocal family obligations via helping the survivors. (p. 170)

Religion

Kalish and Reynolds (1976) observed that the Catholic Church had a significant influence on the ideological constructs of most Mexican Americans, regardless of their sex, age, or religion. Kalish and Reynolds (1976) found that the precepts of the Church have filtered down to affect understandings of daily life and attitudes toward death. For example, Mexican American participants were more likely than were participants of other groups to state that they would call for a priest or minister on their death bed (B 65%, J 51%, M 88%, A 53%). The authors stated that religion is tightly interwoven with the other important aspects of the Mexican American subculture: (a) family, (b) feelings, and (c) women. According to Kalish and Reynolds (1976), the Catholic Church in Mexican and Mexican American cultures does not suppress the outpouring of feelings of grief but validates the gathering of loved ones so that emotions can be publicly and freely expressed. The authors suggested that the free expression of emotions permits the social support system of the extended family to be more functional.

Expression of Feelings About Death

Kalish and Reynolds (1976) found that Mexican American participants tended to acknowledge more conscious death anxiety than did participants from the other ethnic groups. Slightly more Mexican Americans related that they feared dying (B 19%, J 31%, M 33%, A 22%) and indicated that they thought about death at least weekly (B 34%, J 10%, M 37%, A 25%). Mexican American respondents were also the least likely to say that they never thought about their own death (B 14%, J 33%, M 10%, A 22%). The authors found that many Mexican American respondents in their sample acknowledged having experienced death encounters, dreams about death, and unexplainable feelings about dying. Participants who were Mexican American reported having more frequent unexplainable feelings that they were about to die (B 15%, J 12%, M 34%, A 15%) and more frequent feelings that others were about to die (B37%, J 17%, M 38%, A 30%). Mexican American respondents also reported the second highest frequency of having dreams about their own death (B 22%, J 20%, M 36%, A 38%) and the second highest frequency of having paranormal encounters with the already-dead (B 55%, J 29%, M 54%, A 38%). In addition, the Mexican Americans in the study indicated that they had more experiences in which they felt close to dying themselves than did participants of other ethnic groups (B 48%, J 31%, M 49%, A 37%). From the data and from information gathered in interviews, Kalish and Reynolds (1976) asserted that "Mexican Americans find death and dying more pervasive and more likely to enter into their day-to-day living" (p. 175) than do members of the other ethnic groups studied. The authors noted that although they found greater preoccupation with death and dying among the Mexican American respondents, their study findings revealed that Mexican Americans were no more likely than Black or Japanese Americans to have known someone who had recently died, to have attended a funeral, or to have visited a dying individual.

When Kalish and Reynolds (1976) examined their findings concerning expression of emotion, they found that more Mexican American respondents indicated that they would worry if they could not cry at the death of a spouse than would respondents from other ethnic groups (B 42%, J 42%, M 59%, A 42%). Similarly, more Mexican Americans in the sample stated that they would be likely to cry themselves out in private or public (B 64%, J 71%, M 88%, A 60%) and would be more likely to touch (B 51%, J 31%, M 76%, A 51%) or kiss (B 13%, J 12%, M 59%, A 33%) the body at the funeral service. More Mexican Americans than members from other groups also reported that they would try to control their grief in public (B 21%, J 17%, M 36%, A 26%); however, the desire to control public grief was gender and age related. The researchers found that 94% of the middle-aged men (40–59 years old) stated that they would try very hard to control the way they showed their emotions in public. Kalish and Reynolds (1976) suggested that the frequency with which Mexican American middle-aged men advocated emotional control of public grief reactions was a response of the group to dominant cultural norms. Nevertheless, the researchers felt that overall, Mexican American respondents admitted to more fear related to death and dying and greater overt expression of grief than did participants from the other ethnic groups.

Funerals

After gathering information on Mexican American funeral customs through interviews with professionals associated with funerals, observations of funerals, examination of the survey data, and a review of pertinent literature, Kalish and Reynolds (1976) concluded that funerals in the Mexican American community differed substantially from those in the Black, Japanese, or Anglo American communities. The authors felt that the differences between the ethnic groups in funeral customs were obscured when the focus was placed solely on responses to the survey questions.

Kalish and Reynolds (1976) highlighted five points they found to be characteristic of Mexican American funeral behavior. First, the authors noted that according to funeral professionals, Mexican Americans, especially women, tended to be emotional—so much so that it was sometimes necessary to call a physician and to use tranquilizers. In the survey, Kalish and Reynolds (1976) discovered that more Mexican Americans expected tranquilizers to be used at their funeral or wake than did any other group (B 38%, J 16%, M 50%, A 41%). Second, funeral professionals stated that "when death comes, all come" (p. 180), including the merest acquaintance of the deceased. This characteristic was reflected in the greater percentage of Mexican American participants who indicated that they wanted "lots of friends" present at their funeral (B 21%, J 9%, M 33%, A 9%). A third characteristic of the Mexican American culture noted by Kalish and Reynolds (1976) was the tendency for people to show sympathy by attending evening wakes. Study results indicated that more Mexican Americans stated that they wanted a wake than did members of other groups (B 25%, J 41%, M 68%, A 22%), and of these, more desired the wake at the funeral home than at the church or family home. The authors found funeral services (i.e., funeral masses) were usually held in the mornings, thus most people with jobs could not attend. Consequently, many friends and acquaintances paid their respects at the wake.

A fourth characteristic noted was the relative lack of advanced funeral and death preparations. Kalish and Reynolds (1976) found that fewer Mexican Americans than members of other ethnic groups had made advanced funeral arrangements (B 13%, J 11%, M 8%, A 14%), had taken out life insurance (B 84%, J 70%, M 52%, A 65%), made a will (B 22%, J 21%, M 12%, A 36%), or were paying for a cemetery plot (B 22%, J 26%, M 12%, A 25%). The authors suggested that the lack of funeral and death preparations was probably due to economic and educational differences among the groups studied rather than lack of death-related social considerations. The authors found that Mexican American participants were no less likely than some of the other groups to have discussed their eventual death (B 27%, J 16%, M 33%, A 37%) or to have arranged for someone to handle their affairs (B 24%, J 17%, M 25%, A 42%). Finally, Kalish and Reynolds (1976) noted that Mexican Americans, whether Protestant or Catholic, rarely desired cremation. Results of the survey revealed that Mexican Americans were the most likely of the ethnic groups studied to desire burial (B 84%, J 33%, M 89%, A 66%). Furthermore, most Mexican American respondents indicated that they would like to be buried in Los Angeles (B 54%, J 60%, M 67%, A 51%) or Mexico, where loved ones were buried.

Other Work With Mexican Americans

Examination of recent literature on Mexican American attitudes toward death and dying yields a similar pattern to that found in reviewing research on African American and Japanese American death attitudes. Kalish and Reynolds's (1976) study is one of the few projects that have focused on ethnic differences in death attitudes in the United States, and there have been few empirical studies concerning Mexican Americans' attitudes toward death since then. A study by Fiero (1980) compared death concerns of 54 Mexican American and 54 Anglo American undergraduate college students. Fiero's results indicated that Mexican American students showed greater concern for and contemplation of death than did the Anglo American students. Another contribution to the literature was made by Grabowski and Frantz (1993), who examined the intensity of grief reactions among Latinos and Anglo Americans following both sudden and expected deaths. The study employed 50 Anglo Americans and 50 Latinos; however, the composition of the Latino population was predominantly Puerto Rican (82%), with the remaining participants having cultural ties to Mexico, Guatemala, Colombia, the Dominican Republic, and El Salvador. Grabowski and Frantz found that "Latinos grieving sudden death have a significantly greater intensity than Latinos grieving expected death and than Anglos grieving either kind of death" (p. 273). A study by Oltjenbruns (1998) also considered grief responses in college students of different ethnicities. Oltjenbruns compared the results of 39 Mexican American college students with those of 61 Anglo American students using the Grief Experience Inventory. All of the participants had experienced the death of someone close to them in the previous two years. Results indicated that there were significant differences on two scales: (a) Loss of Control and (b) Somatization. The Mexican American respondents had higher scores on both scales, indicating a more intense response. Oltjenbruns pointed out that his findings were consistent with those of Kalish and Reynolds (1976)' study in regard to the observation of greater expression of emotion among the Mexican American participants. Results of the other studies were also consistent with those found by Kalish and Reynolds (1976).

Despite this work, additional research needs to be done using a broad population base to gain further information on multicultural approaches to death and dying. Such research might enable us to understand the changes that have occurred since Kalish and Reynolds's (1976) study dealing with the interaction of ethnicity with attitudes, beliefs, and behaviors toward dying and death.

4

The Impact of Cultural Change on Death Attitudes

Kalish and Reynolds's (1976) study was conducted in the early 1970s when the topic of death began to emerge from its taboo status. Growth of a general death awareness movement occurred in the 1970s, and death returned to public view (Moller, 1996). During the first half of the 20th century, death had faded from the public eye as fewer people died at home and more died in hospitals, the handling of the dead was turned over to funeral directors, mourning customs changed, and references to death were disguised by euphemisms (Kamerman, 1988). That death had reemerged as a public topic was illustrated by Fulton (1976), who estimated that more material concerning death and dying appeared in scholarly journals between 1970 and 1975 than had appeared in the previous one hundred years. Kamerman attributed the surge of popularity in the subject of death to the convergence of several factors, including demographics, developments in medicine and health care, the war in Vietnam, the threat of a nuclear holocaust and environmental catastrophe, and an increase in the perceived amount and coverage of violence in the 1960s. The demographic changes that affected interest in death were related to the swell in the population of individuals living past retirement and then dying in great numbers. Kamerman pointed out that the Baby Boomer generation, who grew up without experiencing the death of a grandparent until adolescence, was unprepared for facing the death of family members, the focus on the increased population of elderly persons, and the media's coverage of both. Advances in medicine and health care caused increased interest in death because of moral questions that arose regarding prolongation of life and the clinical definition of death. The Vietnam war served as a catalyst in increasing awareness of death because media coverage of the war featured regular "body counts" of dead soldiers and news footage that showed dying and dead people on daily television newscasts. As to the threat of megadeath and thoughts of a Hiroshima-type experience, the near catastrophe at the Three Mile Island nuclear power plant diminished Americans' faith in science's ability to control nuclear energy and ecological destruction. Finally, media coverage of urban disturbances and accompanying loss of life in many major American cities made death difficult to avoid. The interest in death was further stimulated and sustained by the publication of Elizabeth Kubler-Ross's (1969) *On Death and Dying,* Herman Feifel's (1959) *The Meaning of Death,* and Robert Fulton's (1965) *Death and Identity.*

The influence of the media has continued to shape perceptions of death in American society (see King & Hayslip, 2002). Fulton and Owen (1988) emphasized the impact of the pervasiveness of television that features death and violence relentlessly, especially among the young, yet only superficially portrays grief and the ruptured lives that death leaves in its wake. The researchers also noted the explicit portrayal of violent deaths in movies and the morbid fascination with death in popular music, such as rap music. Furthermore, they pointed out that violent death is a staple theme of popular fiction. Fulton and Owen asserted that the media predominantly presents death as interference rather than inevitability, and that death is rarely projected as a natural part of human existence. They concluded that, "The media treats death casually and impersonally while denigrating our human responses to it" (p. 384).

There is ample evidence that the American view of death has changed over the last several decades. The euthanasia, hospice, and death awareness movements that began in the 1970s led to a multidisciplinary human effort that promoted books and journals, therapies and organized services for the dying and bereaved, and death education for professional and lay groups (Feifel, 1992). Furthermore, societal changes such as technological innovations, further militarization and medicalization of American society, media coverage of Dr. Jack Kevorkian and court decisions on the right to die, the AIDS epidemic, awareness of women's rights, and the increased focus on wellness because of the aging of the Baby Boomer generation have influenced Americans' current attitudes toward death.

According to Kamerman (1988), "Death has come to be reconceptualized as a technological problem" (p. 34). Technology and medical research have produced cures and preventatives for many of the afflictions of the past leading to the postponement of death and redefinition of treatment of the dying. The medical profession has taken an active-intervention orientation in dying that has prolonged the dying process and placed dying in a bureaucratic, restricted, technical framework. A consequence of the technological mediation of death is public focus on the concerns of the dying, death with dignity, clinical definitions of death, and court decisions regarding patient self-determination. Concern over the inappropriate use of medical life-extending technology has led to public controversy and written guidelines regarding the withdrawal of medical treatment, discontinuation of food and fluids, and decisions on resuscitation (Benoliel, 1997).

There has also been an increased incidence in and awareness of long-term debilitating and terminal diseases such as Alzheimer's disease, cancer, and AIDS. Contemporary changes in family relationships with fewer intact families have made reliance on family support increasingly uncertain. Incapacitated individuals are vulnerable to cost containment, bureaucratic decisions by managed care companies, and moral dilemmas about the use of medical treatments, as well as placement in institutional care and loss of personal control. The identification and media coverage of AIDS has intensified concerns about terminal care and dying. Morgan (1995) stated that he believed the AIDS epidemic to be a cornerstone in our contemporary death system since AIDS typically involves persons who are "significantly younger than the death date anticipated for their age cohort" (p. 41). Morgan asserted that the AIDS epidemic has resulted in greater death anxiety and depression because it has called into question our presuppositions about the reasonableness of the universe.

A few studies have sought to compare attitudes toward death in the 1990s with those of earlier times. Lester and Becker (1993) administered a questionnaire on death attitudes to a group of 63 undergraduate college students in 1991. The same questionnaire had been given to 63 college students in 1935 (Middleton, 1936) and in 1970 (Lester, 1971). Participants in the 1970 and 1991 studies were matched in age (19 to 25 years) and gender (17 men and 46 women) to those in the 1935 study. When Lester (1971) compared the questionnaire results of the 1970 study with results obtained in 1935, he found that students in 1970 did not think about death or fear death more often, although participants more often wished they were dead, were less likely to desire to live after death, and tended to be more depressed by thoughts of death. With the 1991 administration of the questionnaire, Lester and Becker discovered that, compared to the students in 1935, the 1991 students were more concerned with and afraid of death. Results indicated that students in the 1990s (a) thought more often about their own death, (b) were more likely to visualize themselves as dying or dead, (c) were more likely to think about dying from some specific disease and from some specific type of accident, (d) were more likely to dream of dying or of being dead, (e) went to more funerals, (f) were more likely to be depressed by funerals and cemeteries, (g) were more fascinated and more depressed by newspaper stories about death, and (h) were more likely to want to know about the existence of life after death. Lester and Becker concluded that college students in 1991 were more aware of death and dying than they were in 1935 or 1970, but that the 1991 students appeared to lack the belief systems and attitudes that would enable them to come to terms with their mortality.

Lester (1992) also replicated a study conducted by Richard Kalish (1966) concerning prejudice toward deviant and psychiatric groups as well as toward religious and ethnic groups. In the mid-1960s, Kalish found that prejudice directed toward those who are dying, those who are in pain, and those who are suicidal (included in the deviant and psychiatric group) was greater than that directed toward the religious and ethnic groups. The participants in Kalish's study were undergraduate college students; Lester's study also employed 44 college students and both used the same social distance scale. Lester obtained similar results to those found by Kalish. Prejudice was stronger, overall, toward people exhibiting deviant behaviors (criminal and psychiatric) than toward the ethnic and religious groups that have traditionally been the objects of discrimination. The later study extended the finding by Kalish that extraversion was associated with greater acceptance by almost all of the groups toward whom prejudice is directed. Lester found that prejudice toward attempted suicide remained as great in his 1992 study as it was in Kalish's study although prejudice toward dying persons had decreased. Lester suggested that contemporary Americans may have become more tolerant of death and dying because of increased awareness of death through the AIDS epidemic and problems associated with long-term diseases, such as cancer and Alzheimer's disease.

Another comparison study of current death attitudes with those of the 1970s addressed changes in death personifications. Kastenbaum and Herman (1997) repeated a 1971 study (Kastenbaum & Aisenberg, 1972), which explored death personifications of college students, student nurses, nurses, and mortuary science students. The mid-1990s study employed 123 students of nursing and 324 college students enrolled in general study courses. Kastenbaum and Herman also examined the possibility that Dr. Jack Kevorkian may have emerged as a current image of death. The authors found that male personifications of death still predominated, but that female personifications occurred more often than in the earlier study, especially among female participants. The more recent study found that the relationship between age and death personification seemed to have weakened as there was a greater divergence between the sexes in the type of death personification selected most frequently. Women tended to select "kind and gentle" imagery most often, but men tended to view death as a "cold, remote" person. Although there were some grim and terrifying death images mentioned, such images were selected least often by participants. Kastenbaum and Herman reported that they found no evidence of a Kevorkian-type death personification, although Dr. Kevorkian was correctly identified by almost all of the respondents and the majority viewed him favorably.

A final comparison study considered the sympathy card as a means of the cultural assessment of American attitudes toward death, bereavement, and grief. In 1980, McGee surveyed 87 college students to determine their use of and attitudes toward sympathy cards. In 1995, Caldwell, McGee, and Pryor (1998) replicated the study with 93 college students. The researchers in both studies also analyzed sympathy cards on the basis of symbols used, color, length and form of message, and common wording. Comparison of data from the two studies revealed that there have been some changes in attitudes toward sympathy cards. For example, Caldwell, McGee, and Pryor found that (a) more people sent cards in 1995 than in 1980, (b) more people wanted to receive cards in 1995 than before, (c) the use of cards had become an appropriate means of expressing sympathy, and (d) cards using brighter colors and nature scenes had become more popular. The study showed a continued reluctance to confront death in sympathy cards with the use of the words *dead, died, or death*. The researchers concluded that, " Americans, as sympathizers, are not yet ready to confront the survivor with the reality of death; and sympathy card content, form, and appearance reflect this attitude" (p. 131).

Overall, societal changes since the 1970s appear to have influenced American attitudes and responses toward death. The topic of death is now more openly discussed in newspapers and magazines, self-help books, literature, television, movies, and music, to say nothing of the events of September 11, 2001, and the subsequent loss of life in the Iraq war. Moral and ethical discussions concerning euthanasia, physician-assisted suicide, and technological prolongation of life have also increased public awareness. Americans are more conscious of death, although fear of death does not seem to have diminished. A few studies have sought to index the change in death responses, but these studies have mostly considered specific aspects of death attitudes and have involved college students. Furthermore, the studies have largely ignored differences in responses based on the variables of gender, age, or ethnicity. The present research project addresses these limitations by (a) employing a broader-based and larger sample, (b) addressing ethnic, gender, and age factors, and (c) using a more comprehensive survey instrument to assess death attitudes.

5

The Present Study

Our purpose in this study was to assess historical changes in death attitudes and behaviors within the parameters of multiculturalism, age, and gender, since Kalish and Reynolds's (1976) study. Their study compared the responses of participants from four groups, including African Americans, Japanese Americans, Mexican Americans, and Anglo Americans, as well as examining the influence of the variables of age and gender, irrespective of ethnicity. Kalish and Reynolds's study focused on death attitudes and behaviors in the domains of the respondents' own deaths, the deaths of others, the grief and mourning of survivors, and the concept of death in the abstract. To organize data in the present study we used the categories of (a) experience with death; (b) attitudes toward one's own death, dying, and afterlife; and (c) attitudes toward the dying, death, or grief of someone else. As in Kalish and Reynolds's study, participants were grouped along the variables of ethnicity, gender, and age.

Of importance, we contrasted the findings of the present study with those of Kalish and Reynolds (1976) in the aforementioned specific areas, and we tested several hypotheses regarding expected differences. These hypotheses were based on a variety of considerations, to include Kalish and Reynolds's findings, an examination of the literature on death attitudes since the 1970s, and a consideration of the aforementioned changes that have occurred in American society in the last quarter century, especially those influencing attitudes toward death, dying, and bereavement.

Hypotheses

We proposed the following hypotheses.

Hypotheses 1. Regarding comparison between Kalish and Reynolds's (1976) study and our study, we proposed that our analyses of results would indicate that participants in the present study would:

1. Think about death more frequently than those in the Kalish and Reynolds's study.
2. Report greater fear of death than participants in the earlier study.
3. Indicate a more liberal attitude toward death and dying than participants in Kalish and Reynolds's study.

Hypothesis 2. Regarding comparisons between ethnic groups in the present study, we proposed that our analyses of results would indicate:

1. That Asian Americans (a) are more accepting of death, (b) have a greater preference for cremation, and (c) state that they would be the least emotionally expressive in grief compared with members of the other ethnic groups.
2. That Anglo Americans are (a) more resistant to death, (b) have made more practical death preparations (e.g., writing a will, paying on a burial plot, etc.), and (c) report fewer mystical or paranormal experiences compared with members of the other ethnic groups.
3. That Hispanic Americans hold more restrictive views toward mourning practices and indicate they would be more emotionally expressive in response to grief compared with members of the other ethnic groups.
4. That African Americans have encountered death more frequently than have members of the other ethnic groups.

Hypothesis 3. Regarding comparisons within the current study on gender differences irrespective of age and ethnicity, we proposed that our analyses of results would indicate:

1. That men have more liberal attitudes toward bereavement practices and have made more practical preparations for death (e.g., writing a will, paying on a burial plot, etc.) than have women.
2. That women anticipate expressing more open emotional response to grief than do men, and that women have less restrictive attitudes toward the determination of pathological grief than do men.

Hypothesis 4. Regarding comparisons within the present study on age differences irrespective of ethnicity and gender, we proposed that our analyses of results would indicate:

1. That participants in the 60-year-and-older age group would (a) have thought about death more frequently, (b) have shown less death anxiety and more death acceptance, (c) have made more

practical preparations for death, (d) have encountered more deaths, (e) have attended more funerals, and (f) have professed belief in an afterlife more frequently than have members of other age groups.

2. That members in the 20–39 year age group would (a) have made fewer practical preparations for death, (b) have encountered fewer deaths, (c) have attended fewer funerals, and (d) have expected that they would be more emotionally expressive in response to grief than members of other age groups.

METHODOLOGY

Data Collection

This study used a time lag design (see Baltes, 1968; Schaie, 1965) to replicate the survey portion of Kalish and Reynolds's (1976) study. Data were collected in late 1999 and early-mid 2000. However, certain sample modifications were necessary because of population differences between north Texas and Los Angeles as well as to limitations in the resources available to collect data for the current study. For example, the ethnic composition of north Texas differs from that of Los Angeles, particularly regarding the percentage of Japanese American residents. Therefore, it was necessary to survey a broader Asian-American group, including persons of Chinese, Korean, Asian Indian, and Philipino background in addition to Japanese Americans. Similarly, the Hispanic population in the current study is more varied than that of Kalish and Reynolds.

Kalish and Reynolds (1976) used a large number of students and office personnel as research staff, and employed a cadre of skilled interviewers through the University of California at Los Angeles (UCLA) Survey Research Center. A person of the same ethnicity as the interviewee conducted every interview and used the language preferred by the interviewee. The interviewers coded the answers and completed questionnaires for the respondents. The Survey Research Center also carried out the actual sample selection procedure and sampled neighborhoods with high ethnic densities and composed of households in the targeted median income levels.

The current study's resources were limited to a single individual (C. A. Peveto) researcher gathering all data. In contrast to the availability of a Survey Research Center to interview within ethnic neighborhoods, we drew the sample from the community with targeted ethnic group composition, such as church and community center groups. The researcher presented information about the study at meetings and gatherings of these groups, and provided interested participants with the study questionnaire, an informational letter, and informed consent form packets. The researcher encouraged participants to complete the questionnaires upon their receipt, but provided stamped and addressed envelopes for respondents who preferred to return completed questionnaires by mail.

Participants

Composition of the Samples

Participants in Kalish and Reynolds's (1976) study included 101 Anglo Americans, 109 African Americans, 114 Mexican Americans, and 110 Japanese Americans. The sample of 434 individuals was divided almost evenly between men and women (215 and 219, respectively). Approximately 37% of the participants were between 20 and 39 years of age, 35% were between 40 and 59 years of age, and 28% were 60 years of age and older. The educational level of their sample varied with ethnicity. The average number of years of schooling completed for each ethnic group was as follows: Asian Americans, 12.4 years; Anglo Americans, 11.1 years; African Americans, 10.6 years; and Hispanic Americans, 6.5 years.

The current study consists of responses from 164 Caucasian Americans (31.2% of the sample), 100 African Americans (19%), 205 Hispanic Americans (39%), and 57 Asian Americans (10.8%), for a total of 526 participants. The ethnic composition of the Hispanic Americans participants was 85.8% Mexican, 5.4% Spanish, 1.5% Puerto Rican, and 7.3% of "other" Hispanic descent. As to the Asian American respondents, 36.8 % were Indian Asian, 21.1% were Chinese, 19.3% were Korean, 10.5% were Japanese, 3.5% were Philipino, and 8.8% were of other Asian descent. Two hundred and twenty-two participants (42.2%) in the study were male; 304 (57.8%) were female. By age, the sample included 244 respondents (46.4%) aged 20 to 39 years, 136 respondents (25.9%) aged 40 to 59 years, and 146 (27.7%) aged 60 years and older. Educational level also varied with ethnicity. Asian American participants in the study averaged the most years of education (17.0 mean years), followed by Caucasian Americans with 16.2 years, African Americans with 15.1 years, and Hispanic Americans with 9.6 years (Table 5.1).

Comparison of Samples

The data for Kalish and Reynolds's (1976) study ($N = 434$) was gathered in the fall of 1970 in Los Angeles County, California. Data for the present study ($N = 526$) was assembled during the fall of 1999 and

TABLE 5.1   Comparison of Ethnicity, Age, Gender, And Marital Status of the Sample in Kalish and Reynolds's (1976) Study With the Present Sample

Variable	1976 Study (%)	Present Study (%)	Overall χ^2	Post hoc χ^2
Ethnicity			50.87**	
Cau.A.	23.3	31.2		5.50*
Afr.A.	25.1	19.0		4.35*
His.A.	26.3	39.0		11.39**
Asn.A.	25.3	10.8		29.63**
Age group (years)			11.46**	
20–39	36.9	46.4		5.28*
40–59	35.0	25.9		6.16*
60+	28.1	27.7		0.01
Gender			4.9*	
Male	49.5	42.2		2.67
Female	50.5	57.8		2.23
Marital status			44.86**	
Married	65.0	48.2		11.83**
Never married	12.5	29.3		31.18**
Widowed	13.5	11.2		0.86
Divorced/Separated	9.0	11.3		0.99

*$p < .05$. **$p < 01$.

Note. Cau.A = Caucasian American. Afr.A. = African American. His.A. = Hispanic American. Asn.A. = Asian American.

the spring of 2000 in the north Texas area. Thus, differences between the two studies exist in the geographic residence of the participants, in the population from which the samples were drawn, and with respect to historical time. To examine the differences between the sample demographics of Kalish and Reynolds's study and the present study, we calculated chi square statistics on variables of ethnicity, age, gender, and marital status. We found significant differences between the samples along several demographic parameters. Table 1 presents a comparison of the two studies in terms of percentages as well as overall and post hoc chi square calculations for ethnicity, age, gender, and marital status. Mean educational levels by ethnicity for each of the studies were also compared.

Regarding ethnicity comparisons between the two studies, we had proportionately more Caucasian American and Hispanic American participants and proportionately fewer African American and Asian American participants in our study than did the earlier study. There were also significant differences between studies in age group membership, specific to the 20–39 year-old groups and to the 40–59 year-old groups, where the present study had proportionately more participants in the 20–39 year-old group and proportionately fewer participants in the 40–59 year-old group. There were no significant differences between the percentage of participants in the 60 years and older groups. The gender difference between the two studies was also significant at the overall level; however, it was not significantly different for post hoc calculations for men and women. Marital status was significantly different between the two studies for married and never married participants, but not significantly different for widowed or divorced and separated participants (see Table 5.1).

Finally, educational levels indexed by ethnicity were different for the two studies, although the ranking of mean number of years of schooling of each ethnicity was similar for both studies. Kalish and Reynolds (1976) reported that for their sample, Mexican American participants, as a group, and older participants, as a group, had less education than other ethnic and age groups. The same was true for this study. In Kalish and Reynolds's study, Japanese Americans averaged the most number of years of education, with 12.4 years, followed by Anglo Americans with 11.1 years, African Americans with 10.6 years, and Mexican Americans with 6.5 years. In the current study, Asian American respondents were also the most formally educated with 17.0 mean years of schooling, followed by Caucasian Americans with 16.2 years, African Americans with 15.1 years, and Hispanic Americans with 9.6 years. Overall, the participants in the present study had more years of formal education than did the participants in Kalish and Reynolds's study (14.5 mean years vs. 10.2 mean years, respectively).

Comparison of ethnic groups by age within the present study also revealed unequal representation of ethnicities among age groups. The percentage of participants in the 20–39 year-old age group was: Caucasian Americans (Cau.A.), 30.5%; African Americans (Afr.A.), 33%; Hispanic Americans (His.A.), 63.9%; and Asian Americans (Asn.A.), 52.6%. The percentage of respondents in the 40–59 year-old age group was as follows: Cau.A., 29.2%; Afr.A., 26%; His.A., 23.4%; and Asn.A., 24.6%. The percentage of participants within the current study aged 60 years and older was: Cau.A., 40.2%; Afr.A., 41%; His.A., 12.7%; and Asn.A., 22.8%.

Measures

The questionnaire we used in the study was identical to that used by Kalish and Reynolds, with a few exceptions. We omitted eight questions because they were not relevant to the current study. Omitted questions included:

1. Compared to most (insert respondent's religious affiliation here), do you feel you are (a) more devout, (b) about the same, (c) less devout?
2. Where were you born? (a) Los Angeles, (b) elsewhere in CA, (c) elsewhere in US/Canada, (d) outside US/Canada.
3. How old is the oldest person living in this household?
4. In general, do you think that others in *your family* would be more strict, about the same, less strict, or other (don't know, etc.) in their expectations of this widow/widower?
5. In general, do you think that others in *your neighborhood* would be more strict, about the same, less strict, or other (don't know, etc.) in their expectations of this widow/widower?
6. Where would you like your body/ashes to be disposed of? (a) Los Angeles, (b) elsewhere/USA, (c) outside/USA, (d) ocean, (e) other/indifferent.
7. About what percentage of the people on this block would you say are of your own ethnic group? (a) 75–100, (b) 25–74, (c) 0–24.
8. This interview was conducted in (a) English (mostly), (b) Japanese, (c) Spanish.

We altered the response choice for a question regarding expected funeral expenses (Question #107) to reflect price inflation that has occurred since the 1970s. In addition, we included the following questions to provide demographic information:

1. What is your ethnicity?
2. If Latino/a, do you consider yourself of Hispanic or Spanish origin?
3. If Latino/a, are you (a) Mexican, (b) Puerto Rican, (c) Cuban, (d) Other?
4. If Asian, are you (a) Chinese, (b) Philipino, (c) Japanese, (d) Asian Indian, (e) Korean, (f) Vietnamese, (g) Other?
5. Where were you born?
6. If you were born outside of the United States, how many years have you lived in the U.S.?
7. What is your native language?
8. If English, do you speak another language? (a) Yes, (b) No.
9. If English, can you read another language? (a) Yes, (b) No.
11a. You are (a) male, (b) female.
25. How often do you attend religious services? (a) 1 or more times per week, (b) 1 to 2 times per month, (c) 1 to 2 times per year, (d) Less than once per year, (e) Never.

The administered questionnaire totaled 125 questions. With the exception of seven items, the questions elicited nominal and categorical responses. The questionnaire took about 15 to 20 min to complete for most participants.

Kalish and Reynolds (1976) developed the questionnaire over a period of about 12 months, and during its development, they completed three substantial revisions prior to initial pilot testing. The fourth revision was pilot tested on approximately 40 individuals, who included participants from all four ethnic groups, all adult age groups, all social class groups, and both sexes. The fifth revision involved translation of the survey into Japanese and Spanish, and the sixth revision was given to the Survey Research Center at UCLA where additional changes were made, and the questionnaire was field tested in the community in all three languages. Adjustments were made as needed, and the final questionnaire was the eighth version, which (with the above indicated alterations) was the questionnaire we used in the current study.

Data Analysis

Kalish and Reynolds (1976) used four types of comparisons in analyzing their survey data. They collected descriptive data within each subculture group to answer the question, "How did each ethnic group respond?" They conducted comparisons among the groups to answer the question, "How do these groups compare with each other?" The authors further separated results within each group by age, sex, and educational level to answer, "What are the variations within each group by age, sex, and educational level?" Finally, Kalish and Reynolds pooled the data from all groups to determine if dimensions of age, sex, and educational level would show significant differences regardless of ethnicity, thus addressing the question, "What human dimensions cut across the subcultural groups?" (pp. 189–190).

Our study employed similar comparisons to examine findings within the study sample and compared the current sample's results with those of Kalish and Reynolds's (1976) to examine differences between the two studies. Because of the large size of the data set, we analyzed the data in the present study in terms of the variables of ethnicity, gender, and age, without considering educational level. Furthermore, we did not examine results within each ethnic group by age and gender, although we analyzed data by age and gender. Finally, we focused on specific issues of death experience and attitudes in this study, which were addressed by 46 questions, or 37% of the questionnaire. We studied the following topics and questions.

A. Experience with death. This was addressed by the following questions:

16. How many persons that you knew personally died in the past two years? (a) None, (b) 1–3, (c) 4–7, (d) 8 or more.
21. How many funerals have you attended in the past two years? (a) None, (b) 1–3, (c) 4–7, (d) 8 or more.
23. How many persons who were dying did you visit or talk with during the past two years? (a) None, (b) 1, (c) 2 or more.
30. Do you actually know of someone who was dying in circumstances like these, so that a decision was made to tell him/her that he/she would shortly die? (a) Yes, (b) No.
91. Have you ever experienced or felt the presence of anyone after he/she had died? (a) Yes, (b) No.

Attitudes toward one's own death, dying, and afterlife. This was addressed by the following questions:

24. About how often do you think about your own death? (a) Daily, (b) Weekly, (c) Monthly, (d) Yearly/Hardly Ever, (e) Never.
29. If you were dying, would you want to be told? (a) Yes, (b) No.
35. If you were told that you had a terminal disease and had six months to live, how would you want to spend your time until you died? (a) With a marked change in behavior (quit job, travel, etc.), (b) By withdrawing or focusing on Inner Life, (c) By showing concern for others (spending time with family, etc.), (d) By completing projects, (e) With no change in behavior, (f) Other.
36. Would you tend to accept death peacefully or fight death actively? (a) Accept, (b) Fight, (c) Depends.
42. Would you try very hard to control the way you showed your emotions in public? (a) Yes, (b) No.

For questions 55–62: Here are some reasons why people do not want to die. Tell me whether they are important to you, very important to you, or not important to you personally.

55. I am afraid of what might happen to my body after death. (a) Very important, (b) Important, (c) Not important.
56. I could no longer care for my dependents. (a) Very important, (b) Important, (c) Not important.

57. I am uncertain as to what might happen to me.
    (a) Very important, (b) Important, (c) Not important.
58. I could no longer have any experiences.
    (a) Very important, (b) Important, (c) Not important.
59. My death would cause grief to my relatives and friends.
    (a) Very important, (b) Important, (c) Not important.
60. All my plans and projects would come to an end.
    (a) Very important, (b) Important, (c) Not important.
61. The process of dying might be painful.
    (a) Very important, (b) Important, (c) Not important.
62. Some people say they are afraid to die and others say they are
    not. How do you feel? (a) Afraid/Terrified, (b) Neither afraid
    nor unafraid, (c) Unafraid/Eager, (d) Depends.
63. Of the following, which one has influenced your attitudes
    toward death the most? (a) Being or thinking you were close to
    death, (b) Death of someone else, (c) Reading, (d) Conversa-
    tions, (e) Religion/including mystical experiences, (f) Funerals
    and other rituals, (g) Media, (h) Other.
70. Have you taken out life insurance?
    (a) Yes, (b) No.
71. Have you made out a will?
    (a) Yes, (b) No.
72. Have you made arrangements to donate your body or parts of
    it to medicine?
    (a) Yes, (b) No.
73. Have you made funeral arrangements?
    (a) Yes, (b) No.
74. Have you paid for or are you now paying for a cemetery plot?
    (a) Yes, (b) No.
75. Have you seriously talked with anyone about your experienc-
    ing death someday? (a) Yes, (b) No.
86. Do you believe you will live on in some form after death?
    (a) Yes, (b) No.
95. Other than during dreams, have you ever had the unexplain-
    able feeling that you were about to die? (a) Yes, (b) No.
98. How often do you dream about your own death or dying?
    (a) Frequently, (b) Sometimes, (c) Rarely, (d) Never.
114. Would you object to having an autopsy performed on your
    body?
    (a) Yes, (b) No, (c) Indifferent.
115. Would you object to being embalmed?
    (a) Yes, (b) No, (c) Indifferent.

116. How would you like your body to be disposed of?
     (a) Buried, (b) Cremated, (c) Donated, (d) Indifferent/
     Undecided.
119. Where would you like to die?
     (a) At home, (b) In a hospital, (c) Other.
125. What effect has this interview had on you?
     (a) Positive, (b) Neutral, (c) Negative.

Attitudes toward the dying, death, or grief of someone else. This was indexed by the following questions:

For questions 26 and 28: Imagine that a friend of yours is dying of cancer. He/she is about your age and gender. His/her family has been told by the physician that he/she will die soon.

26. Should your friend be told that he/she is going to die?
    (a) Yes, (b) No, (c) Depends.
28. Do you think that a person dying of cancer probably senses he's dying anyway without being told? (a) Yes, (b) No, (c) Depends.
33. Did you ever tell someone he/she was about to die?
    (a) Yes, (b) No.
45. Would you be likely to kiss the body at any of the funeral services?
    (a) Yes, (b) No.
50. An infant's death (up to 1 year old), a child's death (around 7 years old), a young person's death (around 25 years old), a middle-aged person's death (around 40 years old), and an elderly person's death (around 75 years old). Which seems most tragic?
    (a) Infant, (b) Child, (c) Young person, (d) Middle-aged person, (e) Elderly person, (f) Depends.
51. Which seems least tragic?
    (a) Infant, (b) Child, (c) Young person, (d) Middle-aged person, (e) Elderly person, (f) Depends.
53. Which seems most tragic: Natural death, accidental death, suicidal death, homicidal death, or death in war? (a) Natural death, (b) Accidental death, (c) Suicidal death, (d) Homicidal death, (e) Death in war.

For questions 78–81: People may have certain expectations of a widow/widower. The next few questions are about someone of your age, gender, and ethnicity who has just lost his/her spouse. In general, after what period of time would you personally consider it all right for a person like yourself:

78. To remarry:
    (a) Unimportant to wait, (b) 1 week–6 months, (c) 1 year, (d) 2 years, (e) Never, (f) Depends.
79. To stop wearing black?
    (a) Unimportant to wait, (b) 1 day–4 months, (c) 6 months or more, (d) Others/Depends.
80. To return to his/her place of employment?
    (a) Unimportant to wait, (b) 1 day–1 week, (c) 1 month or more, (d) Other/Depends.
81. To start going out with other men/women?
    (a) Unimportant to wait, (b) 1 week–1 month, (c) 6 months, (d) 1 year or more, (e) Other/Depends.
120. Do you feel people should be allowed to die if they want to?
    (a) Yes, (b) No.
121. (If yes) Under what circumstances should they be allowed to die?
    (a) In pain, (b) Dying anyway, (c) Unproductive/Unhappy, (d) No feelings or sensations, (e) Because they want to, (f) Other.

In this study we used the same statistical tools for data analysis as those used by Kalish and Reynolds's (1976), where Chi square calculations, re: frequencies, percentages, and analysis of variance (ANOVA) for continuous data, were employed. For comparison of results between the current study and the earlier study, we used chi square calculations and post hoc tests as appropriate. Sample sizes for the present study varied between 424 and 526, due to missing data for some questions.

6

Analysis of Findings: Intrastudy Variability

EXPERIENCE WITH DEATH

Let us first examine variability across ethnicity, age, and gender in a manner similar to that of Kalish and Reynolds (1976), to lay the groundwork for our central concern: historical shifts in attitudes toward dying, death, and bereavement. Examination of the results in the present study related to experience with death revealed significant differences primarily among ethnic and age groups, with gender differences being minimal. Appendix A presents the summary of questionnaire results for the present study broken down by ethnicity, age, and gender.

Intrastudy Variability: The Effects of Ethnicity

Concerning ethnic differences, our results suggest that Asian American participants in the study had the most experience with a few (1–3) deaths, African Americans with several (4 or more) deaths, and Hispanic Americans had the least experience with death. A larger percentage of Asian Americans than participants from the other ethnic groups in the study indicated that they personally knew one to three persons who died in the last 2 years (75.4%), had attended one to three funerals (64.9%), and had talked with or visited one dying person in the last year (35.7%). More African American respondents than respondents from the other ethnicities related that they personally knew four to seven and eight or more persons who died in the last 2 years (27.3% and 22.2%, respectively) and had attended four to seven and eight or more funerals (19.2% and 18.2 %, respectively).

African Americans and Caucasian Americans were the most likely to have recently visited or talked with two or more persons who were dying (38.5% and 38.8%, respectively). There was a greater percentage of Hispanic Americans in the study who stated that they personally knew no persons who died in the last 2 years (42.3%), had attended no funerals (51.2%), and had talked with or visited no persons who were dying (68.7%). Study results also indicated that Caucasian Americans were the most likely to have known someone who was dying and in a situation in which a decision was made about informing the dying person that he/she would shortly die (61.8%).

Intrastudy Variability: The Effects of Age

We also found significant age differences related to experience with death. Participants in the young age group (20–39 years) were most likely to have personally known no one who died in the last 2 years (30.9%), to have attended no funerals (44.9%), and to have not visited or talked with anyone who was dying (62.2%).

Participants in the oldest age group (60+ years) indicated that they were the most likely to have known eight or more persons who died recently (22.7%), to have attended four to seven funerals in the past 2 years (19.9%), and to have visited or talked with two or more persons who were dying (38.7%) than were participants in the other age groups. Respondents in the 60 years and older group were also the most numerous to report having experienced or felt the presence of someone after he or she had died (62.7%).

ATTITUDES TOWARD ONE'S OWN DEATH, DYING, AND AFTERLIFE

Comparisons between ethnic, age, and gender groups within the study on attitudes toward one's own death, dying, and afterlife revealed a number of significant findings. Only one of the 28 questions examined (question #86: Appendix A) to index attitudes about one's own death, dying, and afterlife was not significantly different across any of the three variables. Differences between ethnic groups were most numerous.

Intrastudy Variability: The Effects of Ethnicity

Regarding differences between ethnic groups, when participants were asked, "If dying, would you want to be told?" more Caucasian and Asian American respondents replied affirmatively (93.9% and 89.3%, respectively) than did respondents in the other ethnic groups. A larger percentage of Caucasian (61.1%), Hispanic (56.2%), and African Americans (46.3%) indicated that if they were told they had a terminal disease, they would want to spend the last 6 months of their lives showing concern for others than did Asian Americans (31%), who were almost equally likely to choose to withdraw or focus on their inner lives (27.3%). More Asian Americans (57.1%) and African Americans (51%) in the study related that they would tend to accept death peacefully, whereas more Hispanic Americans (51.2%) stated that they would fight death actively. Caucasian Americans (41.5) tended to indicate "depends."

There were also differences among the ethnic groups to a series of questions about the personal importance of reasons for not wanting to die. A larger percentage of Hispanic Americans (50.5%) stated that uncertainty as to what might happen to them after death was "very important" as compared with other groups, whereas Asian (53.6%) and Caucasian Americans (53.3%) tended to feel that such uncertainty was "not important." In fact, a larger percentage of Asian Americans than other ethnic group participants indicated "not important" for several of the reasons, including, that one could no longer have experiences, death would cause grief to one's friends and relatives, one's plans and projects would come to an end, and the process of dying may be painful. Hispanic Americans (28.6%) in the study were more likely than others to relate that they were afraid or terrified of dying, whereas Caucasian Americans (64.1%) were the most likely to respond that they were "neither afraid nor unafraid."

Study results concerning preparations for death varied among the ethnic groups. A larger percentage of African Americans indicated that they had taken out life insurance (84.8%), had made funeral arrangements (27.3%), and had paid for cemetery plots (35%) than members of the other ethnic groups. More Caucasian Americans than participants in other groups related that they had made out wills (55.4%) and had made arrangements to donate their bodies or body parts to medicine (35.9%). Results showed that Hispanic Americans were the most likely to have seriously talked with someone about someday experiencing death (55.2%), and more Hispanic Americans than participants in other groups indicated that they had experienced the unexplainable feeling that they were about to die (35%).

In comparison with other ethnic groups, a larger percentage of Asian Americans related that they never dreamed about their own death or dying (50.9%). Asian Americans were also more likely than other participants to state that they were "indifferent" about being autopsied (44.4%) or embalmed (58.5%). With regards to disposal of one's body, Asian Americans tended to choose cremation (46.3%) more often than other ethnic groups, and African Americans chose burial (71.4%) more frequently than did others.

Finally, although the majority of respondents in each ethnic group asserted that they preferred dying at home, a larger percentage of African Americans (28.9%) indicated that they would like to die in a hospital than did members of other ethnic groups.

Intrastudy Variability: The Effects of Age

Significant differences also occurred among age groups in attitudes toward one's own death, dying, and afterlife. The differences tended to occur most between the young (20–39 years) and the older (60+) age groups, with those in the middle-aged group (40–59 years) positioned in between. A larger percentage of participants in the young age group (22.4%) indicated that they never thought about their own death than did participants of other age groups. Young aged participants were also more likely to state that they would fight death actively (40.4%), whereas older aged participants were more likely than others to relate that they would tend to accept death peacefully (53.8%).

In reference to the importance of reasons for not wanting to die, a larger percentage of participants in the older age group asserted that no longer being able to care for dependents was not important (29.5%), nor was the concern that their death would cause grief to friends and relatives (19.9%) when compared with the responses of other age groups. Participants in the older age group were also the most likely to state that they were neither afraid nor unafraid to die (60%).

In addition, older age group members in the study tended to have made the most arrangements for death (i.e., life insurance, will, funeral arrangements, cemetery plot payment), whereas young age group members had made the least. Nevertheless, the percentage of respondents in the 60 years and older group were the most likely to state that they never dreamed about their own death or dying (65.2%).

Intrastudy Variability: The Effects of Gender

There were fewer significant differences between genders concerning attitudes about one's own death, dying, and afterlife. A larger percentage of men (33.8%) than women (22.1%) indicated indifference to the thought that the process of dying might be painful. Attitudes about autopsy and embalming also differed with genders. Men in the study were more likely to indicate indifference about being autopsied (31.8% men vs. 19.8% women) or embalmed (30.3% men vs. 20.3%

women), whereas women (24%) were more likely to object to an autopsy than were men (14.1%) and more likely not to object to being embalmed (57.6% women vs. 51.8% men). In addition, a larger percentage of women (25.2%) than men (17.8%) indicated that they had made arrangements to donate their body or body parts to medicine.

ATTITUDES TOWARD THE DYING, DEATH, OR GRIEF OF SOMEONE ELSE

Examination of the study results related to attitudes toward the dying, death, or grief of someone else revealed that the number of significant differences among ethnic groups was most numerous, with fewer significant differences between age groups, and fewest differences between genders. Two of the questions examined (#45 and #120: Appendix A) were not significantly different based on ethnic, age, or gender group comparisons.

Intrastudy Variability: The Effects of Ethnicity

When we looked at differences in attitudes between ethnic groups, we found that Caucasian American participants were the most likely to state that a friend should be informed if he or she was going to die (78.9%), whereas Hispanic Americans were the least likely to believe that a friend should be told (54.9%). Caucasian (18.1%) and Asian Americans (16.4%) were more likely to have told someone that he or she was about to die than were African American (3.0%) or Hispanic Americans (5.0%). When asked to compare the relative tragedy of various types of death, Asian Americans (33.9%) tended to indicate that accidental deaths were the most tragic, whereas African Americans (41.7%) and Hispanic Americans (35.5%) designated suicidal deaths as the most tragic, and Caucasian Americans (41%) stated that homicidal deaths were the most tragic. On the basis of the age of the deceased, Caucasian Americans (47.5%) felt that the death of a child was the most tragic, Asian Americans (31.5%) and Hispanic Americans (27.8%) felt that the death of a young adult was most tragic, and African Americans (29.9%) tended to respond with "depends."

On a group of questions related to their expectations about the behavior of a person similar to themselves who had just lost a spouse, Asian Americans (26.35) were more likely to believe that one should never remarry compared with study participants in other ethnic groups. Caucasian Americans (78.6%) were the most likely to feel that it was unimportant to wait before ceasing to wear black, and Hispanic

Americans (33.2%) were the most likely to feel that it was unimportant to wait before returning to one's place of employment. In answer to the question when it was appropriate to start going out with other men or women, Hispanic Americans (27%) were the most likely to believe that one should wait a year or more, whereas African Americans (7%) were the least likely to think that one needed to wait that long. The majority of Asian Americans (68.4%) indicated that the appropriate time to begin dating was "other or depends."

When questioned about the circumstances under which people should be allowed to die, Caucasian (38.2%) and African Americans (27.6%) related that the people needed to be dying anyway, Hispanic Americans (28.4%) tended to feel that the people should be in pain, and Asian Americans responded that people should be allowed to die if they had no feelings or sensations (24%), they were dying anyway (24%), or they wanted to die (24%).

Intrastudy Variability: The Effects of Age

There were also some significant differences between age groups in attitudes toward the dying, death, or grief of others. For example, participants in the older age group (30.3%) were more likely than the younger (17.9%) or middle-aged participants (10.9%) to respond with "depends" when asked if a friend should be informed that he or she was going to die. Middle-aged persons in the study were the most likely to feel that a child's death (43.6%) was the most tragic, whereas younger participants were equally divided between feeling that an infant's death (27.2%) and a child's death (27.2%) were most tragic. Those in the older age group were equally divided between responding that a child's death (26.1%) and "depends" (26.1%) were most tragic.

In response to questions concerning their expectations about the behavior of someone who had just lost a spouse, participants in the older age group were more likely to respond "never" (22%) or "depends" (44%) when asked when it was appropriate for the bereaved spouse to remarry. Those who were in the middle-aged group were most likely to indicate that it was unimportant for the bereaved spouse to wait before returning to one's place of employment (29.1%), whereas those in the older age group were most likely to respond with "depends" (38.6%). Finally, young age group participants (27.2%) were more likely to relate that one should wait for a year or more before going out with other men or women than were participants in the other age groups.

Intrastudy Variability: The Effects of Gender

There were few significantly different results between genders related to attitudes about death, dying, and grief of others. However, one notable finding was that a larger percentage of women than men (21.9% vs. 16.4%, respectively) responded with "depends" when asked if a friend should be told that he or she was going to die. In addition, more men than women participants (30.6% vs. 20.7%, respectively) indicated that it was unimportant to wait before returning to one's place of employment after the death of a spouse, and more women than men (18% vs. 11%, respectively) suggested that it was appropriate to wait 1 month or longer before returning to work.

7

Analysis of Findings: Interstudy Variability

INTERSTUDY COMPARISONS REGARDING EXPERIENCE WITH DEATH

Comparison of results concerning experience with death in Kalish and Reynolds's (1976) study with the findings in this study revealed some significant differences, although three of the five questions examined to index experience with death showed no significant interstudy differences (questions #21, #30, #91: see Appendix B). The areas in which significant differences occurred between the two studies related to personally knowing four to seven persons who had died in the past 2 years and the number of dying persons with whom one had spoken or visited in the last 2 years (see below).

Overall Interstudy Differences

Having described the present study's findings in Chapter 6 by ethnicity, age, and gender, we now turn to the central focus of this project, interstudy differences in attitudes toward death, dying, and bereavement (see Appendix B for statistical tests of such comparisons). Such data speak directly to historical shifts in such attitudes. On the basis of the comparison of results, we found that participants in the present study personally knew fewer persons who had died in the previous 2 years than did those in Kalish and Reynolds's (1976) study. Respondents in this study were less likely to know four to seven people who had recently died than were respondents in the 1976 study (16.5% current vs. 22.5% earlier). However, the percentage of participants in the current study who related that they had talked with or visited with dying persons was greater than in the earlier study. More current study respondents indicated that they had visited two or more dying persons (25.9% current vs. 17.5% earlier), and fewer participants related that they had visited or talked with no dying persons (48.8% current vs. 62% earlier) than in Kalish and Reynolds's study.

Interstudy Differences in the Effects of Ethnicity

Compared with Kalish and Reynolds's (1976) results, a larger percentage of Caucasian (21.7% in the current study vs. 14% in the earlier study) and African Americans (27.3% current vs. 23% earlier) in the present study knew several people who died recently whereas a smaller percentage of Hispanic (8% current vs. 29% earlier) and Asian Americans (10.5% current vs. 24% earlier) had personally experienced four to seven deaths. We also found ethnic shifts in the percentage of participants who visited or talked with persons who were dying. Fewer Caucasian (32.7% current vs. 68% earlier) and African Americans (32.2% current vs. 62% earlier) had visited no dying persons than in Kalish and Reynolds's study, and more Caucasian (38.8% current vs. 18% earlier) and African Americans (38.5% current vs. 16% earlier) had visited or talked with two or more persons who were dying. We found little difference in the percentages between the present study and earlier study for Hispanic and Asian American groups.

Interstudy Differences in the Effects of Age

On the basis of age, a smaller percentage of 20–39-year-olds (9.1% current vs. 15% earlier) personally knew several persons who died in the past 2 years as did fewer persons in the 60 and older age group (22% current vs. 33% earlier) as compared with Kalish and Reynolds's (1976) study. Relative to the 1970s, all age groups in the present study also indicated that they had more experience with visiting dying persons.

Interstudy Differences on Effects of Gender

Gender differences between the earlier study and the current study were greatest for women's experience with visiting dying persons. Fewer women in the present study had visited or talked with no one who was dying (47.3% current vs. 65% earlier) and more women had visited two or more dying persons (28.8% current vs. 14% earlier). We found less of a change between this study and Kalish and Reynolds's (1976) study for men's experience with dying persons.

INTERSTUDY COMPARISONS OF ATTITUDES TOWARD ONE'S OWN DEATH, DYING, AND AFTERLIFE

The examination of study results between the present study and Kalish and Reynolds's (1976) study regarding attitudes toward one's own death, dying, and afterlife revealed a number of changes in attitude that occurred across ethnicity, age, and gender variables. These differences suggest shifting trends that have occurred over time, although consideration must be given to the significant differences between the samples from the earlier study and the current study when drawing conclusions.

Overall Interstudy Differences

With regard to awareness of one's own death, the percentage of participants in the present study who indicated that they thought about their own death on a daily basis decreased in comparison with Kalish and Reynolds's (1976) study (10.8% current study vs. 17.5% earlier study), whereas the percentage who indicated they thought about their own death on a weekly (17.3% current vs. 10% earlier) and monthly basis (43.8% current vs. 15% earlier) increased. Respondents in the present study also were more likely to want to be told if they were dying than in the earlier study (82.9% current vs. 71% earlier). Participants in the present study's prediction as to how they would respond if told they had a terminal disease and had only 6 months to live was also different across ethnicities, age groups, and genders than with Kalish and Reynolds's participants. In the present study, fewer people indicated that they would respond with a marked change in behavior, such as quitting their jobs or traveling (8.1% current vs. 17% earlier), withdrawing or focusing on their inner life (9.6% current vs. 20.5% earlier), or with no change in behavior (14.4 % current vs. 26% earlier), whereas more people in the current study related that they would respond by showing concern for others, such as spending time with their families (52.9% current vs. 22.5% earlier). The current study participants were less likely to endorse that they would accept death peacefully (37.1% current vs. 63.5% earlier) and more likely to relate that it "depends" (28.1% current vs. 1.5% earlier). Recent participants also stated that they would be less likely to try very hard to control their emotions in public (35.1% current vs. 25% earlier).

Responses to personal fear of death also differed between the two studies. The percentage of persons who indicated that they were afraid to die was smaller in this study than in Kalish and Reynolds's (1976) study (17.8% current vs. 26.5% earlier), as was the percentage who indicated that they were unafraid of dying (11.1% current vs. 51% earlier). Rather, participants in the recent study were more likely to indicate that they were neither afraid nor unafraid (49.9% current vs. 19% earlier) or "depends" (21.2% current vs. 2.5% earlier). The frequency of dreaming about death also seems to have changed. The percentage of persons in the present study who stated that they never dream about their own death or dying was less than in the earlier study (45.7% current vs. 71% earlier).

The percentage of respondents who indicated no longer being able to care for their dependents if they died was "very important" was greater in the current study (53.1%) in comparison with the earlier study (40.5%), and the percentage of persons who stated that the ability to care for dependents was "not important" was less (14% current vs. 30.5% earlier). Concern for the grief that one's death would cause relatives and friends (based on the percentage who indicated that it was "very important") was also greater in the present study (45.8% current vs. 25% earlier). Another reason people fear death, uncertainty as to what might happen to them when they die, was also endorsed as "very important" (33.4% current vs. 11% earlier) or "important" (25.6% current vs. 19% earlier) by a larger percentage of the participants in the present study than in Kalish and Reynolds's (1976) study.

Responses in each of the studies to a series of questions about preparations for death were also different. More respondents in the present study indicated that they had made arrangements to donate their bodies or body parts to medicine (21.5% current vs. 3.5% earlier), and more persons stated that they had talked seriously with someone about their future death (46.9% current vs. 28% earlier). More participants in the present study also indicated that they preferred to die at home (75.7% current vs. 57.5% earlier).

More recent study participants were more likely to feel "indifferent" about having an autopsy performed on their body (25.8%) than were participants in the study conducted in the 1970s (11%). In addition, there was a decrease in the percentage of respondents in this study who indicated they desired burial (55.5%) as compared with Kalish and Reynolds's (1976) study (68.5%) and an increase in the percentage who stated that they were indifferent or undecided (15.5% current vs. 7% earlier). Furthermore, the percentage of participants in the present study who endorsed the belief that they will live on in some form after death was greater (87.3%) than the percentage endorsing that belief in the previous study (52.5%).

Finally, fewer respondents in the current study felt that participation in the study had a positive effect on them (28.5% current vs. 44% earlier) and more related that it had a neutral effect (65% current vs.

45.5% earlier). We found no significant differences between the present study and Kalish and Reynolds's (1976) study on four of the questions that we examined that were related to attitudes toward one's own death, dying, and afterlife (questions #60, #63, #73, #74: see Appendix B).

We also found notable differences in attitudes toward one's own death, dying, and afterlife occurred across ethnic groups, age groups, and genders between the two studies. Within the ethnic, age group, and gender variables, we also found significant differences in the way the participants in the present study and those in Kalish and Reynolds's (1976) study responded.

Interstudy Differences in the Effects of Ethnicity

With regard to ethnicity, we found marked differences between the present and earlier study in the size of the response within ethnic groups to a number of questions. For example, on the item asking how they would spend their time if told they had a terminal disease and had only 6 months to live, the percentage of participants who were African American and Caucasian American in the current study indicated a greater contrast in their responses in comparison with their respective groups in the earlier study than did the Hispanics or Asian Americans. The percentage of African American and Caucasian respondents who related that they would spend time by showing concern for others increased markedly (Afr.A.: 46.3% current vs. 14% earlier; Cau.A.: 61.1% current vs. 23% earlier), whereas the percentage of African Americans who stated that they would spend their final months by withdrawing or focusing on their inner lives decreased (4.2% current vs. 26% earlier), and the percentage of Caucasian Americans who related that they would spend their final months with no change in behavior decreased from the earlier study (9.6% current vs. 36% earlier).

The percentage of Hispanic Americans in this study who responded that they thought about death on a daily basis decreased markedly from the 1976 study (7.4% current vs. 27% earlier), as did the percentage of Hispanic Americans who stated that they would accept death peacefully (27.3% vs. 65%). The percentage of Caucasian American respondents who indicated "depends" in response to the query of whether they would accept death peacefully or fight increased greatly from the earlier study (41.5% current vs. 4% earlier). A larger percentage of Asian Americans in the present study stated that they would not try very hard to control the way they showed emotion in public than did the Japanese in Kalish and Reynold's (1976) sample (49.1% current vs. 18% earlier). We also found large differences within the ethnic groups between the two studies regarding reasons for fearing death.

Forty-eight percent of African Americans in the 1976 study related that no longer being able to care for their dependents was "not important"; however, only 16.8% of the African Americans in the present study said that it was not important. African American and Hispanic American participants in the earlier study indicated that uncertainty as to what might happen to them when they died was not important (75% and 68%, respectively), but fewer African Americans and Hispanic Americans felt that it was not important in the current study (36.7% and 29.2%, respectively).

The thought that one's death would cause grief to one's relatives and friends was seen as "very important" to a much larger percentage of African Americans and Hispanic Americans in this study (47.4% and 56.9%, respectively) than in the 1976 study (3% and 7%, respectively). Hispanic Americans in the current study were also much more likely to believe that they would live on in some form after death than were the Mexican Americans in Kalish and Reynolds's (1976) study (90.2% current vs. 40% earlier). African Americans in this study were much less likely to indicate that they "never" dreamed about their own death or dying (42% current vs. 78% earlier). Finally, Asian Americans in the present study indicated that they were "indifferent" regarding embalming and autopsy considerably more often than did the Japanese in the 1976 study (embalming: 58.5% current vs. 13% earlier; autopsy: 44.4% current vs. 8% earlier).

Interstudy Differences in the Effects of Age

Marked differences between the present study and that of Kalish and Reynolds (1976) in comparison of age groups' responses also occurred. Regarding how one would spend one's time if only 6 months of life remained, recent respondents in the 60 and older age group were much more likely to indicate that they would show concern for others (50.7% current vs. 12% earlier) and much less likely to state that they would withdraw from life and focus inwardly (9.0% current vs. 37% earlier) than were the respondents in the 1976 study. Young (20–39 years old) and middle-aged (40–59 years old) participants in the present study responded with "depends" more often when asked whether they would accept death peacefully or fight as compared with the same age group participants in the earlier study (young: 32.2% current vs. 1% earlier; middle-aged: 31.1% current vs. 3% earlier).

The young and middle-aged participants in our study were also much more likely to relate that they believed that they would live on in some form after death than were similarly aged participants in Kalish and Reynold's (1976) study (young: 89.8% current vs. 48% earlier;

middle-aged: 88.4% current vs. 48% earlier). The percentage of middle-aged participants in the present study who stated that they had made arrangements to donate their bodies or body parts to medicine was much greater than in the 1976 study (42% vs. 4%, respectively). The middle-aged participants in the recent study were less likely to state that they never dreamed about their own deaths than were those in the earlier study (37.3% vs. 75%), and they were more likely to state that they preferred to die at home (88% current vs. 49% earlier). In addition, a much larger percentage of participants who are 60 and older indicated that they had made out a will than had the oldest group in Kalish and Reynolds' study (75.2% vs. 39%, respectively).

Interstudy Differences in the Effects of Gender

We found fewer response differences between the genders in the present study and the 1976 study, in contrast to those found for ethnic and age group comparisons between the two studies. A much larger percentage of men in our study (52.1%) indicated that they would spend time showing concern for others if they had only 6 months to live than did the men in the earlier study (16%). Men in the present study were also more likely to indicate that they wished to die at home (77.4% current vs. 55% earlier). Female participants in the recent study were more likely to relate that they had made arrangements to donate their bodies or body parts to medicine than were females in the 1976 study (25.2% current vs. 2% earlier).

INTERSTUDY COMPARISONS OF ATTITUDES TOWARD THE DYING, DEATH, OR GRIEF OF SOMEONE ELSE

Comparison of responses between the two studies related to questions about attitudes toward the dying, death, or grief of someone else also revealed differences that occurred across ethnicity, age, and gender variables.

Overall Interstudy Differences

Participants in the present study were less likely to respond "no" when asked if friends should be told that they are going to die (14.7% current vs. 37.5 % earlier) compared with those in Kalish and Reynold's (1976) study. Those in the recent study were also less likely to believe that persons dying of cancer probably sense that they are dying without having been told than were participants in the 1976 study (69% current vs. 82% earlier) and more likely to respond with "depends" (20.6% current vs. 4.2 % earlier).

Attitudes about relative degree of tragedy related to different types of death also differed between the two studies. More respondents in the present study indicated that suicidal death seemed most tragic (34.5%) than did respondents in the earlier study (10%). In contrast, more participants in Kalish and Reynolds's (1976) study viewed death in war as the most tragic (30.0%) as compared with those in this study (4.4%). Fewer persons in the current study ranked the death of a young person (around 25 years old) as most tragic than did participants in the earlier study (21.0% current vs. 42% earlier); rather, a larger percentage of recent study participants responded with "depends" to the question than did those in the 1976 study (22.7% current vs. 2% earlier). Similarly, participants in the recent study indicated "depends" more often than those in Kalish and Reynolds's study when asked at which age death was the least tragic (24.5% current vs. 1.5% earlier).

Comparison between studies on a series of questions relating to expectations about how a person similar to themselves should behave after the death of a spouse revealed additional differences. When asked when it was okay for the spouse to remarry, the percentage of participants in the present study who indicated that it was unimportant to wait (6.7% current vs. 24% earlier) or responded with 1 year (8.8% current vs. 31.5% earlier) was less than in the earlier study. However, the percentage of respondents in the present study who responded with "never" or "depends" was much greater than in the 1976 study (65.2% current vs. 17.5% earlier). More people in the recent study also indicated "other or depends" than in the previous study (25.1% current vs. 7% earlier) when asked when it was okay for the spouse to stop wearing black. Finally, this study's participants were more likely to respond with "other or depends" than those in the earlier study to questions of when it was appropriate for the bereaved spouse to return to his or her place of employment (32.4% current vs. 10% earlier) or when it was okay to start going out with other men or women (53.5% current vs. 18.5% earlier). Comparison between the two studies on two of the focus questions (questions #45 and #120: Appendix B) yielded nonsignificant results.

Interstudy Differences in the Effects of Ethnicity

Regarding ethnicity, we found that differences in responses between the present and earlier study concerning the relative tragedy of types of death were largest for African American and Hispanic American participants. African and Hispanic Americans in the recent study were considerably more likely to rate suicidal death as the most tragic type of death than were their counterparts in the 1976 study (Afr.A.: 41.7% current vs. 9% earlier; His.A.: 35.5% current vs. 8% earlier) and were less likely to rate death in war as most tragic (Afr.A: 1% current vs. 36% earlier; His.A.: 3% current vs. 35% earlier). African and Hispanic Americans in this study were also much less likely to consider a young person's death to be the most tragic than were these groups in the previous study (Afr.A: 9.3% current vs. 45% earlier; His.A.: 27.8% current vs. 48% earlier). In addition, both ethnic groups in the present study were more likely to respond with "depends" when asked to identify at which age death seems most tragic (Afr.A: 29.9% current vs. 1% earlier; His.A.: 23.7% current vs. 3 % earlier) and the age at which death seems least tragic (Afr.A: 29.6% current vs. 1% earlier; His.A.: 32.3% current vs. 1% earlier). Hispanic Americans in this study were also less likely to indicate that a friend should not be told that he or she is going to die than were Mexican Americans in the 1976 study (23.5% current vs. 58% earlier). When asked under what circumstances a person should be allowed to die, a much smaller percentage of Hispanic American participants indicated that the person must be dying anyway than did those in Kalish and Reynolds's (1976) study (26.9% current vs. 57% earlier).

Questions regarding expectations of how a person should behave after the death of a spouse resulted in differences within ethnic responses between the present and earlier studies. A smaller percentage of Hispanic and Asian American respondents indicated that 1 year was an appropriate time to wait before remarrying than had similar participants in the previous study (His.A.: 7.5% current vs. 38% earlier; Asn.A.: 1.8% current vs. 30% earlier), and a much larger percentage of each of the ethnic groups responded with "never or depends" to the question than had similar ethnic groups in the earlier study. Asian and African American participants in the present study were also more likely to respond with "other or depends" to a query about the appropriate length of time to wear black than were Japanese and African Americans in the Kalish and Reynold's 1976 study (Asn.A.: 42.9% current vs. 11% earlier; Afr.A.: 37.2% current vs. 4% earlier). Recent Caucasian American participants were less likely to indicate that it was unimportant to wait before returning to employment after the death of a spouse than were Caucasian American participants in the 1976 study (18.9% current vs. 47% earlier). Finally, African American respondents in this study were less likely to respond that it was unimportant to wait before going out with men or women after the death of one's spouse than were those in the previous study (10% current vs. 30% earlier).

Interstudy Differences in the Effects of Age

A comparison of the present study and Kalish and Reynolds's (1976) study within age groups revealed large differences on some items. Young age group participants in the recent study were much less likely to believe that death in war was the most tragic type of death than were young participants in the earlier study (3.8% current vs. 37% earlier). Young and middle-aged respondents in our study were also less likely to state that it was okay for bereaved persons to remarry 1 year after their spouses' deaths than were similarly aged participants in the 1976 study (young: 8.2% current vs. 32% earlier; middle-aged: 11.1% current vs. 36% earlier). Current study participants in the older age group were less likely to feel that a friend should not be told that he or she is going to die (16.9% current vs. 53% earlier) and more likely to respond with "depends" than older participants in the previous study (30.3% current vs. 5% earlier).

Interstudy Differences in the Effects of Gender

Regarding gender differences between the two studies, we found female respondents in the present study were much less likely to feel that death in war was the most tragic type of death than were female participants in Kalish and Reynolds's (1976) study (2.7% current vs. 37% earlier). Women participants in our study were also less likely to indicate that a person needed to be dying anyway before he or she should be allowed to die than were women in the previous study (31.1% current vs. 54% earlier).

Table 7.1 summarizes the differences in attitudes toward death, dying, and bereavement between the present study and that of Kalish and Reynolds.

TABLE 7.1   Interstudy Findings

Interstudy comparison variable	Relative to Kalish and Reynolds
Experience with death	
Frequency of funeral attendance	No difference
Knowledge of persons who death was imminent	No difference
Feeling the presence of someone who had died	No difference
Knowing 4–7 persons who had died	Less common
Having spoken to and/or visited dying persons	More common
Having spoken to and/or visited no dying person	Less common
Impact of ethnicity on experience with death	Greatest for Causacian and African Americans
Impact of age on experience with death	Greatest for younger and older adults
Impact of gender on experience with death	Greater for women
Attitudes toward one's own death and/or dying	
Thinking about one's death daily	Less common
Thinking about one's death weekly or monthly	More common
Wanting to be told about one's own dying	More common
Accepting death peacefully	Less common
Fearful of one's own death	Less common
Unafraid of dying	Less common
Ambivalent regarding dying	More common
Preparations for death	
Donating organs and/or bodies after death	More common
Talking with someone about future death	More common
Preferring to die at home	More common
Ambivalent about autopsy	More common
Desiring a traditional burial	More common
Belief in an afterlife	More common
Death puts an end to one's goals	No difference
Impact of experience on death attitudes	No difference
Making funeral arrangements	No difference
Paying for a cemetery plot	No difference
Impact of ethnicity on death preparations	Greatest for Caucasian, African, and Hispanic Americans
Impact of age on death preparations	Greatest for middle-aged and oldest
Impact of gender on death preparations	Modest at best

(continued)

TABLE 7.1   Interstudy Findings *(continued)*

Interstudy comparison variable	Relative to Kalish and Reynolds
Orientation toward others' deaths and/or dying:	
Telling a friend about his or her imminent death	Less common
Persons dying are aware of it	Less common
Suicide is most tragic	More common
Death in war is most tragic	Less common
Young person's death is most tragic	Less common
OK to marry soon after spouse's death	Less common
Ambivalent about when to remarry	More common
Ambivalent about when to return to work	More common
Ambivalent about when to date	More common
Kissing the corpse at the funeral	No difference
People should be allowed to die via their choice	No difference
Impact of ethnicity on attitudes toward others' deaths	Greatest for African and Hispanic Americans
Impact of age on attitudes toward others' deaths	Varied by age
Impact of gender on attitudes toward others' deaths	Greater for women

8

Hypotheses Regarding Interstudy and Intrastudy Variability

O n the basis of a review of the literature, we had made numerous intrastudy comparisons regarding what the results would suggest pertaining to the impact of historical change on death attitudes. An examination of the accuracy of the predictions revealed that the proposed hypotheses were often refuted by the study data.

HYPOTHESES COMPARING KALISH AND REYNOLDS'S STUDY WITH PRESENT STUDY RESULTS

We made three predictions concerning anticipated differences between the results from the 1976 study and the current study. We hypothesized that participants in our study would think about death more often than did those in the earlier study. A comparison of results between the two studies indicated that respondents in Kalish and Reynolds's (1976) study tended to think about death more often than respondents in the current study (Question #24).

We also proposed that participants in the present study would report greater fear of death than in the earlier study. However, a comparison of the responses yielded mixed results. A larger percentage of participants in Kalish and Reynolds's study reported that they were afraid of death and reported that they were unafraid of death than did those in our study, but more participants in the present study indicated that they were "neither afraid nor unafraid" or responded with "depends" (Question #62).

Finally, we hypothesized that respondents in the present study would indicate a more liberal attitude toward death and dying than those in the 1976 study. This hypothesis was supported. As compared with participants in Kalish and Reynolds's study, respondents in the current study were more likely to indicate that a friend should be told if he or she were going to die (Question #26) and were more likely to state that they would wish to be informed if they were dying (Question #29). When asked if persons were allowed to die, under what circumstances should it be allowed, those in the earlier study were more likely to respond that the persons must be dying anyway (Question 121). A greater percentage of participants in the current study than in the 1976 study indicated that death should be allowed under the circumstances of "other."

HYPOTHESES COMPARING ETHNIC, AGE, AND GENDER GROUPS WITHIN THE PRESENT STUDY

Hypotheses Comparing Ethnic Groups

We offered several hypotheses concerning expected differences between the ethnic groups in the present study on attitudes toward death and dying, but only a few of these predictions proved to be accurate. We proposed that Asian Americans would be more accepting of death and have a greater preference for cremation than would participants from other ethnicities (Questions #36 & #116). The two hypotheses proved accurate. However, the data failed to support the expectation that Asian Americans would be less emotionally expressive.

In our hypotheses concerning Caucasian Americans, we suggested that Caucasian Americans would be more resistant to death and report fewer mystical or paranormal experiences than participants in other groups. Nonetheless, results indicated that Caucasian Americans were most likely to respond with "depends" when asked if they would accept or fight death (Question #36). Furthermore, participants who were Caucasian American reported experiencing the most, rather than the least number of paranormal experiences (Question #91).

We predicted that Caucasian Americans would have made more preparations for death than respondents from other ethnic groups, which proved partially accurate (Questions #70–75 & #77). More Caucasian Americans indicated that they had completed wills, had donated their bodies or body parts to medicine, and had made arrangements for someone to handle their affairs, but Caucasian Americans were only the second most likely ethnic group to have bought life insurance, to have arranged for funerals, to have purchased cemetery plots, or to have talked with someone seriously about their own deaths.

The hypotheses concerning Hispanic American attitudes and behavior regarding death were not strongly supported by our findings. We proposed that Hispanic Americans would hold more restrictive views toward mourning practices. Results indicated that Hispanic Americans' attitudes were the most liberal on only one of the four questions related to expectations of the bereaved (Questions #78–81). Hispanic Americans were the most likely to state that it was unimportant to wait before returning to one's place of employment after the death of a spouse, but Hispanic Americans' responses to expectations concerning remarriage, wearing black, and dating were more conservative. In another hypothesis we predicted that Hispanic Americans would indicate that they would be the most emotionally expressive concerning death, but results showed that Asian Americans reported that they would be the least likely to struggle to maintain emotional control (Question #42).

The single hypothesis we proposed concerning African American attitudes and experience with death was supported by the data in our study. We predicted that African Americans would have encountered death more frequently than members of the other ethnic groups. The results showed that African American respondents personally knew more people who had died recently than did respondents from the other ethnicities.

Hypotheses Comparing Age Groups

Most of the hypotheses we offered concerning expected within-study differences between age group participants in relation to death experience and attitudes were supported by our results. Our predictions that participants in the older age group would (a) think about death more frequently (Question #24), (b) have less death anxiety and more death acceptance (Questions #62 & #36), (c) have made more practical preparations for death (Questions #70–75 & #77), have encountered more deaths (Question #16), and (e) have attended more funerals (Question #21) proved accurate based on our study's findings. However, the hypothesis that older age group participants would be more likely to profess belief in an afterlife than would members of other age groups was not supported (Question #86).

Our predictions concerning participants in the young age group were, for the most part, supported. Hypotheses that participants in the 20–39 year age group would (a) have made fewer practical preparations for death (Questions #70–75 & #77), (b) have encountered fewer deaths (Question #16), (c) have attended fewer funerals (Question #21), and (d) have reported being more emotionally expressive about death (Questions #42 & #43) than would participants in other age groups proved correct based on the data. On only one of the seven questions related to practical preparations made for death were young age respondents not the least prepared (Question #72), and that item addressed donating one's body or body parts to medicine.

Hypotheses Comparing Gender Groups

Hypotheses related to gender differences were not consistently supported by the data. The prediction that men would have more liberal attitudes toward bereavement than would women was accurate (Questions #78–81), whereas the hypothesis that men would have made more practical preparations for death was supported only by their more frequent purchase of life insurance (Question #70). Women in the study indicated that they had made more practical preparations for death than had men on the other items (Questions #71–75, & #77).

We hypothesized that women would be more emotionally expressive about death, but our findings indicated that men and women responded similarly in this respect (Question #42). Finally, the prediction that women would have less restrictive attitudes toward the determination of pathological grief than would men was supported (Question #85)

9

Discussion

OVERVIEW OF INTERSTUDY AND INTRASTUDY VARIABILITY

The results of our study supported slightly more than half of the hypotheses we proposed. The hypotheses and their outcomes are as follows.

Hypothesis 1. Regarding comparison between Kalish and Reynolds's (1976) study and our study, we proposed that our analyses of results would indicate that participants in the present study would:

1. Think about death more frequently than those in the Kalish and Reynolds's study (indeterminant).
2. Report greater fear of death than participants in the earlier study (indeterminant).
3. Indicate a more liberal attitude toward death and dying than participants in Kalish and Reynolds's study (supported).

Hypothesis 2. Regarding comparisons between ethnic groups within the present study, we proposed that our analyses of results would indicate:

1. That Asian Americans (a) are more accepting of death (supported), (b) have a greater preference for cremation (supported), and (c) state that they would be the least emotionally expressive in grief (not supported) as compared with members of the other ethnic groups.
2. That Caucasian Americans are (a) more resistant to death (not supported), (b) have made more practical death preparations (not supported) and (c) report fewer mystical or paranormal experiences (not supported) compared with members of the other ethnic groups.

3. That Hispanic Americans hold more restrictive views toward mourning practices (not supported) and indicate they would be more emotionally expressive in response to grief compared with members of the other ethnic groups (not supported).
4. That African Americans have encountered death more frequently than have members of the other ethnic groups (supported).

Hypothesis 3. Regarding comparisons within the current study on gender differences irrespective of age and ethnicity, we proposed that our analyses of results would indicate:

1. That men have more liberal attitudes toward bereavement practices (supported) and have made more practical preparations for death (not supported) than have women.
2. That women anticipate expressing more open emotional response to grief than do men (not supported) and that women have less restrictive attitudes toward the determination of pathological grief than do men (supported).

Hypothesis 4. Regarding comparisons within this study on age differences irrespective of ethnicity and gender, we proposed that our analyses of results would indicate:

1. That participants in the 60-year-and-older age group would (a) have thought about death more frequently (supported), (b) have shown less death anxiety (supported) and more death acceptance (supported), (c) have made more practical preparations for death (supported), (d) have encountered more deaths (supported), (e) have attended more funerals (supported), and have professed belief in an afterlife (not supported) than have members of other age groups.
2. That members in the age group 20–39-year-old would (a) have made fewer practical preparations for death (supported), (b) have encountered fewer deaths (supported), (c) have attended fewer funerals (supported), and (d) have expected that they would be more emotionally expressive in response to grief (supported) than have members of other age groups.

Hypotheses Comparing Kalish and Reynolds's Study With the Present Study Results

Only one of the hypotheses concerning predicted differences between Kalish and Reynolds's (1976) study and this study was clearly supported, and the status of the other two hypotheses was unclear based on the data. Although attention to death has increased in American society over the past quarter of a century through the media, and the euthanasia, hospice, and death awareness movements, and because of the increased incidence and awareness of long-term debilitating and terminal diseases, participants in the current study indicated that they were less likely to think about their own death on a daily basis and more likely to think about death on a weekly or monthly basis as compared with those in the earlier study. Yet, the difference between the two studies in the percentage of participants who responded with "yearly/hardly ever" or "never" was not significant. The findings suggest that current study respondents often thought about death (weekly or monthly), but not as often as had those in Kalish and Reynolds's study (daily). Little clarity in this respect was gained by examining Lester and Becker's (1993) study comparing recent attitudes toward thinking about death with those in the 1930s and 1970s. Although Lester and Becker found that college students in 1991 thought about their own deaths more frequently than did college students in 1970 or 1935, the sample was differentially composed versus the current study (college students vs. adults in the community) and "frequently" was not defined by a time period (i.e., daily, weekly, or monthly). The present findings regarding the frequency with which persons thought about death might also be explained by the fact that at present, purposeful exposure to death is not a daily event in most persons lives. Most individuals in fact, are quite insulated from death on a routine basis. The fact that the present sample reported thinking about death on a weekly or monthly basis could thus simply reflect the success with which persons avoid thinking about their own death daily, and indeed might choose to do so less frequently because they are inundated by it daily via the media (see King & Hayslip, 2002), wherein such exposure likely heightens persons' fears about their own death.

It was also difficult to clearly determine if respondents in the present study were more overtly afraid of death than those in Kalish and Reynolds's (1976) study because a greater percentage of participants in our study indicated that they were "neither nor unafraid" to die or "depends" rather than indicating that they were afraid or that they were not afraid. In Kalish and Reynolds's study, 51% of the respondents stated that they were unafraid of death. In our study, 11.1% of the participants stated that they were unafraid, but 49.9% reported that they were neither afraid nor unafraid as compared with 19% of Kalish and Reynolds's participants. Although a 1991 Gallup Poll found that 75% of adults declared that they did not fear death (Kastenbaum, 2001), respondents in the present study tended to respond with more ambivalence, suggesting a more neutral or ambiguous attitude toward one's own death. These findings might be explained in the context of fear of death being best measured along a continuum, versus the dichotomous, forced choice nature of the survey questions utilized in both the Kalish and Reynolds and the present study. Such an approach may restrict the range of potential responses, attenuating the variability across persons. Likewise, the choice of the word "afraid" in this context may also dampen persons' willingness to report how they really felt, wherein an open-ended approach may yield richer information.

It is however, interesting to note that historical shifts in death attitudes pertaining to oneself are less reliably affected by historical change than are such attitudes that are about others' deaths or about "conditional" death, (i.e., if one were dying, would he/she wish to be told such).

Such ambivalence regarding the frequency of thoughts about death or such fears may therefore be understood in light of the more threatening nature of such questions, perhaps eliciting more anxiety about one's mortality, especially in light of the salience of cues about death in present culture, (i.e., the physician-assisted suicide and euthanasia controversies of recent years, and the AIDS epidemic). Being reminded of one's mortality via such events might at the minimum elicit more ambivalence about death and/or a more episodic response to one's mortality. Such speculation, of course, would be best tested via research examining the power of such stimuli to heighten one's defenses about one's own death, in part based on the assumption that persons in varying degrees need to defend themselves against the reality of their own deaths (see Kastenbaum, 2001).

The third hypothesis regarding comparison between the two studies, (that participants would have a more liberal attitude toward death and dying than those in the 1976 study) was supported. Participants in the current study were more likely to state that a friend should be told if he or she were going to die and were more likely to state that they would want to be told if they were dying. Respondents in the present study were also more liberal in indicating under what circumstances a person should be allowed to die than were those in the earlier study. The change toward wanting to be more informed and have more control over dying is probably influenced by societal changes that have increased death awareness and by the technological innovations that have provided greater control over the process of dying. Until recently, medicine seemed obsessed with using new technology and biomedical advances with the sole purpose of fighting death and prolonging life (Connelly, 1998). Dying became medicalized and removed from everyday life to the hospital and funeral home (Cloud, 2000). Depersonalization was part of the biomedical model (DeSpelder &

Strickland, 2002). As health care expenditures rapidly increased, and medical coverage was extended to more people, managed care companies rationed or limited the amount of health care a person could receive. Physicians often served as "gatekeepers" in providing access to treatments and procedures that serve the patient's welfare (DeSpelder & Strickland). However, society has begun to recognize the need to place limits on the unfettered technical progress in saving lives and natural death legislation has been enacted (Connelly). The natural death laws have promoted awareness of the holistic needs of the dying patient and given patients, rather than physicians, the primary responsibility for deciding when to refuse life-sustaining treatments. The desire to be informed that one is going to die is part of the individual's expectation of greater personal involvement in end-of-life decisions. The evolution toward "dying well" has also been reflected in the hospice movement and controversy over physician-assisted suicide.

Hypotheses Comparing Ethnic Groups

Hypotheses related to predictions on ethnic differences were frequently unsupported by the data. It was correctly anticipated that Asian Americans would indicate more acceptance of death and would prefer cremation for body disposal more frequently than participants in the other ethnic groups in this study. However, the hypothesis that Asian Americans would be the least emotionally expressive in grief was not supported. In their study, Kalish and Reynolds (1976) found that the Japanese Americans were the most likely to state that they would try very hard to control their emotions in public. Yet, in the current study, Asian American participants indicated that they would be the least likely, to do so, although the percentages were not significantly different. The contrast between this study and the earlier one may be due to the more varied composition of Asian American participants in the current study as compared with the exclusively Japanese sample used by Kalish and Reynolds or may be due to changes over time concerning the acceptable levels of public emotional expression.

None of the three suggested hypotheses concerning the death attitudes of Caucasian Americans was supported. Although Caucasian Americans in the earlier study were the most likely of the ethnic groups to state that they would fight death actively, those in the current study more frequently responded with "depends" (41.5%) than stating that they would accept (35%) or actively fight death (24%). "Depends" was also a frequent response of the other ethnic group members, suggesting that participants in the present study were more interested in considering the situation in relation to a number of factors.

The prediction that Caucasian Americans would have made more practical preparations for death than participants in other ethnic groups was based on the earlier findings of Kalish and Reynolds. In the 1976 study, the researchers found that, with the exception of purchasing life insurance, Caucasian Americans were the most likely to (a) have made a will, (b) have arranged to donate their body parts to medicine, (c) have made funeral arrangements, (d) have talked seriously with someone about experiencing death, and (e) have arranged for someone to handle their affairs. In our study, Caucasian Americans were the most likely to (a) have made a will, (b) have arranged to donate their body or body parts to medicine, and (c) have arranged for someone to handle their affairs, but African and Hispanic Americans were more likely to have made other practical death preparations.

The hypothesis that Caucasian Americans would report fewer mystical or paranormal experiences than participants from other ethnic groups was also refuted. In the earlier study, Kalish and Reynolds found that African Americans (55%) and Mexican Americans (54%) were more likely to have experienced the presence of someone after he or she had died, whereas Caucasian and Asian Americans were less likely to have done so (38% & 29%, respectively). Nevertheless, in the present study, Caucasian Americans were the most likely to have reported such mystical or paranormal experiences (Cau.A., 58.2%; Afr.A., 55.7%; His.A., 40.3%, Asn.A., 47.3%).

Neither of the hypotheses regarding Hispanic Americans was supported. Even though Kalish and Reynolds found that Mexican and Japanese Americans held the most conservative mourning attitudes, Hispanic Americans in the current study were generally not more conservative than other ethnic groups. We also hypothesized that Hispanic Americans would indicate that they would be more emotionally expressive in response to grief, as was found in the 1976 study; however, results of the current study found that differences between the ethnic groups were not statistically significant.

The hypothesis regarding African Americans was supported. African Americans indicated that they personally knew more people who had died in the previous 2 years than did respondents from the other ethnic groups. Kalish and Reynolds's (1976) findings were similar. The results from both studies corresponded with the findings of Rogers et al.'s (1996) study that compared ethnic differences in mortality rates in the United States. On the basis of statistics from the National Health Interview Survey–National Death Index, Rogers et al. found that African Americans had the highest mortality rates, which likely explains why African Americans personally knew the most people who had died.

In that these data are purely descriptive, it might be tempting to guess about the reasons for the predominant nonsupport of the hypotheses. In this respect, it may be that there is indeed more variability within the ethnic groups studied in the present study and that of Kalish and Reynolds than one might otherwise assume. Indeed, it might be argued that except for mourning practices, when one considers matters regarding one's own death as well as the deaths of others, individual life histories and the quality of their relationships with others who have yet to die, or have since died are paramount. Clearly, these data suggest that we have a great deal more to learn about the intersection of individual and ethnicity-related factors in understanding persons' attitudes toward death, dying, and bereavement.

It is interesting to note that there is more similarity across studies regarding predictions about death attitudes with age, versus those for example, regarding gender or ethnicity. This may reflect the universally differential experience that younger and older adults continue to have regarding death and dying. It therefore appears that death issues, fairly or not, are nevertheless perceived as matters for the most part that pertain to older persons. Older adults clearly have more experience with death than do younger adults, and hold different attitudes toward grief, bereavement and mourning than do younger adults, whose knowledge and experience with death are generally more limited, and whose experiences with death are grounded in their upbringing (Hayslip, Servaty & Guarnaccia, 1999). Unfortunately, the present data also reinforce (at least at the attitudinal level) the implicit linking of age and death (see Kastenbaum, 1978), often with dehumanizing consequences for older persons. Thus, we have "a ways to go" regarding the uncoupling of perceptions linking the salience or appropriateness of death with increased chronological age.

Hypothesis Comparing Gender Groups

Regarding comparison of genders, we hypothesized that men would have more liberal attitudes toward bereavement practices than would women, a hypothesis which was supported by the data. Four questions addressed accepted mourning behavior, and men's responses were more liberal on three of the items (appropriate time to wear black, return to work, and begin dating). Male responses concerning the acceptable period before remarrying also tended to be more liberal, but the difference was not statistically significant. Kalish and Reynolds (1976) also found that men tended to have less conservative views than women toward bereavement practices.

The hypothesis that more men than women would have made practical preparations for death was not supported. In fact, a larger percentage of women than men in the current study had made arrangements to donate their bodies or body parts to medicine and arranged for others to handle their affairs. These results are in contrast to those of Kalish and Reynolds (1976) who found that male participants in their study had made more practical preparations for death than had women. The increase in women's preparations for death may be reflective of the increased number of women with careers as well as the increased divorce rate and number of single parent households since the 1970s when Kalish and Reynolds's data were collected.

The hypothesis that a larger percentage of women than men would anticipate that they would publicly express emotions of grief was not supported. Results of the present study revealed that men and women responded similarly concerning efforts to control emotions in public. In the 1976 study, more men than women stated that they would try very hard to control the way they showed their emotions in public (earlier, men: 80%, women: 70%; current, men: 64.1%, women: 65.8%). The lack of difference in control of emotional expression between genders is likely due to the greater acceptance of emotional expression in men in today's culture.

The final hypothesis (that women would have less restrictive attitudes toward the determination of pathological grief) was supported by the data. Results indicated that women were more likely than men to feel that normal grieving may occur for as long as 6 or more months or to respond with "other." These findings are similar to those of the earlier study except that a larger percentage of the respondents in the current study indicated "other."

In considering these gender differences, it is relevant to consider the fact that women most likely (at present) still outlive men, and thus, issues of grief and bereavement are likely to be most relevant to women, and thus, we know considerably less about men's attitudes toward such matters. Thus, men's relative liberality may reflect a lack of experience with issues pertaining to grief and bereavement. Likewise, women are more likely to have cared for an ailing spouse before his death, and thus, will have been more likely to have funeral arrangements and interacted with others in the context of their anticipation and subsequent experience with widowhood. They may be more conservative having "been there" emotionally, and therefore come to value the importance of tradition and ritual in dealing with very painful experiences. It is also possible that women in these studies are simply more generally conservative in their response styles than are men. On the other hand, the lack of gender differences in many cases in the present study may reflect a less gendered orientation toward grief and bereavement, borne of more liberal times regarding men's and women's roles.

Hypotheses Comparing Age Groups

Of the eleven hypotheses concerning differences among age groups, ten were supported. Results from the current study revealed that participants aged 60 years and older had more experience with death and were more likely to be prepared for death emotionally and practically than were participants aged 20 to 39 years. Those in the older age group (a) had encountered more deaths, (b) had attended more funerals, (c) had thought more frequently about death, had shown less overt death anxiety, (e) had shown more death acceptance, and (f) had made more practical preparations for death. Kalish and Reynolds found similar results in the 1970s.

One hypothesis, that participants in the older age group would be more likely to profess belief in an afterlife than would members of other age groups, was not supported. In fact, data revealed that participants in the young age group were the most likely to believe that they would live on in some form after death, but the difference was not statistically significant. In the 1976 study, significantly more respondents in the older age group expressed belief in an afterlife than did those in the other age groups. However, the disparity between the findings in the two studies may be influenced by sample bias in the present study. We recruited many of the older age respondents in the current study from the Senior Citizens of Greater Dallas, a nonreligious organization, whereas we recruited many of the participants in the younger group through a variety of churches.

The four hypotheses concerning participants in the young age group were also supported. As predicted, those who were in the 20–39 year-old group (a) had encountered fewer deaths, (b) had attended fewer funerals, and (c) had made fewer practical preparations for death than had those in the other age groups. The young respondents related that they were also less likely to try very hard to control grief-related emotions in public. Kalish and Reynolds (1976) reported similar findings.

Differences Between the Two Studies Concerning Experience With Death

Two main differences emerged when the results of the present study were contrasted with those of Kalish and Reynolds concerning experience with death. Participants in this study were less likely to have personally known as many persons who had died in the previous 2 years than were participants in the earlier study. This trend was particularly applicable to respondents who were 20 to 39 years of age. The decrease in personal exposure to death may be due to a number of factors, including increased life expectancy and lower mortality rates, greater geographic mobility that has tended to separate and isolate family groups, and the impact of medical technology that has prompted the displacement of death from the home to the hospital or nursing home (DeSpelder & Strickland, 2002). Currently three-fourths of Americans die in medical institutions (Cloud, 2000). Therefore, people in today's society are more likely to have gained their death lessons from television, cinema, newspapers, and the arts rather than from direct exposure to death (Keal, 1989; King & Hayslip, 2002). Consequently, contact with death has become secondhand, and knowledge of death has become filtered by intermediaries and social interpreters.

Nonetheless, comparison between the studies revealed that participants in the current study were more likely to have visited or talked with persons who were dying than were those in the 1976 study. The contrast with the earlier study was most notable for Caucasian and African Americans. The greater contact with dying persons likely reflects increased cultural acceptance of dying persons (Lester, 1992). Lester suggested that contemporary Americans may have become more tolerant of death and dying because of increased awareness of death through media concerning the AIDS epidemic and problems associated with long-term diseases, such as cancer and Alzheimer's disease. An explanation for the greater likelihood of Caucasian and African Americans to have had contact with dying persons is that a larger percentage of Caucasian and African Americans, as compared with Hispanic and Asian Americans, indicated that they personally knew several persons who had died recently, and we speculate that they may have visited with those who died.

Another explanation for this finding is that of sampling bias. A larger percentage of Caucasian and African Americans participants in the present study were in the older age group as compared with the percentage of Hispanic and Asian American participants in the 60-years-and-older group, and results showed that older people personally knew more people who had died in the previous 2 years.

Differences Between the Two Studies Concerning Attitudes Toward One's Own Death, Dying, and Afterlife

An examination of differences between the findings of the present study and those of Kalish and Reynolds' (1976) study revealed a number of differences. As addressed previously in the comparison between

our study and that of 1976, there has been a shift to a more liberal attitude toward death and dying, as evidenced in the results of the present
study. A larger percentage of participants in the current study indicated that they wanted to be informed if they were dying, and fewer
participants related that they would accept death peacefully than had
those in the 1976 study. The increased desire to know about one's
imminent mortality may be considered as a way of seeking greater control of death, and consequently, such findings express a more active
and less passive stance toward death. People today expect physicians
and health care workers to provide more information about their
health status and expect to be more actively involved in decisions
related to their health care (DeSpelder & Strickland, 2002). Present
study respondents were more likely to respond with "depends" rather
than accepting dying. This trend was especially true for Caucasian and
Hispanic Americans, as well as participants in the younger age group.
The contingency, or depends, response indicates a desire to consider
the context or broader implications of the situation before making a
decision and suggests a more flexible response.

As discussed earlier, participants in the present study were less likely
to think about their own deaths on a daily basis than were participants
in the 1976 study and were more likely to think about death on a
weekly or monthly basis. Present study participants were also less likely
to acknowledge overt fear of death; rather, current participants tended
to respond that they were neither afraid nor unafraid of death or
depends. However, a smaller percentage of the respondents in this
study related that they never dreamed about their own death. One
might speculate that the reduced frequency in thoughts of death and
diminished acknowledgement of death fear are related to the current
study participants' lower levels of direct death experience. The out-
come of limited direct experience with death may be decreased overt
death anxiety, reinforcing its denial. The indication that present study
participants are more likely to dream about their own death than were
those in the earlier study may connote increased covert or unconscious
death anxiety (see Hayslip, Guarnaccia, Radika, & Servaty, 2002).

Differences emerged between the studies in the relative status of the
importance of reasons for not wanting to die. Participants in the current study versus the earlier study were more likely to indicate that no
longer being able to care for dependents, concern about the grief that
their deaths would cause friends and relatives, and concern about what
might happen to them when they died were important or very important considerations. The shift from the earlier study to the current
study was greatest among African Americans. Hispanic Americans in
this study were also particularly concerned about the grief that their

death would cause to friends and relatives. These findings suggest that relationships with others, especially family members, have become a more important focus for contemporary north Texas residents than they were for Los Angeles residents in the 1970s. The movement toward greater focus on the family among African Americans may be a response to counteracting the high percentage of single parent homes found in the African American culture. For example, the Million Man March on Washington, DC, symbolized the movement in the African American community to strengthen family ties.

Another area suggesting a trend toward greater focus on family and relationships was found in the contrast between the two studies in the way respondents stated that they would choose to spend their last 6 months of life if told they were terminally ill. A larger percentage of participants in the present study indicated that they would spend their final months showing concern for others than had participants in Kalish and Reynolds's (1976) study. The shift to spending more time with others was greatest for Caucasian and African Americans, older age group respondents, and men. Current study participants were less likely to indicate that they would withdraw (especially older aged participants), respond with a marked change of behavior, or make no change in behavior than had participants in the previous study. The increased importance of spending time with one's family during the final 6 months of life is reflected by the growth of the Hospice Movement. Hospice programs are intended to provide care, comfort, and a sense of security for terminally ill people and their families (Kastenbaum, 2001). The first hospice program was established in the United States in 1974, and there are now more than 3000 hospice programs in operation in the United States (National Hospice Foundation, 2004). Hospice care functions to provide an alternative to an isolated, depersonalized, technological death by centering care around the needs and wishes of the dying person and family. With hospice, family members and volunteers become part of the care-giving system.

Another area of significant change from the earlier study was in preparations for death. Participants in this study, particularly middle-aged and women participants, were more likely to have made arrangements to donate their bodies or body parts to medicine than were those in the earlier study. This increase in body and body part donation is likely due to awareness concerning advances in technology, which make possible the use of organ transplants and biological research resulting in significant medical breakthroughs. Current participants were more likely to have talked seriously with others about their future deaths as compared with those in the 1976 study, perhaps indicating a greater awareness of death through its prevalent coverage

in the media and because of the increased focus on family relationships posited earlier. Present study respondents were also more likely
to feel "indifferent" about having their bodies embalmed or autopsied
at death. The indifference was especially true for Asian Americans.
Asian Americans in the current study seemed more detached or indifferent to death than were the Japanese in the 1976 study. The difference may be due to the more diverse background of this study's group
of Asian participants as compared with the specifically Japanese ethnic
group in Kalish and Reynolds's (1976) study. The difference between
the two studies in the percentage of participants who had made funeral
arrangements or paid for a cemetery plot was not significant.

In addition, a larger percentage of participants in the present study
indicated that they preferred to die at home. This finding corresponds with the results of a recent poll by Time/CNN (as cited in
Cloud, 2000). According to the poll, 7 out of 10 Americans stated
that they want to die at home (Cloud, 2000). The preference for
dying at home is evident in the growth of hospice programs, as was
discussed earlier.

Another area of change concerned belief in an afterlife. A greater
percentage of participants in this study indicated that they believed
they would live on in some form after death than did those in the previous study. The shift from the earlier study was greatest for Hispanic
Americans and those in the young and middle-aged groups. Whereas
Kalish and Reynolds found that participants in the older age group
were the most likely to profess belief in an afterlife, results from the
current study indicated no statistically significant differences between
ethnic, age, or gender groups. In a 1993 study, Harley and Firebaugh
examined trends over the previous 2 decades in Americans' beliefs in
the existence of an afterlife and found no evidence that belief in an
afterlife increased notably with age. The increased percentage of
those professing belief in an afterlife among participants in the present study may reflect regional and time differences between a more
liberal attitude of residents in California in the 1970s and a more conservative approach of residents in north Texas (the "Bible Belt") in
1999–2000.

In a related vein, the fact that beliefs in the afterlife and in reincar-
nation are more common in the president study perhaps reflects a
greater association between dying and the presence of others at home,
and especially the attention given to near death and/or out-of-body
experiences by the media. Likewise, greater direct experience with
dying persons and more ambivalence about one's own dying could eas-
ily elicit concerns about what might happen after one dies. Clearly,
these issues reflect a less traditional orientation over time toward what

might lie beyond death, necessarily accompanied by uncertainty and even curiosity about what death is and when persons really die, and a more conflicted attitude about communicating with others about dying.

Finally, results indicated a trend toward less restriction of emotions in response to grief. Current study respondents indicated that they would expend less effort to control their emotions in public than had participants in the 1976 study. As mentioned earlier, there has been a shift in cultural acceptance of showing emotion in public (e.g., the tears shed publicly by Presidents Clinton and George W. Bush).

Differences Between the Two Studies Concerning Attitudes Toward the Dying, Death, or Grief of Someone Else

Comparison of the present study with that of Kalish and Reynolds's study suggests three areas of change. Participants in the current study were more likely to indicate that persons should be told when they are dying. The shift toward a person's right to be informed was greatest among Hispanic Americans and older age group participants as contrasted with their respective groups in the 1976 study. The finding corresponds with the larger percentage of participants in this study who stated that they would want to be informed if they were dying. These findings reflect the changes that have occurred regarding end-of-life decision making. The responsibility for decisions concerning those who were dying was previously in the hands of physicians and the health care system; however, now there is more opportunity for patients and their families to participate in decision making (Kastenbaum, 2001). Indeed, the right-to-die movement, the prevalence of illnesses such as AIDS or Alzheimer's disease, and debates about physician-assisted suicide have all fueled such concerns in recent years.

Examination of the differences between the two studies also revealed changes in attitudes concerning the comparative extent of tragedy of different kinds of death. Participants in the present study, especially those who were African or Hispanic American, were more likely to indicate that suicidal deaths were the most tragic. Current study participants were less likely than those in the 1976 study to state that deaths in war were the most tragic, particularly among African and Hispanic Americans, women, and young age group respondents. The reduction in the belief that deaths in war were most tragic is apt to be due to the decreased number of deaths among Americans that have occurred in wars in the last 25 to 30 years. In contrast, the suicide rate in the United States has increased to become the ninth most common cause of death, according to national data from 1996 (Kastenbaum, 2001). Regarding the age of the deceased, fewer participants in the present study related that deaths of young adults were most tragic and more indicated "depends" when compared with respondents in Kalish and Reynolds's study. In a similar way, current study participants were more likely than those in the earlier study to respond with "depends" concerning the age at which death is least tragic. There was a frequent tendency among participants in the present study to choose the "depends" response on several items in the questionnaire and suggests a broader consideration of contextual factors (e.g., whether a death was due to illness, suicide, accidental, or via war or homicide) than was exhibited by participants in the 1976 study.

Another area of movement between the two studies concerned attitudes toward bereavement practices. Comparison of responses between the two studies revealed additional examples of the inclination of participants in this study to consider attitudes from a relative viewpoint, considering the context of the situation. Participants in the current study were more likely than those in the earlier study to respond with "depends" regarding the appropriate period for remarriage, wearing black, returning to one's place of employment, and dating. The predilection of our study's participants to regard situations in light of a contextual viewpoint was evident in their responses to numerous items, and contrasts with the more "black or white," "yes or no," or concrete thinking reflected by the participants in the 1976 study and may suggest a cultural shift to greater flexibility of thinking regarding matters pertaining to death and dying. With regard to some grieving persons, this is likely to ease their self or other-imposed isolation, and such shifts will hopefully facilitate such persons' asking for help when they indeed need it most, rather than being constrained by others' expectations regarding what is and is not appropriate.

Differences Within the Present Study Concerning Experience With Death

Differences between ethnic groups. As discussed earlier, African Americans in the present study had the most experience with death, which corresponds with the results of Kalish and Reynolds's (1976) study. However, Hispanic American participants in our study had the least experience with death, which differed from the results in the 1976 study. Kalish and Reynolds's results indicated that Caucasian Americans in their study personally knew the fewest number of persons who had died. In 1996, Rogers et al. found that Asians had the lowest mortality rate of the four ethnic groups in the United States. Consequently, Asians would be expected to have the least experience with death, not Hispanic Americans. An explanation for the relatively low death experience of Hispanic Americans in the current study may be due to the large percentage of Hispanic Americans in this study who were in the young age group (131 out of 205 persons, or 63.9%). Study results revealed that those in the 20–39-year-old age group had the least experience with death; thus, the young age of the majority of Hispanic American participants likely influenced the comparison between ethnic groups concerning death experience.

Another significant difference among ethnic groups was found regarding which groups were more likely to have visited or talked with persons who were dying. Results revealed that Caucasian and African Americans were more likely to have visited with dying persons than were Hispanic or Asian Americans. Kalish and Reynolds (1976) found little difference between Caucasian, African, and Mexican Americans in their frequency of visitation. Again, the difference indicated in the current study may be due to a confounding of ethnicity with age. In this study, there were a greater percentage of participants in the older age group who were Caucasian (40.2%) and African American (41%) than were Hispanic (12.7%) or Asian American (22.8%). Furthermore, comparison of this study's findings regarding the effects of age indicated that those in the older age group were more likely to have visited the dying than were those in the other age groups.

Differences between age groups. Comparison of differences between age groups in this study indicated that participants in the 20–39-year-old age group had the least experience with death, and those in the 60-years-and-older group had the most experience with death. Kalish and Reynolds (1976) found similar results in the 1970s. In addition, older respondents in the present study were the most likely to have visited persons who were dying, and participants from the young age group were least likely to have visited or talked with the dying. This finding also corresponds with those of the earlier study. Another significant result concerned the mystical or paranormal experience of feeling the presence of someone after he or she had died. Participants in the older age group were more likely to report that they had had such experiences than were those in the other age groups. Kalish and Reynolds found similar results, but the differences were not statistically significant.

There were no notable gender differences within the current study related to experience with death.

Differences Concerning Attitudes Toward One's Own Death, Dying, and Afterlife

Differences between ethnic groups. In the current study, Caucasian Americans were the most likely of the studied ethnic groups (a) to indicate that they would want to be informed if they were dying, (b) to have actually known of someone who was dying about whom such a decision was made, and (c) to have told someone that he or she was about to die. Kalish and Reynolds found a similar desire to know rather than be protected from the facts among Caucasian Americans in their study. When asked if they would accept death or actively fight it, Caucasian American participants were the most likely to respond with "depends." Caucasian Americans were also the most likely to state that they were "neither afraid nor unafraid" of dying as compared with respondents in the other ethnic groups. Regarding how they would spend the last 6 months of their lives if told that they had a terminal disease, Caucasian Americans in the current study were the most likely to relate that they would spend time showing concern for others. Finally, Caucasian Americans were also the most likely to have made arrangements to donate their bodies or body parts to medicine.

African Americans in the present study indicated that they had made more practical applications for death than had participants in the other ethnic groups. African Americans were the most likely (a) to have purchased life insurance, (b) to have made funeral arrangements, and (c) to have purchased cemetery plots. African American respondents in the 1976 study were not as well prepared. Although the majority of participants from each of the ethnic groups related that they preferred to die at home, more African Americans indicated that they wanted to die in the hospital than did participants from other ethnicities. African Americans were also the most likely to chose burial for the disposal of their bodies at death. Study participants who were African and Asian Americans were the most likely to state that they would accept death peacefully.

Hispanic American respondents in this study were the most likely to state that they would fight death actively; however, the finding may be confounded by the large percentage of Hispanic Americans who were in the young age group because members of the younger age group were also the most likely to indicate that they would fight death actively. Nonetheless, Kalish and Reynolds also found that Mexican Americans were the most likely to state that they would fight death actively. A characteristic quality of the Hispanic American culture is the focus on the family and extended family relationships as resources for support and assistance (Shapiro, 1995). The assistance customarily includes involving others, particularly immediate kin, in major decisions concerning the individual's well-being, such as the advisability of surgery, hospitalization, or referral to hospice care (Salcido, 1990). Thus, a pattern of group consultation often exists that provides the individual with support and direction in fighting death.

Kalish and Reynolds also related that the Mexican American participants in their study tended to acknowledge more conscious death anxiety than did participants from other ethnic groups. The present study found similar results. Hispanic Americans in the current study were the most likely to indicate that they were afraid to die. This finding was probably not confounded by age of the respondents because an almost equal percentage of participants who were middle-aged also stated that they were afraid of dying. As found in the 1976 study, Hispanic Americans in this study were the most likely to report that they experienced the unexplainable feeling that they were about to die. Again, the finding was not likely due to age because the difference between groups by age was not statistically significant. In addition, Hispanic Americans were the most likely of the ethnic group participants to indicate that being uncertain about what might happen to them after they died was an important or very important reason for not wanting to die.

Asian American participants in the current study were the most likely to state that they never dreamed about dying when compared with other ethnic group participants. Asian Americans were also the most likely to have responded with "not important" to a number of reasons for not wanting to die, including fear of what might happen to their bodies after death, fear of what might happen to them, that they could no longer have any experiences, that all of their projects and plans would come to an end, that the process of death might be painful, and that their deaths would cause grief to friends and relatives. Asian Americans in the present study were also more likely than respondents of other ethnic groups to indicate indifference regarding autopsy and embalming procedures and the most likely to relate that they preferred cremation for disposal of their bodies. Asian and African American participants were the most likely to state that they would accept death peacefully. However, Asian Americans indicated that they wanted to be informed about their own deaths. Like Caucasian Americans, almost 90% of Asian Americans asserted that they wanted to be told if they were dying. Asian Americans seemed to exhibit an attitude of neutrality or indifference toward death, yet they wanted to be informed of their health status.

Differences between age groups. Comparison of within-study differences between age groups revealed similar findings to those of Kalish and Reynolds (1976) in that the greatest differences were between the young and older age groups. With regard to attitudes toward their own death, dying, and afterlife, participants in the 20–39-year-old group were the least likely to have thought about their own deaths or to have made practical arrangements for death and were the most likely to state that they would fight death actively.

Older age participants in the current study were the most likely to state that they would accept death peacefully and to have made practical preparations for death. The 1976 study reported the same findings. Current study participants aged 60 years and older were also more likely to state that they were "neither afraid nor unafraid" of death than were respondents from other age groups. This finding is in accordance with the results of a study by Gesser, Wong, and Reker (1987) who found that general fear of death and dying declined in old age. Older age participants in our study were also the most likely to indicate that they never dreamed about their own deaths. The findings may suggest a greater readiness for death by the older than by the younger age participants.

Differences between gender groups. There were few significant differences between gender groups in the current study related to attitudes toward their own deaths and dying. More men than women indicated that the fear of dying being painful was not an important concern for them. Men also tended to express more indifference about being autopsied or embalmed at their deaths than did women. Additionally, results revealed that a larger percentage of women than men had made arrangements to donate their bodies or body parts to medicine. The results may indicate that women have greater concern with respect to what happens to their bodies after death than do men.

Differences Concerning Attitudes Toward the Dying, Death, or Grief of Someone Else

Differences between ethnic groups. In regards to attitudes toward the dying, death, or grief of others by participants within the present study, Caucasian Americans were the most likely to state that others should be told if they are going to die, and Caucasian and Asian Americans were the most likely to state that they had told someone that he or she was about to die. When asked to compare the relative tragedy of different kinds of death, Caucasian Americans were more likely of feel that homicidal deaths and the deaths of children were most tragic. Caucasian Americans in our study also were the most likely to indicate that it was unimportant to wait before a bereaved spouse should stop wearing black for mourning.

African American participants within the study were the most likely to respond with "depends" when asked at what age death is most tragic. African and Hispanic Americans related that suicidal deaths were the most tragic type of death.

Respondents belonging to the Hispanic American ethnic group were the least likely to state that a friend should be told if he or she was about to die. Kalish and Reynolds (1976) similarly found Mexican Americans to be the most protective about informing others of their dying. Hispanic and Asian Americans indicated that they believed the death of a young adult to be the most tragic. With regard to mourning behavior, Hispanics were the most likely to state that a bereaved spouse should wait a year or more before beginning to date, but were also the most likely to relate that it was unimportant for the bereaved to wait before returning to work. The latter finding may be influenced by the large percentage of Hispanic Americans in the young age group. Kalish and Reynolds reported that Mexican Americans in their study were consistently more likely to suggest longer mourning periods prior to remarriage, dating, and returning to work, as well as being the least likely to feel that waiting was unimportant.

The Asian American participants in our study were the most likely to feel that accidental deaths were the most tragic. Asian Americans also indicated some conservative attitudes toward appropriate mourning behavior. They were more likely than participants in other ethnic groups to relate that a bereaved spouse should never remarry, but Asian Americans were also the most likely to respond with "depends" or "other" concerning the appropriate time for the bereaved to wait before dating.

Differences between age groups. There were only a few significant differences between the age groups regarding attitudes toward the death, dying, or grief of others. Participants in the young age group indicated that an infant's death and a child's death were the most tragic. The death of a child is complex because the deaths of babies and children are not expected in Western society. Thus, the death seems to represent some failure of family or society, as well as a loss of hope for the future (Raphael, 1995, p. 261). A child's death is accompanied by the belief "that it should not have happened" and tends to evoke intense bereavement and a wide range of reactions (Raphael, p. 262). Furthermore, a child's death may affect the parent's worldview and raise questions concerning the parent's core assumptions about the nature and purpose of life (Kastenbaum, 2001). Young age respondents were also more likely than those of other age groups within the study to indicate that a bereaved spouse should wait 1 year or more before dating; however, this finding is confounded by the large percentage of Hispanic Americans within the young age group.

Middle-aged respondents were the most likely to believe that a child's death was the most tragic. This may reflect the assumption that they will likely die before their children, who would most likely be adolescents or young adults. In this context the death of a child is especially non-normative. Participants who were in the 40–59-year-old age group were also the most likely to indicate that it was unimportant for a bereaved spouse to wait before returning to work. The latter finding was possibly influenced by the established work positions of many of the middle-aged who may be very involved in their careers.

Those in the 60-years-and-older group were the most likely to respond with "depends" when asked if a friend should be informed if he or she were about to die. Considering which type of death seemed the most tragic, older participants were equally likely to respond with a child's death or "depends." Finally, older aged participants tended to respond with "depends" to when it was appropriate for a bereaved spouse to remarry or return to work. The tendency to respond with "depends" implies a predilection among those in the older age group to consider the salience of the immediate situation in relationship to the wider context in which death occurs and suggests more flexibility in this respect.

Differences between gender groups. Among the limited number of gender differences found within the current study, it was revealed that women were more likely than men to respond with "depends" concerning whether to inform others that they were about to die. It was also found that men were more likely than women to state that it was unimportant to wait before a bereaved spouse returned to his or her place of employment, whereas women were more likely to indicate that the bereaved should wait 1 month before returning to work.

IMPLICATIONS OF THESE FINDINGS

Experience With Death and Death Anxiety

What do these findings mean? What do they tell us about cultural and/or historical shifts in our responses to death? Most important, as persons who are at once grievers and helpers, and as persons who will ultimately die, how can we best learn from them?

Although fewer participants in the present study indicated that they personally knew as many people who had died in the previous 2 years as those in Kalish and Reynolds's study, direct experience with death will likely increase in the future. With the aging of the Baby Boomers, the number of deaths will, probabilistically speaking, be more likely to escalate, and persons will therefore have more direct experience with death. Furthermore, because of the recent (September 11, 2001) tragedy of the terrorism of the New York City Twin Towers and Washington Pentagon buildings, death awareness and death fear has likely increased among Americans and many others in the world. Indeed, the media has focused on the grief and anxiety associated with the terrorist acts as well as on the potential of further terrorism and war. The tragedy of the situation and future uncertainty create an atmosphere that predisposes the populace to question life's predictability, a central thesis in Terror Management Theory's attempt to understand death anxiety (Pyszczynski et al., 2003). Thus a probable consequence of the current environment is an increased level of overt death anxiety. An important response to such increased anxiety is the encouragement of persons to discuss and address their fears and concerns. Mental health workers and others benefit from knowledge about normal responses of grief and fear to help those who are having difficulties working through their feelings as well as to recognize those who need professional help. That persons might be more comfortable in tolerating the expression of such feelings might enhance the likelihood of their asking for help to cope with loss.

Informing Dying Persons and Acceptance of Death

The preference for being informed that one is dying suggests that health care workers and family members of the dying should seriously consider discussing prognoses and health care options with dying persons. This finding is underscored by the failure of Project SUPPORT (see Enck, 2003) to enhance the quality of dying persons' lives by improving the communication skills of physicians. Although there was some variation between cultural groups in the percentage of persons who stated that they would want to be told if they were going to die, over 75% of the participants in each ethnic group indicated preference for knowledge about one's own dying. With the increased technological developments and pharmaceutical advancements, more options for treatment are now available. However, managed care restrictions and considerations of quality of life are also important considerations. The trend toward more active involvement in dying, as well as the shift toward considering situations in light of the context, indicate the need for more open discussion of medical and health conditions with the dying and their families.

Importance of Relationships With Others and Practical Preparations for Death

Results from the current study revealed the importance of relationships with family and friends to study participants. These findings emphasize the salience of including family members in working with and in planning for those who are dying, as dying for many persons is still an isolating, depersonalizing experience. When possible, hospital personnel should facilitate inclusion of family members during treatments and periods of hospitalization when requested by dying patients. In addition, development of further social services and financial support to enable dying persons to die at home is needed. Indeed, it may be necessary that insurance companies will need to reimburse clients for more kinds of palliative care. Moreover, the use of Medicare's hospice benefit needs to be clarified and broadened, and more general end-of-life health insurance plans need to become available (Cloud, 2000). Greater provision of accessible assistance for making practical preparations for death would also help family members and the dying contend with arrangements for death. Indeed, increased awareness and use of advanced directives would better ensure that the wishes of dying persons are fulfilled.

Mourning Practices and Contextualism

Our study's findings indicated that respondents tended to approach bereavement practices, as well as a number of issues related to death and dying, from a relativistic viewpoint. Participants in the present study were likely to respond with "depends" to questions regarding appropriate time before a bereaved spouse should remarry, date, return to work, or cease wearing black for mourning. The inclination to regard grieving persons' situations based on their context suggests that flexibility is essential in working with persons concerning issues of death, dying, and bereavement. Preconceptions of appropriate behavior are often not applicable in contemporary situations concerning death and dying. Counselors, health workers, and others also need to employ a contextual vantage point in working with dying and bereaved persons and in death-related issues. This shift toward more flexibility regarding grief and bereavement practices suggests that grieving, generally speaking is less disenfranchised (Doka, 1989), and therefore reflects greater attention to the individual needs of grieving persons.

IMPLICATIONS FOR PRACTITIONERS

Perhaps the most sweeping implication of our findings for grief counselors, death educators, for those professionals in the funeral industry, and for professionals and family members making end-of-life decisions is to recognize the tremendous importance of cultural change and/or cohort effects in shaping attitudes toward death, dying, and bereavement.

For this reason, persons who are born at different historical times are not likely to share similar values, attitudes, behaviors, or feelings about a variety of issues relating to beliefs about the afterlife, the acceptability of suicide, funeral preparations, fears about death and dying, personal experience with dying persons, orientation toward the deaths of others, and expectations regarding what constitutes appropriate grieving behavior. Recognizing these differences, and most important, not allowing them to impede communication (especially when such communication involves persons from different birth cohorts) empowers professionals in recognizing and respecting the uniqueness of individuals who are faced with the necessity of making life-changing and emotionally heart-wrenching decisions.

Clearly, individuals change as they age in terms of such values (see Hayslip & Hansson, 2003), but cultures change as well (see Aries, 1981; Moore & Williamson, 2003; Wood & Williamson, 2003). These cultural changes may or may not complement the individual life changes persons experience, creating choices and difficulties for counselors, death educators, physicians, hospice personnel, funeral directors, and patient advocates in understanding patients' and families' wishes regarding such issues as physician-assisted suicide, euthanasia, funeral arrangements, and end-of-life care. Moreover, such professionals' values may differ from those of their patients as a function of differences between persons of different genders, ethnicities, and age. In many respects, professionals play out roles that represent dominant cultural values, and such persons must reconcile conflicts between such values and those of not only their patients, but also with those that they hold personally. Thus, historical change forces professionals to redefine their roles as players in our culture's death system.

While these findings should reflect some cautions in interpreting their worth (see below), they nevertheless challenge us at many levels to reflect upon our own mortality as well as that of others.

With regard to the former cautions, not only might the data in Table 5.1 regarding differences across the two studies in sample composition reflect cultural shifts in the extent to which persons volunteer for survey research, but such sampling differences need to be given serious consideration in interpreting the apparent cultural shifts in attitudes toward death, dying, and bereavement found here (see Table 7.1), as well as interstudy differences in the impact of ethnicity, age and gender on such attitudes.

More generally speaking, regarding the latter challenges, the above discussed conflict between societal change and individuals' timing of life experiences, their personal values, and the role-specific obligations, behaviors, and biases they hold regarding death and dying is a given, representing necessary asynchrony and/or structural lag between individual life experiences and cultural change (see Brofenbrenner, 1977; Riegel, 1976). Such conflict indeed can produce both positive (in causing individuals to change their attitudes and behaviors) and negative (by reinforcing previously held biases and/or attenuating opportunities for attitudinal changes) consequences in both laypersons and professionals.

These data strongly suggest that cultural changes in our attitudes toward death, dying, and bereavement are likely to continue to evolve. How will we respond to such changes? Will our everyday behaviors change for the better or worse when we interact with those who are dying or grieving? Will we behave more planfully regarding our own eventual deaths? Will we behave differently at a funeral? Will we respond differently when those we love or when we ourselves receive a terminal diagnosis? To what extent will we consider someone's age, ethnicity, or gender in responding to the news of that person's death or to the news about the death of a loved one in his or her family? These questions are those which these data force us to contemplate.

LIMITATIONS OF THE PRESENT STUDY

Sampling Difficulties

Caution should be used when applying findings from this study to the broader population because various sampling problems were encountered in collecting the data. Although we contacted a wide range of community organizations and church groups to recruit study participants, the initial response was minimal. Therefore, we offered donations to groups (not individuals) that participated in the study. Once again, although an appeal was made to a range of groups, the response between groups was unequal. In spite of much effort to replicate the sample proportions used in Kalish and Reynolds's (1976) study, the final sample of the current study was uneven in these respects in relation to ethnic group membership, age, and gender. The disparity was greatest among Hispanic (too many) and Asian American (too few) participants. Furthermore, the majority of Hispanic and Asian American respondents (64% and 53%, respectively) were in the young age group, whereas a greater percentage of Caucasian and African Americans (40% and 41%, respectively) were in the older age group.

Another sampling bias related to recruitment involved the nature of the participating groups. Many of the participants in the 60-years-and-older age group were recruited from the Senior Citizens of Greater

Dallas, a nonreligious organization. However, we recruited many of the other participants through various church groups. Therefore, the older population in the sample may be composed of less religious persons than those in the other age groups. In addition, the Asian and Hispanic American sample populations in the present study consisted of ethnically diverse groups. The respondents in Kalish and Reynolds's study were more homogeneous Japanese and Mexican American samples. In this study, however, Asian American participants included Indian Asians, Chinese, Koreans, Japanese, and Philipinos, and Hispanic American participants included Mexicans, Spanish, Puerto Ricans and others of Hispanic descent.

Despite this awareness of varying degrees of diversity within each study's ethnic group, attention to ethnicity in this context can be seen in positive terms. Clearly, given the increased attention to the quality of life among such ethnic and racial groups as Native Americans (see Cox, 2003) and Jews (see Schindler, 2003), as well as persons who may immigrate into the United States, for example, Hindus (see Rambachan, 2003), Muslims (see Sultan, 2003), Chinese (see Crowder, 2003), and Japanese (Suzuki, 2003), as well as those who have left the Middle East and the Soviet Union to come to America, it is clear that there is much that we do not know about racial and ethnic differences in attitudes toward death, dying, and bereavement. Each subculture has unique values regarding the meaning of death, the afterlife, grieving, preparation for death, and funeralization. Despite their limitations in this respect, in light of the present findings, it would not be unusual to see such differences both reflect and influence future cultural changes in our death system (see Kastenbaum, 2001). Thus, an emphasis on diversity across the multiple parameters of culture, race, ethnicity, age, and gender may help to frame our understanding of death and dying to an even greater extent in the future. Such diversity, as noted above, may also work against the expression of group differences in attitudes toward death, dying, and bereavement. Simply put, an individual's unique experiences with death may outweigh gender, age, or ethnic influences.

In addition to the diverse nature of both samples, disparity in education among the participants within the present study and between this study and Kalish and Reynolds's study is another concern bearing on these findings' worth. Although the educational levels of Hispanic respondents in the current study and the Mexican respondents in the 1976 study were similar, participants of the other ethnic groups in the present study had more formal education than did those of Kalish and Reynolds's study. Nonetheless, the ranking of ethnicities according to education was the same in both studies (i.e., Japanese and Asian Americans, most educated; Caucasian Americans, next most; then African Americans; and Mexican and Hispanic Americans, least educated).

Another sampling problem exists with regard to differences in the socioeconomic status of participants of different ethnic groups. Although we made efforts to recruit participants from similar socioeconomic levels, the final sample was composed of comparatively more affluent Caucasian Americans and comparatively less affluent Hispanic Americans in relation to African American and Asian American participants.

Although strictly speaking, the two studies differed in the above respects, such variations must be understood in light of historical shifts in the parameters themselves that differentiate the samples, (i.e., greater access to increased educational opportunities for those in the present study, greater acceptance of multiculturalism). Thus, what may be perceived as a limitation may reflect a genuine cultural shift in factors that otherwise influence sample characteristics.

Geographic and Cohort Differences

We recruited participants for the present study from the north Texas area, whereas respondents in Kalish and Reynolds's study were recruited from the Los Angeles area. Differences between the two studies doubtlessly exist because of cultural and regional differences between the two sets of participants. Californians are reputed to have more liberal attitudes whereas north Texans are considered more conservative.

Strictly speaking, in a time lag analysis, historical change effects are confounded with cohort effects as dimensions of cultural change (Baltes, 1968; Schaie, 1965). Consequently, although our emphasis has been on the discussion of historical change effects in death attitudes from the 1970s until 2000, cohort effects nevertheless remain an alternative interpretation of these findings. For example, on the assumption that cohorts by definition, are characterized by persons sharing common sets of experiences, single events, or a series of events that predispose one cohort versus another to acquire certain attitudes relevant to death and dying (e.g., that dying is natural; that most people die of certain illnesses, accidentally, or in war; that dying persons should be avoided), this might differentiate those interviewed by Kalish and Reynolds from persons in the present study. Changes in patterns of mortality, the availability of hospice care, changes in life expectancy because of cures for degenerative or communicative diseases, the advantages (or disadvantages) of managed care, the presence of public health measures to lessen infant mortality and control disease, and the prevention of disease via changes in our lifestyle might all characterize a culture's shift in the death system (see Corr, Nabe, & Corr, 2003; Kastenbaum, 2001).

In this context, cohort effects could also be defined in terms of discrete events (or patterns of events) whose impact on persons as a function of year of birth (or a range of years of birth) is distinct. Such events might be exemplified by the publicity given to Jack Kevorkian, the establishment of the first hospice in North America in New Haven, Connecticut, the passage of the Oregon Death with Dignity Act, the Columbine High School shootings, the Challenger disaster, the regulation of the funeral industry by the Federal Trade Commission, the Oklahoma City bombing, the San Francisco earthquake, the dropping of the Atomic bomb on Japan, the attack on Pearl Harbor, the deaths of high profile persons (e.g., John F. Kennedy, John Lennon, Princess Diana, Robert F. Kennedy, and Martin Luther King), the Vietnam War, or more recently, the Columbia disaster or the terrorist attacks of September 11, 2001. Each of these events, in isolation or in combination, might have a powerfully differentiating effect on the death experiences, feelings about one's own death, one's own grief, or the attitudes toward the deaths and grief of others, separating persons from others born at different historical times. For example, it may be that traditional college age students' knowledge of and attitudes toward American war involvement is less critical than it was in the 1970s (the Iraq war not withstanding), with the latter cohort having literally grown up with the Vietnam War. The impact of such events might therefore affect each age cohort's response to survey questions.

Although the veracity of cohort effects is not without its detractors (see Rosow, 1978), the possibility nevertheless exists, especially in light of the reliable age effect found in both our study and that of Kalish and Reynolds, that the historical changes effects discussed here as possible explanations for the differences between Kalish and Reynolds's findings and our own, are also in part attributable to age cohort effects in the nature of death itself and death experiences unique to the life experiences of some persons and not others. Complicating matters further in this respect are the interaction of historical changes in attitudes toward death, dying, and bereavement with the unique experiences and values of persons of various ethnicities and cultural backgrounds (see Corr et al., 2003, for a discussion), as well as for persons varying by gender. As suggested by the data, it is entirely possible that the above discussed historical changes are uniquely experienced by persons of difference ethnicities.

Measurement Limitations

Finally, the present study was limited by the use of Kalish and Reynolds's questionnaire and by the use of analysis of categorical data. To compare the two studies in the examination of their differences, it was necessary to use the same measurement instrument and a similar data analysis. Thus, exploration of specific bereavement or death concerns was hindered by confinement to the original questionnaire. Moreover, restriction of the analysis to categorical data limited the possibility of employing more powerful and sophisticated statistical tools. Indeed, asking persons to make forced choices, i.e., agree/disagree, on matters of death where contextual and individual difference factors are influential may underestimate the variability and richness in persons' attitudes about very powerful and emotionally salient issues in their lives. At the same time asking questions in this manner may actually relieve some persons in that they are not forced to think about such issues too deeply, and are therefore more likely to respond more superficially, or with more concern for what might be socially desirable.

DIRECTIONS FOR FUTURE RESEARCH

In light of the present findings, future research in death, dying, and bereavement needs to continue to explore the ways in which beliefs and attitudes have changed as we enter a new millennium, (i.e., will the trend toward an increased concern for the context in which death occurs affect such attitudes?). In light of the ethnicity effects found in both studies, a challenge for research in the next decade will be to improve researchers' understanding of the grieving process in relation to the influence exerted by the growing diversity within North America (Doka, 2000). Research in effective interventions to meet the needs of different populations is especially necessary; this is significant in light of the fact that not all bereaved persons express themselves in the same ways or share the same experiences in managing their grief. Thus, research needs to include bereaved persons from a much broader spectrum of the population, to include persons who vary along the age continuum.

Because of the increasing ethnic diversity of the population, "bereavement studies should systematically test for cross-cultural and ethnic comparisons" (Lund & Caserta, 1998, p. 295). Such studies especially need to include more heterogeneous samples with sufficient numbers of African, Hispanic, Asian, and Native Americans to consider the effects of ethnic differences. As noted above, it is important to incorporate our knowledge of cultural similarities and differences in addition to individual ones to more fully understand the grieving process. There also needs to be increased sophistication in the study of interventions emphasizing what strategies work best with which populations (Doka, 2000). In this light, the goal of such interventions should be to assist dying persons and their families in experiencing an appropriate death within the context of cultural diversity and individual differences across both age and gender.

A last challenge for the future, in light of our findings, is to improve our understanding of the changing processes involved in life-threatening illnesses and dying in light of the growth in hospice and palliative medicine (Doka, 2000). Prolongation of the dying process through medical advances and movement toward greater consideration of a more holistic approach to death calls forth the need for new theoretical models, innovative research, and interventions at different points in the illness experience and at different points across the lifespan. Regarding end-of-life decisions, contemporary American culture is in transition from the previous physician-oriented approach to one which considers the needs of patients and families (Kastenbaum, 2001). This underscores the importance of continuing to examine both culturally relevant and idiosyncratic influences on individuals' attitudes toward not only their own deaths, but also the deaths and bereavement of others.

Appendix A

Summary of Results by Ethnicity, Age, and Gender for the Present Study

1. What is your ethnicity?
Caucasian:	31.2%	($N = 164$)
African American:	19%	($N = 100$)
Hispanic American:	39%	($N = 205$)
Asian American:	10.8%	($N = 57$)
Total		($N = 526$)

2. If Latino/a, do you consider yourself of Hispanic or Spanish origin?
   Hispanic: 94.6%
   Spanish: 5.4%

3. If Latino/a, are you
Mexican:	90.7%
Puerto Rican:	1.5%
Cuban:	0
Other:	7.8%

4. If Asian, are you
Chinese:	21.1%
Filipino:	3.5%
Japanese:	10.5%
Asian Indian:	36.8%
Korean:	19.3%
Vietnamese:	0
Other:	8.8%

5. Where were you born?
   United States: 55.9%
   Outside U.S.:   44.1%

6. If you were born outside of the United States, how many years have you lived in the U.S.?

Less than 2 years:	17.0%
2–5 years:	32.6%
5–10 years:	15.2%
10–20 years:	17.0%
More than 20 years:	18.3%

7. What is your native language?

English:	54.3%
Spanish:	33.3%
Asian Language:	10.1%
Other:	2.1%

8. If English, do you speak another language?

Yes:	28.3%
No:	71.7%

9. If English, can you read another language?

Yes:	28.3%
No:	71.7%

	Ethnicity, M (SD)				Age, M			Sex, M	
	Cau.A.	Afr.A.	His.A.	Asn.A.	20–39	40–59	60+	Male	Female
10. How many years of school did you finish?									
20–39 years old:									
Male:									
	15.9	15.0	10.3	18.4					
	(3.20)	(2.65)	(4.61)	(4.21)					
Female:									
	15.3	16.0	10.4	16.8					
	(2.13)	(2.15)	(4.83)	(1.23)					
Total:									
	15.6	15.5	10.4	17.6	14.8			14.9	14.6
40–59 years:									
Male:									
	17.7	19.1	10.8	17.3					
	(4.14)	(3.40)	(5.30)	(3.01)					
Female:									
	15.9	18.0	7.9	15.9					
	(3.12)	(3.21)	(2.88)	(4.14)					
Total:									
	16.8	18.6	9.4	16.6		15.3		16.2	14.4

	Ethnicity, M (SD)			Age, M			Sex, M	
	Cau.A.	Afr.A.	His.A.	Asn.A.	20–39	40–59	60+	Male	Female
60+ years:									
Male:									
	17.7	12.0	10.9	20.0					
	(3.64)	(3.27)	(6.40)	(.00)					
Female:									
	14.5	10.5	7.3	13.6					
	(2.90)	(1.05)	(6.38)	(5.08)					
Total:									
	16.1	11.3	9.1	16.8			13.7	15.2	12.2
Composite Total:									
	16.2	15.1	9.6	17.0				15.4	13.7

11. What is your current occupation?
   Unskilled: 12.7%
   Skilled: 11.5%
   Housewife: 10.9%
   Professional/Managerial: 35.3%
   Other: 29.6%

	Ethnicity, % (n)			Age, % (n)			Sex, % (n)	
	Cau.A.	Afr.A.	His.A.	Asn.A.	20–39	40–59	60+	Male	Female
11a. You are:									
Male:									
	11.0	7.0	18.3	5.9	19.6	12.0	10.6	42.2	
	(58)	(37)	(96)	(31)	(103)	(63)	(56)	(222)	
Female:									
	20.2	12.0	20.7	4.9	26.8	13.9	17.1		57.8
	(106)	(63)	(109)	(26)	(141)	(73)	(90)		(304)

12. What is your current age group?
   20–39 years old:

	Ethnicity, % (n)			Age, % (n)			Sex, % (n)	
Male:									
	3.6	2.3	11.2	2.5				19.6	
	(19)	(12)	(59)	(13)				(103)	
Female:									
	5.9	4.0	13.7	3.2					26.8
	(31)	(21)	(72)	(17)					(141)
Total:									
	9.5	6.3	24.9	5.7	46.4				
	(50)	(33)	(131)	(30)	(244)				

	Ethnicity, % (n)				Age, % (n)			Sex, % (n)	
	Cau.A.	Afr.A.	His.A.	Asn.A.	20–39	40–59	60+	Male	Female

12. What is your current age group *(cont'd)*?
40–59 years old:
Male:

	Ethnicity, % (n)				Age, % (n)			Sex, % (n)	
	Cau.A.	Afr.A.	His.A.	Asn.A.	20–39	40–59	60+	Male	Female
	3.4	2.5	4.8	1.3				12.0	
	(18)	(13)	(25)	(7)				(63)	

Female:

	5.7	2.5	4.4	1.3					13.9
	(30)	(13)	(23)	(7)					(73)

Total:

	9.1	5.0	9.1	2.7	25.9				
	(48)	(26)	(48)	(14)	(136)				

60+ years old:
Male:

	4.0	2.3	2.3	2.1				10.6	
	(21)	(12)	(12)	(11)				(56)	

Female:

	8.6	5.5	2.7	0.4					17.2
	(45)	(29)	(14)	(2)					(90)

Total:

	12.5	7.8	4.9	2.5			27.7		
	(66)	(41)	(26)	(13)			(146)		

13. What is your religious affiliation?
    Buddhist: 1.5%
    Catholic: 21.9%
    Protestant: 48.7%
    Other: 22.3%
    None: 5.6%

14. Compared to most people of your religion, do you feel you are:
    More devout: 26.3%
    About the same: 61.5%
    Less devout: 12.1%

15. Which of these fits your marital status?
    Married: 48.2%
    Never married: 29.3%
    Widowed: 11.2%
    Divorced/separated: 11.3%

	Ethnicity, %				Age, %			Sex, %	
	Cau.A.	Afr.A.	His.A.	Asn.A.	20–39	40–59	60+	Male	Female

16. How many persons that you knew personally died in the past two years?
    None:

| | 9.6 | 6.1 | 42.3 | 12.3 | 30.9 | 18.1 | 9.9 | 21.0 | 22.8 |

1–3 persons:

| | 53.6 | 44.4 | 48.3 | 75.4 | 57.6 | 49.3 | 45.4 | 55.7 | 48.7 |

4–7 persons:

| | 21.7 | 27.3 | 8.0 | 10.5 | 9.1 | 23.2 | 22.0 | 16.9 | 16.1 |

8 or more persons:

| | 15.1 | 22.2 | 1.5 | 1.8 | 2.5 | 9.4 | 22.7 | 6.4 | 12.4 |

Ethnicity:
$$\chi^2 \text{ (df = 9)} = 129.75, p < .01$$
Age:
$$\chi^2 \text{ (df = 6)} = 73.98, p < .01$$
Gender:
$$\chi^2 \text{ (df = 3)} = 6.09$$

17. Of those who died in the past two years, how many died by accident?
    None:

| | 79.4 | 77.6 | 83.7 | 73.2 | 81.4 | 74.6 | 82.9 | 75.5 | 83.7 |

1–2 persons:

| | 20.6 | 22.4 | 16.3 | 26.8 | 18.6 | 25.4 | 17.1 | 24.5 | 16.3 |

Ethnicity:
$$\chi^2 \text{ (df = 3)} = 3.72$$
Age:
$$\chi^2 \text{ (df = 2)} = 3.49$$
Gender:
$$\chi^2 \text{ (df = 1)} = 5.43, p < .05$$

18. How many died in war/military action?
    None:

| | 99.4 | 98.0 | 99.5 | 100 | 99.6 | 100 | 97.8 | 98.6 | 99.7 |

1–2 persons:

| | 0.6 | 2.0 | 0.5 | 0 | 0.4 | 0 | 2.2 | 1.4 | 0.3 |

Ethnicity:
$$\chi^2 \text{ (df = 3)} = 2.75$$
Age:
$$\chi^2 \text{ (df = 2)} = 4.96$$
Gender:
$$\chi^2 \text{ (df = 1)} = 1.77$$

19. How many died by suicide?
    None:

| | 89.7 | 89.0 | 91.5 | 98.2 | 92.1 | 92.0 | 88.6 | 92.2 | 90.9 |

1–2 persons:

| | 10.3 | 11.0 | 8.5 | 1.8 | 7.9 | 8.0 | 11.4 | 7.8 | 9.1 |

	Ethnicity, %				Age, %			Sex, %	
	Cau.A.	Afr.A.	His.A.	Asn.A.	20–39	40–59	60+	Male	Female

19. How many died by suicide *(cont'd)*?
    Ethnicity:
       χ^2 (df = 3) = 4.51
    Age:
       χ^2 (df = 2) = 1.50
    Gender:
       χ^2 (df = 1) = 0.27

20. How many died by homicide?
    None:

	Cau.A.	Afr.A.	His.A.	Asn.A.	20–39	40–59	60+	Male	Female
	98.2	71.9	86.1	94.6	90.1	82.6	90.6	86.2	89.6

    1–2 persons:

	Cau.A.	Afr.A.	His.A.	Asn.A.	20–39	40–59	60+	Male	Female
	1.8	28.1	13.9	5.4	9.9	17.4	9.4	13.8	10.4

    Ethnicity:
       χ^2 (df = 3) = 43.79, $p < .01$
    Age:
       χ^2 (df = 2) = 5.79, $p < .01$
    Gender:
       χ^2 (df = 1) = 1.38, $p < .01$

21. How many funerals have you attended in the past two years?
    None:

	Cau.A.	Afr.A.	His.A.	Asn.A.	20–39	40–59	60+	Male	Female
	17.5	18.2	51.2	29.8	44.9	25.4	15.6	33.5	30.9

    1–3 funerals:

	Cau.A.	Afr.A.	His.A.	Asn.A.	20–39	40–59	60+	Male	Female
	59.0	44.4	41.9	64.9	48.6	53.6	50.4	46.6	52.7

    4–7 funerals:

	Cau.A.	Afr.A.	His.A.	Asn.A.	20–39	40–59	60+	Male	Female
	16.3	19.2	5.9	5.3	4.5	15.9	19.9	12.2	11.4

    8 or more funerals:

	Cau.A.	Afr.A.	His.A.	Asn.A.	20–39	40–59	60+	Male	Female
	7.2	18.2	1.0	0	2.0	5.1	14.2	7.7	5.0

    Ethnicity:
       χ^2 (df = 9) = 100.78, $p < .01$
    Age:
       χ^2 (df = 6) = 70.11, $p < .01$
    Gender:
       χ^2 (df = 3) = 2.73, $p < .01$

22. How often have you visited someone's grave, other than during a burial service, during the past two years?
    Never:

	Cau.A.	Afr.A.	His.A.	Asn.A.	20–39	40–59	60+	Male	Female
	36.7	39.4	70.4	75.4	67.8	47.1	38.3	62.0	49.3

    1–3 times:

	Cau.A.	Afr.A.	His.A.	Asn.A.	20–39	40–59	60+	Male	Female
	41.6	34.3	20.2	19.3	22.4	37.0	34.8	28.1	30.2

    4–10 times:

	Cau.A.	Afr.A.	His.A.	Asn.A.	20–39	40–59	60+	Male	Female
	18.1	16.2	7.4	5.3	7.3	10.9	22.0	6.8	16.1

	Ethnicity, %			Age, %			Sex, %	
Cau.A.	**Afr.A.**	**His.A.**	**Asn.A.**	**20–39**	**40–59**	**60+**	**Male**	**Female**

11 or more times:

Cau.A.	Afr.A.	His.A.	Asn.A.	20–39	40–59	60+	Male	Female
3.6	10.1	2.0	0	2.4	5.1	5.0	3.2	4.4

   Ethnicity:
$$\chi^2 \, (df = 9) = 71.09, \, p < .01$$
   Age:
$$\chi^2 \, (df = 6) = 42.37, \, p < .01$$
   Gender:
$$\chi^2 \, (df = 3) = 13.47, \, p < .01$$

23. How many persons who were dying did you visit or talk with during the past two years?

None:

Cau.A.	Afr.A.	His.A.	Asn.A.	20–39	40–59	60+	Male	Female
32.7	32.3	68.7	51.8	62.2	39.0	34.3	50.2	47.3

1 person:

28.5	29.2	18.2	35.7	18.7	35.3	27.0	26.7	24.0

2 or more persons:

38.8	38.5	13.1	12.5	19.1	25.7	38.7	23.0	28.8

   Ethnicity:
$$\chi^2 \, (df = 6) = 70.65, \, p < .01$$
   Age:
$$\chi^2 \, (df = 4) = 40.16, \, p < .01$$
   Gender:
$$\chi^2 \, (df = 2) = 2.15, \, p < .01$$

24. About how often do you think about your own death?

Daily:

Cau.A.	Afr.A.	His.A.	Asn.A.	20–39	40–59	60+	Male	Female
8.4	19.4	7.4	16.1	7.3	6.6	21.4	11.5	10.0

Weekly:

25.1	17.3	12.9	10.7	11.8	24.8	20.0	17.9	16.7

Monthly:

29.2	20.4	16.3	19.6	20.0	19.0	27.9	21.1	22.7

Yearly/Hardly ever:

31.1	25.5	35.6	48.2	38.4	37.2	22.1	31.2	35.8

Never:

5.4	17.3	27.7	5.4	22.4	12.4	8.6	18.3	14.7

   Ethnicity:
$$\chi^2 \, (df = 12) = 67.35, \, p < .01$$
   Age:
$$\chi^2 \, (df = 8) = 51.69, \, p < .01$$
   Gender:
$$\chi^2 \, (df = 4) = 2.31, \, p < .01$$

	Ethnicity, %				Age, %			Sex, %	
	Cau.A.	Afr.A.	His.A.	Asn.A.	20–39	40–59	60+	Male	Female

25. How often do you attend religious services?
1 or more times per week:

	Cau.A.	Afr.A.	His.A.	Asn.A.	20–39	40–59	60+	Male	Female
	41.8	77.6	51.0	56.1	51.2	46.7	65.0	48.9	57.9

1–2 times per month:

	19.4	18.4	26.2	26.3	24.2	27.0	15.7	21.9	22.9

1–2 times per year:

	22.4	1.0	16.8	5.3	15.6	18.2	8.6	19.2	10.1

Less than once per year:

	9.7	1.0	1.5	8.8	2.9	5.8	7.1	4.1	5.4

Never:

	6.7	2.0	4.5	3.5	6.1	2.2	3.6	5.9	3.7

Ethnicity:
$$\chi^2 \, (df = 12) = 62.66, \, p < .01$$
Age:
$$\chi^2 \, (df = 8) = 21.40, \, p < .01$$
Gender:
$$\chi^2 \, (df = 4) = 11.18, \, p < .05$$

26. Should your friend be told that he/she is going to die?
Yes:

	Cau.A.	Afr.A.	His.A.	Asn.A.	20–39	40–59	60+	Male	Female
	78.9	70.0	54.9	61.4	68.7	74.6	52.8	68.6	63.8

No:

	4.2	11.0	23.5	19.3	13.4	14.5	16.9	15.0	14.3

Depends:

	16.9	19.0	21.6	19.3	17.9	10.9	30.3	16.4	21.9

Ethnicity:
$$\chi^2 \, (df = 6) = 34.61, \, p < .01$$
Age:
$$\chi^2 \, (df = 4) = 20.46, \, p < .01$$
Gender:
$$\chi^2 \, (df = 2) = 2.51, \, p < .01$$

27. (If yes or if depends) Who should tell him/her?
Physician:

	Cau.A.	Afr.A.	His.A.	Asn.A.	20–39	40–59	60+	Male	Female
	74.2	57.5	54.4	53.1	50.0	69.1	75.9	64.8	59.4

Family:

	21.9	32.5	30.2	40.8	41.7	19.1	15.2	22.5	33.6

Clergy:

	2.0	6.3	13.4	4.1	6.3	9.1	6.3	9.9	4.9

Other:

	2.0	3.8	2.0	2.0	1.9	2.7	2.7	2.7	2.0

Ethnicity:
$$\chi^2 \, (df = 9) = 27.10, \, p < .01$$

	Ethnicity, %			Age, %			Sex, %	
Cau.A.	**Afr.A.**	**His.A.**	**Asn.A.**	**20–39**	**40–59**	**60+**	**Male**	**Female**

Age:
$$\chi^2 \, (df = 6) = 33.05, \, p < .01$$
Gender:
$$\chi^2 \, (df = 3) = 8.80, \, p < .05$$

28. Do you think a person dying of cancer probably senses he's dying anyway without being told?

Yes:

75.9	72.0	66.8	60.0	63.5	77.9	73.2	63.8	74.9

No:

3.7	9.0	11.9	20.0	13.5	6.6	5.8	13.3	6.8

Depends:

20.4	19.0	21.3	20.0	23.0	15.4	21.0	22.9	18.3

Ethnicity:
$$\chi^2 \, (df = 6) = 15.27, \, p < .05$$
Age:
$$\chi^2 \, (df = 4) = 12.54, \, p < .05$$
Gender:
$$\chi^2 \, (df = 1) = 9.13, \, p < .05$$

29. If you were dying, would you want to be told?

Yes:

93.9	76.5	76.5	89.3	82.3	88.3	80.1	80.8	84.9

No:

6.1	23.5	23.5	10.7	17.7	11.7	19.9	19.2	15.1

Ethnicity:
$$\chi^2 \, (df = 3) = 24.80, \, p < .01$$
Age:
$$\chi^2 \, (df = 2) = 3.67, \, p < .01$$
Gender:
$$\chi^2 \, (df = 1) = 1.50, \, p < .01$$

30. Do you actually know of someone who was dying in circumstances like these, so that a decision was made to tell him/her or not to tell him/her that he/she would shortly die?

Yes:

61.8	44.4	26.7	36.8	29.2	50.4	56.3	35.6	48.0

No:

38.2	55.6	73.3	63.2	70.8	49.6	43.7	64.4	52.0

Ethnicity:
$$\chi^2 \, (df = 3) = 46.71, \, p < .01$$
Age:
$$\chi^2 \, (df = 2) = 32.18, \, p < .01$$
Gender:
$$\chi^2 \, (df = 1) = 7.89, \, p < .01$$

	Ethnicity, %				Age, %			Sex, %	
	Cau.A.	Afr.A.	His.A.	Asn.A.	20–39	40–59	60+	Male	Female

31. (If yes) Was he/she actually told he/she was going to die?

Yes:

| 85.5 | 73.2 | 61.8 | 64.0 | 75.0 | 80.0 | 69.1 | 73.0 | 75.9 |

No:

| 14.5 | 26.8 | 38.2 | 36.0 | 25.0 | 20.0 | 30.9 | 27.0 | 24.1 |

Ethnicity:
χ^2 (df = 3) = 14.26, $p < .01$

Age:
χ^2 (df = 2) = 2.70, $p < .01$

Gender:
χ^2 (df = 1) = 0.28, $p < .01$

32. (If yes) Who told him/her?

Physician:

| 87.9 | 61.7 | 80.4 | 66.7 | 69.6 | 84.1 | 82.6 | 74.7 | 80.5 |

Family:

| 8.8 | 25.5 | 15.2 | 33.3 | 24.6 | 12.7 | 10.1 | 15.2 | 17.1 |

Other:

| 3.3 | 12.8 | 4.3 | 0 | 5.8 | 3.2 | 7.3 | 10.1 | 2.4 |

Ethnicity:
χ^2 (df = 6) = 18.37, $p < .01$

Age:
χ^2 (df = 4) = 7.27, $p < .01$

Gender:
χ^2 (df = 2) = 5.53, $p < .01$

33. Did you ever tell someone he/she was about to die?

Yes:

| 18.1 | 3.0 | 5.0 | 16.4 | 6.6 | 14.0 | 12.1 | 10.5 | 9.8 |

No:

| 81.9 | 97.0 | 95.0 | 83.6 | 93.4 | 86.0 | 87.9 | 89.5 | 90.2 |

Ethnicity:
χ^2 (df = 3) = 25.68, $p < .01$

Age:
χ^2 (df = 2) = 6.27, $p < .05$

Gender:
χ^2 (df = 1) = .08

34. (If no) Could you tell someone he/she was about to die?

Yes:

| 74.0 | 58.3 | 34.2 | 58.0 | 58.0 | 55.7 | 50.4 | 62.3 | 47.1 |

No:

| 26.0 | 41.7 | 65.8 | 42.0 | 46.1 | 44.3 | 49.6 | 37.7 | 52.9 |

	Ethnicity, %				Age, %			Sex, %	
	Cau.A.	Afr.A.	His.A.	Asn.A.	20–39	40–59	60+	Male	Female

Ethnicity:
χ^2 (df = 3) = 54.33, $p < .01$
Age:
χ^2 (df = 2) = 0.76
Gender:
χ^2 (df = 1) = 10.82, $p < .01$

35. If you were told that you had a terminal disease and had six months to live, how would you want to spend your time until you died?

With a marked change in behavior (quit job, travel, etc.):

	12.7	11.6	9.0	9.1	15.5	6.7	6.0	3.7	12.5

By withdrawing or focusing on inner life:

	2.5	4.2	11.9	27.3	10.5	7.5	9.0	11.2	8.0

By showing concern for others (spending time with family, etc.):

	61.1	46.3	56.2	31.0	52.7	56.0	50.7	52.1	53.6

By completing projects:

	8.9	7.4	4.0	12.7	4.6	9.0	9.7	6.1	7.6

With no change in behavior:

	9.6	22.1	12.9	16.4	9.2	15.7	20.9	16.3	12.5

Other:

	5.1	8.4	6.0	3.6	7.5	5.2	3.7	6.0	5.9

Ethnicity:
χ^2 (df = 15) = 55.40, $p < .01$
Age:
χ^2 (df = 10) = 26.16, $p < .01$
Gender:
χ^2 (df = 5) = 5.05

36. Would you tend to accept death peacefully or fight death actively?

Accept:

	35.0	51.0	27.3	57.1	27.3	37.7	53.8	36.1	38.1

Fight:

	24.0	23.5	51.2	19.6	40.4	31.2	25.9	39.3	30.5

Depends:

	41.5	25.5	21.5	23.2	32.2	31.1	20.3	24.7	31.5

Ethnicity:
χ^2 (df = 6) = 60.41, $p < .01$
Age:
χ^2 (df = 4) = 27.98, $p < .01$
Gender:
χ^2 (df = 2) = 5.07

	Ethnicity, %				Age, %			Sex, %	
	Cau.A.	Afr.A.	His.A.	Asn.A.	20–39	40–59	60+	Male	Female

37. Would you tend to endure pain in silence or tell someone of your pain?
    Endure:

	19.3	23.5	32.7	29.8	28.7	32.6	16.7	32.6	21.8

Tell:

	48.8	46.1	27.8	38.6	34.4	37.7	47.9	39.4	38.9

Depends:

	31.9	30.4	39.5	31.6	36.8	29.7	35.4	28.1	39.3

    Ethnicity:
$$\chi^2 \ (df = 6) = 21.24, \ p < .01$$
    Age:
$$\chi^2 \ (df = 4) = 13.35, \ p < .01$$
    Gender:
$$\chi^2 \ (df = 2) = 10.32, \ p < .01$$

38. Would you encourage your family to spend time with you even if it was a little inconvenient for them?
    Yes:

	45.5	52.9	27.1	35.1	40.2	40.9	34.0	41.6	36.2

No:

	35.2	25.5	33.7	43.9	30.3	36.5	36.9	31.5	34.2

Depends:

	19.4	21.6	39.2	21.1	29.5	22.6	29.1	26.9	28.5

    Ethnicity:
$$\chi^2 \ (df = 6) = 34.20, \ p < .01$$
    Age:
$$\chi^2 \ (df = 4) = 4.32$$
    Gender:
$$\chi^2 \ (df = 2) = 1.56$$

39. Would you call for a priest/minister?
    Yes:

	68.9	68.9	77.5	42.1	72.0	70.3	63.7	66.5	71.7

No:

	19.8	11.7	10.8	33.3	16.7	19.6	12.3	17.6	14.5

Depends:

	11.4	19.4	11.8	24.6	11.4	10.1	24.0	15.8	13.8

    Ethnicity:
$$\chi^2 \ (df = 6) = 32.57, \ p < .01$$
    Age:
$$\chi^2 \ (df = 4) = 15.74, \ p < .01$$
    Gender:
$$\chi^2 \ (df = 2) = 1.67$$

	Ethnicity, %				Age, %			Sex, %	
	Cau.A.	Afr.A.	His.A.	Asn.A.	20–39	40–59	60+	Male	Female

40. Would you allow children under 10 years of age to visit you?
Yes:

| | 73.1 | 60.8 | 67.3 | 63.2 | 72.5 | 70.8 | 55.9 | 71.4 | 63.9 |

Yes with qualifications:

| | 21.6 | 28.4 | 25.1 | 31.6 | 23.0 | 23.4 | 31.5 | 18.6 | 30.8 |

No:

| | 5.39 | 10.8 | 7.5 | 5.3 | 4.5 | 5.8 | 12.6 | 10.0 | 5.4 |

   Ethnicity:
      χ^2 (df = 6) = 6.71
   Age:
      χ^2 (df = 4) = 15.57 $p < .01$
   Gender:
      χ^2 (df = 2) = 12.08, $p < .01$

41. Would you worry if you could not cry?
Yes:

| | 28.3 | 27.5 | 37.9 | 15.8 | 32.0 | 34.3 | 24.5 | 21.7 | 37.5 |

No:

| | 53.6 | 52.0 | 38.9 | 57.9 | 44.1 | 49.6 | 53.1 | 53.8 | 42.9 |

Depends:

| | 18.1 | 20.6 | 23.2 | 26.3 | 23.9 | 16.1 | 22.4 | 24.4 | 19.6 |

   Ethnicity:
      χ^2 (df = 6) = 16.18, $p < .05$
   Age:
      χ^2 (df = 4) = 6.76
   Gender:
      χ^9 (df = 2) = 14.96, $p < .01$

42. Would you try very hard to control the way you showed your emotions in public?
Yes:

| | 68.7 | 65.3 | 65.3 | 50.9 | 57.2 | 67.2 | 75.5 | 64.1 | 65.8 |

No:

| | 31.3 | 34.7 | 34.7 | 49.1 | 42.8 | 32.8 | 24.5 | 35.9 | 34.2 |

   Ethnicity:
      χ^2 (df = 3) = 5.79
   Age:
      χ^2 (df = 2) = 13.70, $p < .01$
   Gender:
      χ^2 (df = 1) = 0.16

	Ethnicity, %				Age, %			Sex, %	
	Cau.A.	Afr.A.	His.A.	Asn.A.	20–39	40–59	60+	Male	Female

43. Would you let yourself go and cry yourself out (in private or in public or both)?
    Yes:

	54.8	40.6	45.5	30.4	51.6	45.7	36.4	36.5	52.7

No:

	16.9	20.8	15.8	17.9	14.2	18.8	20.7	22.4	13.0

Depends:

	28.3	38.6	38.6	51.8	34.1	35.5	42.9	41.1	34.3

Ethnicity:
χ^2 (df = 6) = 14.38, $p < .05$
Age:
χ^2 (df = 4) = 8.90
Gender:
χ^2 (df = 2) = 15.31, $p < .01$

44. Would you be likely to touch the body at any of the funeral services?
    Yes:

	41.3	47.5	43.8	21.1	38.7	44.9	42.4	36.4	44.7

No:

	46.7	40.6	40.8	50.9	42.0	44.2	45.8	48.2	41.0

Depends:

	12.0	11.9	15.4	28.1	19.3	10.9	11.8	15.5	14.3

Ethnicity:
χ^2 (df = 6) = 16.72, $p < .05$
Age:
χ^2 (df = 4) = 6.79
Gender:
χ^2 (df = 2) = 3.72

45. Would you be likely to kiss the body at any of the funeral services?
    Yes:

	22.2	25.0	45.0	12.3	37.9	29.4	18.8	27.7	31.9

No:

	77.8	75.0	55.0	87.7	62.1	70.6	81.2	72.3	68.1

Ethnicity:
χ^2 (df = 3) = 35.77, $p < .01$
Age:
χ^2 (df = 2) = 15.69
Gender:
χ^2 (df = 1) = 1.04

46. Would you carry out your husband's/wife's last wishes even if they seemed to be senseless to you and caused some inconvenience?
    Yes:

	78.0	65.7	54.2	69.6	63.1	77.5	57.7	63.9	66.0

	Ethnicity, %			Age, %			Sex, %	
	Cau.A.	Afr.A.	His.A.	Asn.A.	20–39	40–59	60+	Male	Female
No:									
	3.7	8.8	6.4	5.3	4.1	5.1	9.8	6.8	5.3
Depends:									
	18.3	25.5	39.4	25.0	32.8	17.4	32.5	29.2	28.7

Ethnicity:
$$\chi^2 (df = 6) = 26.04, p < .01$$
Age:
$$\chi^2 (df = 4) = 18.10, p < .01$$
Gender:
$$\chi^2 (df = 2) = 0.58$$

47. Who would you be likely to turn to for comfort?

	Cau.A.	Afr.A.	His.A.	Asn.A.	20–39	40–59	60+	Male	Female
Family member:									
	50.3	33.3	44.4	57.8	49.1	45.7	39.2	43.8	46.2
Clergy/God:									
	34.5	52.2	43.9	40.0	37.7	41.9	49.6	43.3	42.0
Friend:									
	13.1	12.2	10.7	2.2	12.3	11.6	8.0	11.9	9.9
Physician/Funeral Director:									
	0	0	0	0	0	0	0	0	0
No one:									
	2.1	2.2	1.1	0	0.9	0.8	3.2	1.0	1.9

Ethnicity:
$$\chi^2 (df = 12) = 15.02$$
Age:
$$\chi^2 (df = 8) = 8.99$$
Gender:
$$\chi^2 (df = 4) = 1.25$$

48. Who would be most likely to help you with such problems as preparing meals, baby-sitting, shopping, cleaning house, and things like that?

	Cau.A.	Afr.A.	His.A.	Asn.A.	20–39	40–59	60+	Male	Female
Family member:									
	78.8	69.5	88.5	81.5	85.6	81.5	73.9	81.6	81.0
Friend:									
	19.9	26.3	9.0	11.1	11.9	18.5	19.6	15.1	16.3
No one:									
	1.3	4.2	2.5	7.4	2.5	0	6.5	3.3	2.8

Ethnicity:
$$\chi^2 (df = 6) = 23.60, p < .01$$
Age:
$$\chi^2 (df = 4) = 15.47, p < .01$$
Gender:
$$\chi^2 (df = 2) = 0.23$$

	Ethnicity, %				Age, %			Sex, %	
	Cau.A.	Afr.A.	His.A.	Asn.A.	20–39	40–59	60+	Male	Female

49. Sudden death or slow death. Which seems more tragic?

Sudden:

| | 28.5 | 35.9 | 38.7 | 41.1 | 35.1 | 38.7 | 32.4 | 29.5 | 39.4 |

Slow:

| | 37.6 | 36.9 | 39.7 | 51.8 | 36.7 | 41.6 | 42.8 | 42.7 | 37.7 |

Equal:

| | 33.9 | 27.2 | 21.6 | 7.1 | 28.2 | 19.7 | 24.8 | 27.7 | 22.8 |

Ethnicity:
$$\chi^2 \ (df = 6) = 19.42, \ p < .01$$
Age:
$$\chi^2 \ (df = 4) = 4.31$$
Gender:
$$\chi^2 \ (df = 2) = 5.52$$

50. An infant's death (up to 1 year old), a child's death (around 7 years old), a young person's death (around 25 years old), a middle-aged person's death (around 40 years old), and an elderly person's death (around 75 years old). Which seems most tragic?

Infant:

| | 14.6 | 28.9 | 24.7 | 14.8 | 27.2 | 13.5 | 17.9 | 22.5 | 21.0 |

Child:

| | 47.5 | 26.8 | 19.7 | 22.2 | 27.2 | 43.6 | 26.1 | 27.7 | 30.9 |

Young person:

| | 13.9 | 9.3 | 27.8 | 31.5 | 17.6 | 22.6 | 23.1 | 23.9 | 18.1 |

Middle-aged person:

| | 3.8 | 3.1 | 4.0 | 7.4 | 2.9 | 6.0 | 4.5 | 4.7 | 3.8 |

Elderly person:

| | 1.3 | 2.1 | 0 | 1.9 | 0.8 | 0 | 2.2 | 1.4 | 0.7 |

Depends:

| | 19.0 | 29.9 | 23.7 | 22.2 | 24.3 | 18.8 | 26.1 | 19.7 | 25.7 |

Ethnicity:
$$\chi^2 \ (df = 15) = 58.84, \ p < .01$$
Age:
$$\chi^2 \ (df = 10) = 22.35, \ p < .05$$
Gender:
$$\chi^2 \ (df = 5) = 5.39$$

51. Which seems least tragic?

Infant:

| | 1.8 | 11.2 | 14.9 | 9.1 | 9.6 | 9.6 | 8.6 | 11.0 | 8.5 |

Child:

| | 1.8 | 3.1 | 2.0 | 3.6 | 0.8 | 3.7 | 3.6 | 1.4 | 2.7 |

Young person:

| | 0.6 | 1.0 | 2.5 | 3.6 | 2.5 | 0.7 | 1.4 | 0.5 | 2.7 |

	Ethnicity, %			Age, %			Sex, %	
Cau.A.	Afr.A.	His.A.	Asn.A.	20–39	40–59	60+	Male	Female

Middle-aged person:

0.6	3.1	1.0	3.6	1.3	0.7	2.9	2.3	1.0

Elderly person:

79.1	52.0	47.3	63.6	57.1	67.6	57.9	61.9	59.0

Depends:

15.6	29.6	32.3	16.4	28.8	17.6	25.7	22.9	26.1

Ethnicity:

χ^2 (df = 15) = 53.84, $p < .01$

Age:

χ^2 (df = 10) = 14.42

Gender:

χ^2 (df = 5) = 7.51

52. Which seems more tragic? Death of a man or woman?

Man:

1.2	3.9	1.5	5.4	2.8	0	3.4	2.7	2.0

Woman:

13.2	10.8	2.4	0	4.1	8.7	10.3	5.9	7.6

Equal:

85.6	85.3	96.1	94.6	93.1	91.3	86.3	91.4	90.4

Ethnicity:

χ^2 (df = 6) = 27.25, $p < .01$

Age:

χ^2 (df = 4) = 10.78, $p < .05$

Gender:

χ^2 (df = 2) = 0.86

53. Which seems most tragic: Natural death, accidental death, suicidal death, homicidal death, or death in war?

Natural death:

1.2	6.3	2.0	1.2	1.7	1.5	5.1	0.5	4.1

Accidental death:

20.5	15.6	26.5	33.9	25.8	23.0	19.7	24.2	21.9

Suicidal death:

31.7	41.7	35.5	26.8	31.7	30.4	43.1	32.3	36.6

Homicidal death:

41.0	35.4	33.0	28.6	37.1	40.7	27.7	36.9	34.6

War death:

5.6	1.0	3.0	8.9	3.8	4.4	4.4	6.0	2.7

Ethnicity:

χ^2 (df = 12) = 25.33, $p < .05$

Age:

χ^2 (df = 8) = 14.12

Gender:

χ^2 (df = 4) = 10.89, $p < .05$

	Ethnicity, %			Age, %			Sex, %	
Cau.A.	Afr.A.	His.A.	Asn.A.	20–39	40–59	60+	Male	Female

54. Which seems least tragic: Natural death, accidental death, suicidal death, homicidal death, or death in war?
Natural death:

91.4	87.1	90.0	73.2	85.8	91.1	89.8	86.1	90.0

Accidental death:

2.5	2.2	1.0	3.6	0.8	2.2	3.6	3.2	0.7

Suicidal death:

1.2	3.2	1.5	14.3	5.8	1.5	0	1.9	4.1

Homicidal death:

0	0	1.5	0	0.8	0	0.7	0.9	0.3

Death in war:

4.9	7.5	6.0	8.9	6.7	5.2	5.8	7.9	5.2

     Ethnicity:
$$\chi^2 \,(df = 12) = 35.64, \, p < .01$$
   Age:
$$\chi^2 \,(df = 8) = 16.43, \, p < .05$$
   Gender:
$$\chi^2 \,(df = 4) = 8.92$$

55. I am afraid of what might happen to my body after death.
Very important:

4.8	11.5	19.0	3.5	14.2	8.7	8.6	7.7	14.4

Important:

15.6	11.5	18.0	14.0	15.8	15.9	15.1	18.1	13.4

Not important:

79.6	77.1	62.9	82.5	70.0	75.4	76.3	74.1	72.2

     Ethnicity:
$$\chi^2 \,(df = 6) = 26.63, \, p < .01$$
   Age:
$$\chi^2 \,(df = 4) = 4.15$$
   Gender:
$$\chi^2 \,(df = 2) = 6.81, \, p < .05$$

56. I could no longer care for my dependents.
Very important:

49.4	50.5	58.9	48.2	57.8	57.2	40.4	52.3	54.2

Important:

30.7	32.6	32.2	39.3	33.6	33.3	30.1	35.3	30.2

Not important:

19.9	16.8	8.9	12.5	8.6	9.5	29.5	12.4	15.6

     Ethnicity:
$$\chi^2 \,(df = 6) = 11.33$$
   Age:
$$\chi^2 \,(df = 4) = 35.49, \, p < .01$$

Ethnicity, %				Age, %			Sex, %	
Cau.A.	Afr.A.	His.A.	Asn.A.	20–39	40–59	60+	Male	Female

Gender:

χ^2 (df = 2) = 2.02

57. I am uncertain as to what might happen to me.

Very important:

14.4	39.8	50.5	16.1	36.3	31.9	28.8	33.8	32.9

Important:

32.3	23.5	20.3	30.4	25.7	23.9	28.1	25.6	25.5

Not important:

53.3	36.7	29.2	53.6	38.0	44.2	43.1	40.6	41.6

Ethnicity:

χ^2 (df = 6) = 63.60, $p < .01$

Age:

χ^2 (df = 4) = 3.14

Gender:

χ^2 (df = 2) = 0.06

58. I could no longer have experiences.

Very important:

13.3	21.9	11.4	1.8	12.2	13.2	13.2	12.4	13.6

Important:

34.5	28.1	26.9	28.6	32.2	27.9	27.2	29.8	29.3

Not important:

52.1	50.0	61.7	69.6	55.5	58.9	59.6	57.8	57.1

Ethnicity:

χ^2 (df = 6) = 17.46, $p < .01$

Age:

χ^2 (df = 4) = 1.37

Gender:

χ^2 (df = 2) = 0.17

59. My death would cause grief to my relatives and friends.

Very important:

35.9	47.4	56.9	33.9	53.9	47.4	30.5	43.8	47.8

Important:

53.3	37.1	37.2	46.4	39.6	43.8	49.6	45.7	41.5

Not important:

10.8	15.5	5.9	19.6	6.5	8.8	19.9	10.5	10.7

Ethnicity:

χ^2 (df = 6) = 27.97, $p < .01$

Age:

χ^2 (df = 4) = 28.35, $p < .01$

Gender:

χ^2 (df = 2) = 0.95

	Ethnicity, %				Age, %			Sex, %	
	Cau.A.	Afr.A.	His.A.	Asn.A.	20–39	40–59	60+	Male	Female

60. All my plans and projects would come to an end.

Very important:

	Cau.A.	Afr.A.	His.A.	Asn.A.	20–39	40–59	60+	Male	Female
Very important:	16.8	26.8	13.8	14.0	17.1	12.4	21.4	16.9	17.1
Important:	24.0	21.6	36.0	22.8	32.5	28.5	20.0	32.0	25.4
Not important:	59.3	51.5	50.2	63.2	50.4	59.1	58.6	51.1	57.5

Ethnicity:
$$\chi^2 \,(df = 6) = 16.73, p < .05$$
Age:
$$\chi^2 \,(df = 4) = 9.99, p < .05$$
Gender:
$$\chi^2 \,(df = 2) = 2.86$$

61. The process of dying might be painful.

	Cau.A.	Afr.A.	His.A.	Asn.A.	20–39	40–59	60+	Male	Female
Very important:	24.8	35.4	25.5	30.4	22.4	27.5	36.7	24.2	30.4
Important:	55.2	43.4	43.1	28.6	49.2	39.9	44.6	42.0	47.5
Not important:	20.0	21.2	31.4	41.1	28.5	32.6	18.7	33.8	22.1

Ethnicity:
$$\chi^2 \,(df = 6) = 20.15, p < .01$$
Age:
$$\chi^2 \,(df = 4) = 13.70, p < .01$$
Gender:
$$\chi^2 \,(df = 2) = 9.03, p < .05$$

62. Some people say they are afraid to die and others say they are not. How do you feel?

	Cau.A.	Afr.A.	His.A.	Asn.A.	20–39	40–59	60+	Male	Female
Afraid/Terrified:	10.8	10.0	28.6	12.5	20.2	18.8	12.1	17.2	18.4
Neither afraid nor unafraid:	64.1	60.0	33.5	51.8	43.3	52.9	60.0	49.3	50.5
Unafraid/Eager:	7.8	1.0	17.2	14.3	15.0	8.7	5.7	11.8	10.4
Depends:	17.4	29.0	20.7	21.4	21.5	19.6	22.2	21.7	20.7

Ethnicity:
$$\chi^2 \,(df = 9) = 64.63, p < .01$$
Age:
$$\chi^2 \,(df = 6) = 16.75, p < .05$$
Gender:
$$\chi^2 \,(df = 3) = 0.42$$

Ethnicity, %				Age, %			Sex, %	
Cau.A.	Afr.A.	His.A.	Asn.A.	20–39	40–59	60+	Male	Female

63. Of the following, which one has influenced your attitudes toward death the most?

Being or thinking you were close to death:

| 8.8 | 17.8 | 18.7 | 20.0 | 12.4 | 18.0 | 18.1 | 16.1 | 13.6 |

Death of someone else:

| 40.3 | 24.4 | 43.4 | 16.4 | 36.5 | 33.8 | 37.8 | 32.3 | 39.8 |

Reading:

| 4.4 | 1.1 | 2.5 | 7.3 | 2.9 | 0.8 | 7.1 | 4.6 | 2.5 |

Conversations:

| 2.2 | 10.0 | 1.5 | 5.5 | 4.1 | 5.3 | 1.6 | 3.7 | 3.9 |

Religion/including mystical experiences:

| 27.2 | 32.2 | 23.2 | 41.8 | 29.9 | 31.6 | 22.0 | 29.5 | 27.6 |

Funerals and other rituals:

| 5.0 | 6.7 | 3.5 | 5.5 | 3.7 | 6.0 | 5.5 | 4.6 | 5.0 |

Media:

| 1.9 | 2.2 | 2.0 | 0 | 2.9 | 0 | 1.6 | 1.8 | 1.8 |

Other:

| 9.4 | 5.6 | 5.1 | 3.6 | 7.5 | 4.5 | 6.3 | 7.4 | 5.7 |

Ethnicity:
$$\chi^2 \ (df = 21) = 49.67, \ p < .01$$
Age:
$$\chi^2 \ (df = 14) = 22.21$$
Gender:
$$\chi^2 \ (df = 7) = 4.71$$

64. Have you ever felt you were close to dying?

Yes:

| 33.1 | 41.4 | 48.0 | 40.4 | 39.2 | 45.7 | 40.1 | 45.4 | 37.4 |

No:

| 66.9 | 58.6 | 52.0 | 59.6 | 60.8 | 44.3 | 59.9 | 54.6 | 62.6 |

Ethnicity:
$$\chi^2 \ (df = 3) = 8.41, \ p < .05$$
Age:
$$\chi^2 \ (df = 2) = 1.61$$
Gender:
$$\chi^2 \ (df = 1) = 3.35$$

65. (If yes) Did that experience affect your way of living or philosophy of life?

Yes:

| 54.5 | 69.2 | 45.3 | 75.0 | 53.4 | 56.3 | 57.3 | 57.3 | 53.2 |

No:

| 45.5 | 30.8 | 54.7 | 25.0 | 46.6 | 43.7 | 42.7 | 42.7 | 46.8 |

Ethnicity:
$$\chi^2 \ (df = 3) = 13.24, \ p < .01$$

	Ethnicity, %				Age, %			Sex, %	
	Cau.A.	Afr.A.	His.A.	Asn.A.	20–39	40–59	60+	Male	Female

65. (If yes) Did that experience affect your way of living or philosophy of life (cont'd)?
    Age:
        χ^2 (df = 2) = 0.32
    Gender:
        χ^2 (df = 1) = 0.43

66. People can hasten or slow their own death through a will to live or a will to die.

	Cau.A.	Afr.A.	His.A.	Asn.A.	20–39	40–59	60+	Male	Female
Agree:	92.8	86.3	66.0	71.4	73.3	85.4	82.0	76.9	80.2
Disagree:	7.2	13.7	34.0	28.6	26.7	14.6	18.0	23.1	19.8

    Ethnicity:
        χ^2 (df = 3) = 44.38, $p < .01$
    Age:
        χ^2 (df = 2) = 8.91, $p < .05$
    Gender:
        χ^2 (df = 1) = 0.84

67. Death may someday be eliminated.

	Cau.A.	Afr.A.	His.A.	Asn.A.	20–39	40–59	60+	Male	Female
Agree:	5.5	10.5	16.7	16.1	16.0	8.0	9.0	12.1	12.2
Disagree:	94.5	89.5	83.3	83.9	84.0	92.0	91.0	87.9	87.8

    Ethnicity:
        χ^2 (df = 3) = 11.89, $p < .01$
    Age:
        χ^2 (df = 2) = 6.96, $p < .05$
    Gender:
        χ^2 (df = 1) = .00

68. Accidental deaths show the hand of God working among men.

	Cau.A.	Afr.A.	His.A.	Asn.A.	20–39	40–59	60+	Male	Female
Agree:	31.2	33.7	55.6	73.7	57.9	38.8	32.8	47.6	45.0
Disagree:	68.8	66.3	44.4	26.3	42.1	61.2	67.2	52.4	55.0

    Ethnicity:
        χ^2 (df = 3) = 44.49, $p < .01$
    Age:
        χ^2 (df = 2) = 25.66, $p < .01$
    Gender:
        χ^2 (df = 1) = .33

	Ethnicity, %			Age, %			Sex, %	
	Cau.A.	Afr.A.	His.A.	Asn.A.	20–39	40–59	60+	Male	Female

69. Most people who lived to be 90 years old or older must have been morally good people.
    Agree:

	10.9	29.5	21.0	27.3	17.7	17.2	26.3	23.5	16.8

Disagree:

	89.1	70.5	79.0	72.7	82.3	82.8	73.3	76.5	83.2

   Ethnicity:
   χ^2 (df = 3) = 15.79, $p < .01$
   Age:
   χ^2 (df = 2) = 4.87
   Gender:
   χ^2 (df = 1) = 3.56

70. Have you taken out life insurance?
    Yes:

	76.5	84.8	39.3	51.8	44.0	73.7	78.0	63.8	59.1

No:

	23.5	15.2	60.7	48.2	56.0	26.3	22.0	36.2	40.9

   Ethnicity:
   χ^2 (df = 3) = 82.30, $p < .01$
   Age:
   χ^2 (df = 2) = 55.90, $p < .01$
   Gender:
   χ^2 (df = 1) = 1.17

71. Have you made out a will?
    Yes:

	55.4	43.9	11.9	49.1	9.0	42.3	75.2	34.9	36.5

No:

	44.6	56.1	88.1	50.9	90.1	57.7	24.8	65.1	63.5

   Ethnicity:
   χ^2 (df = 3) = 85.32, $p < .01$
   Age:
   χ^2 (df = 2) = 174.18, $p < .01$
   Gender:
   χ^2 (df = 1) = 0.14

72. Have you made arrangements to donate your body or parts of it to medicine?
    Yes:

	35.9	16.3	11.3	31.6	22.4	42.0	17.7	17.8	25.2

No:

	64.1	83.7	88.7	68.4	77.6	58.0	82.3	82.2	74.8

	Ethnicity, %				Age, %			Sex, %	
	Cau.A.	Afr.A.	His.A.	Asn.A.	20–39	40–59	60+	Male	Female

72. Have you made arrangements to donate your body or parts of it to medicine *(cont'd)*?
    Ethnicity:
        χ^2 (df = 3) = 37.13, $p < .01$
    Age:
        χ^2 (df = 2) = 3.32
    Gender:
        χ^2 (df = 1) = 4.07, $p < .05$

73. Have you made funeral arrangements?

Yes:									
	15.1	27.3	8.9	3.5	2.8	11.6	35.0	14.6	12.7

No:

	84.9	72.7	91.1	96.5	97.2	88.4	65.0	85.4	87.3

    Ethnicity:
        χ^2 (df = 3) = 24.68, $p < .01$
    Age:
        χ^2 (df = 2) = 78.56, $p < .01$
    Gender:
        χ^2 (df = 1) = 0.41

74. Have you paid for or are you now paying for a cemetery plot?

Yes:

	25.5	35.0	11.2	1.8	3.6	13.0	52.1	16.7	20.8

No:

	74.5	65.0	88.8	98.2	96.4	87.0	47.9	83.3	79.2

    Ethnicity:
        χ^2 (df = 3) = 40.16, $p < .01$
    Age:
        χ^2 (df = 2) = 141.81, $p < .01$
    Gender:
        χ^2 (df = 1) = 1.36

75. Have you seriously talked with anyone about your experiencing death someday?

Yes:

	47.9	43.1	55.2	22.8	42.9	50.7	51.0	45.5	48.2

No:

	52.1	56.9	44.8	77.2	57.1	49.3	49.0	54.5	51.8

    Ethnicity:
        χ^2 (df = 3) = 19.49, $p < .01$
    Age:
        χ^2 (df = 2) = 3.39
    Gender:
        χ^2 (df = 1) = 0.38

	Ethnicity, %				Age, %			Sex, %	
	Cau.A.	Afr.A.	His.A.	Asn.A.	20–39	40–59	60+	Male	Female
76. (If yes) Who?									
Family member:									
76.7	69.6	53.1	58.3	45.0	75.4	81.1	53.5	71.1	
Friend:									
19.2	26.1	44.2	33.3	49.5	21.3	17.6	41.6	26.1	
Clergy:									
1.4	0	0.9	8.3	1.8	1.6	0	2.0	0.7	
Other:									
2.7	4.3	1.8	0	3.7	1.6	1.3	3.0	2.1	

Ethnicity:
$$\chi^2 \text{ (df = 9)} = 20.34, p < .05$$
Age:
$$\chi^2 \text{ (df = 6)} = 30.38, p < .01$$
Gender:
$$\chi^2 \text{ (df = 3)} = 8.22, p < .05$$

77. Have you arranged for someone to handle your affairs?									
Yes:									
55.6	51.0	18.3	35.1	15.4	39.0	76.4	31.5	42.9	
No:									
44.4	49.0	81.7	64.9	84.6	61.0	23.6	68.5	57.1	

Ethnicity:
$$\chi^2 \text{ (df = 3)} = 63.42, p < .01$$
Age:
$$\chi^2 \text{ (df = 2)} = 144.11, p < .01$$
Gender:
$$\chi^2 \text{ (df = 1)} = 8.28, p < .05$$

78. Regarding the respondent personally if he/she had lost a spouse through death, how important would it be to remarry?

Unimportant to wait:									
11.0	9.0	3.5	3.5	5.7	5.2	10.6	6.4	7.0	
1 week–6 months:									
3.7	6.0	3.0	0	2.9	1.5	6.4	5.5	2.0	
1 year:									
14.6	7.0	7.5	1.8	8.2	11.1	8.5	6.9	10.7	
2 years:									
14.6	9.0	20.5	15.8	20.1	16.3	8.5	12.4	18.7	
Never:									
6.7	9.0	12.5	26.3	5.3	11.9	22.0	12.4	10.7	
Depends:									
49.4	60.0	53.0	52.6	57.8	54.1	44.0	56.4	50.8	

Ethnicity:
$$\chi^2 \text{ (df = 15)} = 44.87, p < .01$$

	Ethnicity, %			Age, %			Sex, %	
Cau.A.	Afr.A.	His.A.	Asn.A.	20–39	40–59	60+	Male	Female

78. Regarding the respondent personally if he/she had lost a spouse through death, how important would it be to remarry *(cont'd)*?
    Age:
    χ^2 (df = 10) = 42.29, $p < .01$
    Gender:
    χ^2 (df = 5) = 10.74

79. To stop wearing black?
    Unimportant to wait:

Cau.A.	Afr.A.	His.A.	Asn.A.	20–39	40–59	60+	Male	Female
78.6	45.7	50.0	39.3	52.3	61.9	58.5	57.7	55.2

1 day–4 months:

10.9	12.8	14.8	12.5	15.8	14.9	5.9	10.7	14.1

6 months or more:

3.6	4.3	10.2	5.4	7.5	3.7	7.4	3.3	9.0

Other/Depends:

10.0	37.2	25.0	42.9	24.5	19.4	28.2	28.4	21.7

   Ethnicity:
   χ^2 (df = 9) = 54.33, $p < .01$
   Age:
   χ^2 (df = 6) = 12.85, $p < .05$
   Gender:
   χ^2 (df = 3) = 9.67, $p < .05$

80. To return to his/her place of employment?
    Unimportant to wait:

18.9	20.4	33.2	22.8	23.9	29.1	22.9	30.6	20.7

1 day–1 week

29.3	26.5	26.6	24.6	24.3	29.1	30.7	27.9	27.1

1 month or more:

13.4	14.2	14.1	22.8	19.3	14.2	7.9	11.0	18.0

Other/Depends:

38.4	38.8	26.1	29.8	32.5	27.6	38.6	30.6	34.2

   Ethnicity:
   χ^2 (df = 9) = 17.34, $p < .05$
   Age:
   χ^2 (df = 6) = 13.31, $p < .05$
   Gender:
   χ^2 (df = 3) = 9.62, $p < .05$

81. To start going out with other men/women?
    Unimportant to wait:

11.0	10.0	11.5	8.8	9.1	8.8	15.1	12.9	8.8

1 week–1 month:

2.5	7.0	3.0	0	2.1	3.6	5.0	4.1	2.7

Ethnicity, %				Age, %			Sex, %	
Cau.A.	Afr.A.	His.A.	Asn.A.	20–39	40–59	60+	Male	Female

6 months:

| 18.4 | 12.0 | 7.0 | 1.8 | 8.6 | 13.9 | 12.2 | 12.0 | 10.4 |

1 year or more:

| 19.0 | 7.0 | 27.0 | 21.1 | 27.2 | 21.2 | 13.7 | 16.1 | 25.9 |

Other/Depends:

| 49.1 | 54.0 | 51.5 | 68.4 | 53.1 | 52.6 | 54.0 | 54.8 | 52.2 |

Ethnicity:

χ^2 (df = 12) = 29.71, $p < .01$

Age:

χ^2 (df = 8) = 15.98, $p < .05$

Gender:

χ^2 (df – 4) = 8.81

82. What do you feel is the fewest number of times he/she should visit his/her spouse's grave during the first year—not counting the burial service?

Unimportant:

| 39.4 | 25.8 | 18.4 | 28.1 | 23.3 | 28.9 | 33.8 | 26.9 | 27.9 |

1–2 times:

| 7.9 | 11.3 | 17.4 | 5.3 | 11.4 | 12.6 | 12.2 | 13.7 | 10.8 |

3–5 times:

| 4.8 | 11.3 | 15.9 | 10.5 | 12.7 | 10.4 | 8.6 | 14.6 | 8.0 |

6 or more times:

| 15.2 | 12.4 | 18.9 | 8.8 | 13.5 | 16.3 | 18.0 | 9.1 | 20.2 |

Other/Depends/Don't know:

| 32.7 | 39.2 | 29.4 | 47.4 | 39.2 | 31.9 | 27.3 | 35.6 | 22.9 |

Ethnicity:

χ^2 (df = 12) = 43.18, $p < .01$

Age:

χ^2 (df = 8) = 10.36

Gender:

χ^2 (df = 4) = 16.11, $p < .01$

83. What do you feel is the fewest number of times he/she should visit his/her spouse's grave during the fifth year after the death?

Unimportant:

| 47.9 | 26.7 | 24.8 | 29.8 | 26.5 | 33.6 | 43.7 | 35.5 | 31.4 |

1–2 times:

| 9.7 | 19.8 | 18.3 | 12.3 | 17.1 | 16.1 | 11.3 | 13.2 | 16.4 |

3–5 times:

| 3.6 | 3.0 | 9.4 | 5.3 | 6.1 | 7.3 | 4.2 | 6.4 | 5.4 |

6 or more times:

| 7.9 | 4.0 | 13.9 | 8.8 | 9.8 | 8.0 | 10.6 | 5.5 | 12.7 |

	Ethnicity, %				Age, %			Sex, %	
	Cau.A.	Afr.A.	His.A.	Asn.A.	20–39	40–59	60+	Male	Female

83. What do you feel is the fewest number of times he/she should visit his/her spouse's grave during the fifth year after the death *(cont'd)*?

Other/Depends/Don't know:

	Cau.A.	Afr.A.	His.A.	Asn.A.	20–39	40–59	60+	Male	Female
	30.1	46.5	33.7	43.9	40.4	35.0	30.3	39.5	34.1

Ethnicity:

χ^2 (df = 12) = 43.35, $p < .01$

Age:

χ^2 (df = 8) = 14.38

Gender:

χ^2 (df = 4) = 9.66, $p < .05$

84. How do you know when someone is NOT grieving normally and needs help?

Withdrawal/Apathy:

	Cau.A.	Afr.A.	His.A.	Asn.A.	20–39	40–59	60+	Male	Female
Withdrawal/Apathy:	27.7	24.7	22.4	30.9	20.7	27.6	32.3	23.2	27.5
Death preoccupation:	9.7	4.5	5.1	9.1	9.3	5.5	3.8	6.6	7.1
Exaggerated expression of grief:	5.8	9.0	9.7	3.6	7.6	7.1	7.7	9.0	6.8
Abnormal behavior:	21.9	29.2	36.7	27.3	31.2	25.2	31.5	34.1	26.4
No reaction:	29.7	21.3	16.8	20.0	20.3	31.5	16.2	19.9	23.9
Other:	5.2	11.2	9.2	9.1	11.0	3.1	8.5	7.1	8.2

Ethnicity:

χ^2 (df = 15) = 24.75

Age:

χ^2 (df = 10) = 23.67, $p < .01$

Gender:

χ^2 (df = 5) = 5.13

85. When would you begin worrying that someone had been crying, grieving, and sorrowful for too long?

	Cau.A.	Afr.A.	His.A.	Asn.A.	20–39	40–59	60+	Male	Female
2 weeks or less:	2.5	4.1	7.1	7.0	7.1	3.6	2.9	5.6	4.8
1–3 months:	11.7	18.6	17.7	21.1	17.9	8.0	21.9	20.8	13.0
6 or more months:	36.2	35.1	45.5	36.8	37.5	51.8	30.7	37.0	41.3
Other/Depends/Don't know:	49.7	42.3	29.8	35.1	37.5	36.5	44.5	36.6	41.0

Ethnicity:

χ^2 (df = 9) = 20.22, $p < .05$

	Ethnicity, %				Age, %			Sex, %	
	Cau.A.	Afr.A.	His.A.	Asn.A.	20–39	40–59	60+	Male	Female

Age:
$$\chi^2 \, (df = 6) = 22.12, \, p < .01$$
Gender:
$$\chi^2 \, (df = 3) = 6.04$$

86. Do you believe you will live on in some form after death?

Yes:

| 87.7 | 83.5 | 90.2 | 81.8 | 89.8 | 88.4 | 81.5 | 87.1 | 87.5 |

No:

| 12.3 | 16.5 | 9.8 | 18.2 | 10.2 | 11.6 | 18.5 | 12.9 | 12.5 |

Ethnicity:
$$\chi^2 \, (df = 3) = 4.31$$
Age:
$$\chi^2 \, (df = 2) = 5.63$$
Gender:
$$\chi^2 \, (df = 1) = 0.02$$

87. (If yes) What form?

Through children/works/memory:

| 14.7 | 14.5 | 4.8 | 2.2 | 5.4 | 13.2 | 13.2 | 7.8 | 10.6 |

Return to earth in Spirit Form:

| 6.3 | 10.8 | 4.3 | 26.1 | 7.2 | 6.6 | 12.3 | 8.3 | 8.4 |

In Heaven/Paradise:

| 72.7 | 69.9 | 86.6 | 45.7 | 82.1 | 71.9 | 64.9 | 74.6 | 76.0 |

Other:

| 6.3 | 4.8 | 4.3 | 26.1 | 5.4 | 8.3 | 9.6 | 9.3 | 4.9 |

Ethnicity:
$$\chi^2 \, (df = 9) = 70.75, \, p < .01$$
Age:
$$\chi^2 \, (df = 6) = 15.71, \, p < .05$$
Gender:
$$\chi^2 \, (df = 3) = 4.15$$

88. (If heaven) Do you believe those in heaven watch over earth or have no concern for earth?

Watch over:

| 81.1 | 81.3 | 63.3 | 60.0 | 70.6 | 75.5 | 72.2 | 64.0 | 78.3 |

No concern:

| 18.9 | 18.7 | 36.7 | 40.0 | 29.4 | 24.5 | 27.8 | 36.0 | 21.7 |

Ethnicity:
$$\chi^2 \, (df = 3) = 18.23, \, p < .01$$
Age:
$$\chi^2 \, (df = 2) = 0.84$$
Gender:
$$\chi^2 \, (df = 1) = 10.54, \, p < .01$$

	Ethnicity, %				Age, %			Sex, %	
	Cau.A.	Afr.A.	His.A.	Asn.A.	20–39	40–59	60+	Male	Female

89. (If no to #86) What is death to you?
   Nothingness:

	Cau.A.	Afr.A.	His.A.	Asn.A.	20–39	40–59	60+	Male	Female
	31.9	14.3	25.0	45.5	25.8	24.2	29.1	33.3	22.4

   Other:

	Cau.A.	Afr.A.	His.A.	Asn.A.	20–39	40–59	60+	Male	Female
	68.1	85.7	75.0	54.5	74.2	75.8	70.9	66.7	77.6

   Ethnicity:
   χ^2 (df = 3) = 7.87, $p < .05$
   Age:
   χ^2 (df = 2) = 0.29
   Gender:
   χ^2 (df = 1) = 2.21

90. Regardless of your *belief* about life after death, what is your wish about it?
   Wish there were:

	Cau.A.	Afr.A.	His.A.	Asn.A.	20–39	40–59	60+	Male	Female
	84.6	61.3	82.8	60.4	79.3	80.0	72.0	75.7	78.4

   Indifferent:

	Cau.A.	Afr.A.	His.A.	Asn.A.	20–39	40–59	60+	Male	Female
	14.2	34.7	11.8	34.0	16.3	17.7	23.7	20.8	17.5

   Wish there were not:

	Cau.A.	Afr.A.	His.A.	Asn.A.	20–39	40–59	60+	Male	Female
	1.2	4.0	5.4	5.6	4.4	2.3	4.3	3.5	4.1

   Ethnicity:
   χ^2 (df = 6) = 34.07, $p < .01$
   Age:
   χ^2 (df = 4) = 4.07
   Gender:
   χ^2 (df = 2) = 0.87

91. Have you ever experienced or felt the presence of anyone after he/she had died?
   Yes:

	Cau.A.	Afr.A.	His.A.	Asn.A.	20–39	40–59	60+	Male	Female
	58.2	55.7	40.3	47.3	38.6	56.9	62.7	40.3	57.1

   No:

	Cau.A.	Afr.A.	His.A.	Asn.A.	20–39	40–59	60+	Male	Female
	41.8	44.3	59.7	52.7	61.4	43.1	37.3	59.7	42.9

   Ethnicity:
   χ^2 (df = 3) = 13.37, $p < .01$
   Age:
   χ^2 (df = 2) = 23.99, $p < .01$
   Gender:
   χ^2 (df = 1) = 14.13, $p < .01$

92. (If yes) What type of experience?
   Dream:

	Cau.A.	Afr.A.	His.A.	Asn.A.	20–39	40–59	60+	Male	Female
	50.0	38.3	59.8	76.9	61.0	48.8	48.4	54.7	52.0

   Visit:

	Cau.A.	Afr.A.	His.A.	Asn.A.	20–39	40–59	60+	Male	Female
	27.0	46.7	10.3	3.8	18.0	25.0	29.0	21.1	25.4

	Ethnicity, %			Age, %			Sex, %	
Cau.A.	Afr.A.	His.A.	Asn.A.	20–39	40–59	60+	Male	Female

Séance:

| 0 | 3.3 | 14.9 | 7.7 | 6.0 | 8.8 | 4.3 | 2.1 | 8.5 |

Other:

| 23.0 | 11.7 | 14.9 | 11.5 | 15.0 | 17.4 | 18.3 | 22.1 | 14.1 |

Ethnicity:

χ^2 (df = 9) = 52.28, $p < .01$

Age:

χ^2 (df = 6) = 6.10

Gender:

χ^2 (df = 3) = 6.92

93. (If yes to #91) What was the quality of the experience?

Appeared/Spoke:

| 37.9 | 32.7 | 45.8 | 48.0 | 41.8 | 36.5 | 42.5 | 29.5 | 46.0 |

Psychologically felt:

| 52.6 | 49.0 | 37.3 | 48.0 | 38.8 | 56.8 | 46.3 | 53.4 | 42.9 |

Sensed by touch:

| 9.5 | 18.4 | 16.9 | 4.0 | 19.4 | 6.7 | 11.2 | 17.0 | 11.0 |

Ethnicity:

χ^2 (df = 6) = 8.64

Age:

χ^2 (df = 4) = 8.80

Gender:

χ^2 (df = 2) = 6.76, $p < .05$

94. (If yes to #91) How did you feel at the time?

Pleasant:

| 75.2 | 50.9 | 29.8 | 57.7 | 47.5 | 56.4 | 59.8 | 44.6 | 59.1 |

Fearful:

| 4.0 | 5.7 | 35.7 | 3.8 | 14.1 | 16.7 | 12.6 | 21.7 | 10.5 |

Mystical:

| 5.0 | 26.4 | 10.7 | 11.5 | 12.1 | 12.8 | 10.3 | 13.0 | 11.1 |

Other:

| 15.8 | 17.0 | 23.8 | 26.9 | 26.3 | 14.1 | 17.2 | 20.7 | 19.3 |

Ethnicity:

χ^2 (df = 9) = 72.80, $p < .01$

Age:

χ^2 (df = 6) = 5.77

Gender:

χ^2 (df = 3) = 7.78

95. Other than during dreams, have you ever had the unexplainable feeling that you were about to die?

Yes:

| 17.6 | 28.9 | 35.0 | 14.3 | 24.5 | 27.4 | 27.5 | 28.0 | 25.1 |

	Ethnicity, %			Age, %			Sex, %	
Cau.A.	Afr.A.	His.A.	Asn.A.	20–39	40–59	60+	Male	Female

95. Other than during dreams, have you ever had the unexplainable feeling that you were about to die *(cont'd)*?
    No:

82.4	71.1	65.0	85.7	75.5	72.6	72.5	72.0	74.9

  Ethnicity:
  χ^2 (df = 3) = 18.83, $p < .01$
  Age:
  χ^2 (df = 2) = 0.59
  Gender:
  χ^2 (df = 1) = 0.56

96. Have you ever had this feeling about someone else?
    Yes:

40.9	55.7	34.7	19.6	32.4	47.4	42.0	33.5	42.7

    No:

59.1	44.3	65.3	80.4	67.6	52.6	58.0	66.5	57.3

  Ethnicity:
  χ^2 (df = 3) = 21.92, $p < .01$
  Age:
  χ^2 (df = 2) = 8.91, $p < .05$
  Gender:
  χ^2 (df = 1) = 4.41, $p < .05$

97. (If yes) Did they actually die subsequently?
    Always:

17.9	11.5	9.0	0	9.7	7.8	20.9	11.8	12.5

    Sometimes:

41.7	41.0	43.8	21.4	33.0	41.6	52.2	35.5	44.7

    No:

40.5	47.5	47.2	78.6	57.3	50.6	26.9	52.7	42.8

  Ethnicity:
  χ^2 (df = 6) = 9.96
  Age:
  χ^2 (df = 4) = 17.93, $p < .01$
  Gender:
  χ^2 (df = 2) = 2.44

98. How often do you dream about your own death or dying?
    Frequently:

1.2	4.0	1.0	0	1.2	0.7	2.8	1.8	1.4

    Sometimes:

9.1	13.0	24.6	12.3	16.3	19.4	12.8	15.1	17.2

    Rarely:

43.6	41.0	29.1	36.8	44.1	42.5	19.2	36.1	37.2

	Ethnicity, %				Age, %			Sex, %	
	Cau.A.	Afr.A.	His.A.	Asn.A.	20–39	40–59	60+	Male	Female

Never:

| 46.1 | 42.0 | 45.2 | 50.9 | 38.4 | 37.3 | 65.2 | 47.0 | 44.3 |

Ethnicity:
$\chi^2 \ (df = 9) = 26.79, \ p < .01$
Age:
$\chi^2 \ (df = 6) = 37.58, \ p < .01$
Gender:
$\chi^2 \ (df = 3) = 0.80$

99. Would you want a big, elaborate funeral?

Yes:

| 6.1 | 16.5 | 8.9 | 0 | 9.4 | 8.9 | 6.5 | 10.1 | 6.8 |

No:

| 71.3 | 61.9 | 60.9 | 78.6 | 57.1 | 71.1 | 77.5 | 56.2 | 74.7 |

Indifferent:

| 22.6 | 21.6 | 30.2 | 21.4 | 33.5 | 20.0 | 16.0 | 33.6 | 18.6 |

Ethnicity:
$\chi^2 \ (df = 6) = 19.58, \ p < .01$
Age:
$\chi^2 \ (df = 4) = 19.84, \ p < .01$
Gender:
$\chi^2 \ (df = 2) = 19.50, \ p < .01$

100. Do you expect that many of your friends and/or relatives will help share the expense of your funeral?

Yes:

| 21.0 | 31.7 | 51.0 | 17.9 | 46.5 | 24.1 | 22.4 | 37.3 | 32.3 |

No:

| 64.6 | 56.4 | 29.7 | 67.9 | 30.0 | 67.2 | 69.9 | 44.1 | 54.3 |

Indifferent:

| 14.4 | 11.9 | 19.3 | 14.3 | 24.5 | 8.7 | 7.7 | 18.6 | 13.3 |

Ethnicity:
$\chi^2 \ (df = 6) = 60.85, \ p < .01$
Age:
$\chi^2 \ (df = 4) = 83.83, \ p < .01$
Gender:
$\chi^2 \ (df = 2) = 5.85$

101. Would you rather have a large funeral with lots of friends and acquaintances or one in which only relatives and close acquaintances attended?

Lots of friends:

| 29.7 | 46.8 | 24.6 | 5.4 | 26.1 | 24.6 | 34.1 | 29.5 | 26.6 |

Only close relatives:

| 32.1 | 24.5 | 43.2 | 53.6 | 35.7 | 41.0 | 36.2 | 35.0 | 39.2 |

	Ethnicity, %				Age, %			Sex, %	
Cau.A.	Afr.A.	His.A.	Asn.A.	20–39	40–59	60+	Male	Female

101. Would you rather have a large funeral with lots of friends and acquaintances or one in which only relatives and close acquaintances attended (*cont'd*)?

Indifferent/Neither:

| 38.2 | 28.7 | 33.2 | 41.0 | 38.2 | 34.4 | 29.7 | 35.5 | 34.1 |

Ethnicity:

χ^2 (df = 6) = 37.30, $p < .01$

Age:

χ^2 (df = 4) = 5.19

Gender:

χ^2 (df = 2) = 1.03

102. Do you want the selection of a priest/minister for the funeral to be made by your family after you've gone?

Yes:

| 49.7 | 56.6 | 63.7 | 54.4 | 57.6 | 50.4 | 61.7 | 56.9 | 57.4 |

No:

| 21.8 | 23.2 | 11.9 | 14.0 | 13.6 | 24.1 | 17.7 | 15.1 | 18.8 |

Indifferent:

| 28.5 | 20.2 | 24.4 | 31.6 | 28.8 | 25.5 | 20.6 | 28.0 | 23.8 |

Ethnicity:

χ^2 (df = 6) = 13.35, $p < .05$

Age:

χ^2 (df = 4) = 9.53, $p < .05$

Gender:

χ^2 (df = 2) = 1.83

103. Do you want the priest/minister to be of your own ethnic group?

Yes:

| 35.0 | 71.1 | 62.2 | 50.9 | 48.1 | 55.6 | 62.8 | 54.6 | 53.8 |

No:

| 3.1 | 5.2 | 3.0 | 9.1 | 3.3 | 6.7 | 2.9 | 4.1 | 3.8 |

Indifferent:

| 62.0 | 23.7 | 34.8 | 40.0 | 48.6 | 37.7 | 34.3 | 41.3 | 42.5 |

Ethnicity:

χ^2 (df = 6) = 49.24, $p < .01$

Age:

χ^2 (df = 4) = 11.59, $p < .05$

Gender:

χ^2 (df = 2) = 0.10

104. Do you feel that a large percentage of your life insurance should go toward paying your funeral expenses?

Yes:

| 18.8 | 29.6 | 30.0 | 14.3 | 28.1 | 16.8 | 26.1 | 22.4 | 26.3 |

	Ethnicity, %				Age, %			Sex, %	
	Cau.A.	Afr.A.	His.A.	Asn.A.	20–39	40–59	60+	Male	Female
No:									
	63.1	60.2	37.0	60.7	44.6	65.0	53.0	54.8	50.5
Indifferent:									
	18.1	10.2	33.0	25.0	27.3	18.2	20.9	22.8	23.2

Ethnicity:
$$\chi^2 \, (df = 6) = 39.78, \, p < .01$$
Age:
$$\chi^2 \, (df = 4) = 15.16, \, p < .01$$
Gender:
$$\chi^2 \, (df = 2) = 1.22$$

105. Would you prefer to have your casket open provided there were no disfigurement?

	Cau.A.	Afr.A.	His.A.	Asn.A.	20–39	40–59	60+	Male	Female
Yes:									
	36.1	57.4	47.0	25.5	45.9	39.4	42.1	41.6	44.4
No:									
	28.3	20.8	28.5	34.5	25.0	30.7	29.3	28.3	27.3
Indifferent:									
	35.5	21.8	24.5	40.0	29.1	29.9	28.6	30.1	28.3

Ethnicity:
$$\chi^2 \, (df = 6) = 21.96, \, p < .01$$
Age:
$$\chi^2 \, (df = 4) = 2.15$$
Gender:
$$\chi^2 \, (df = 2) = 0.44$$

106. Would you prefer that your funeral director be of your own ethnic group?

	Cau.A.	Afr.A.	His.A.	Asn.A.	20–39	40–59	60+	Male	Female
Yes:									
	21.2	62.2	49.5	39.3	37.4	44.9	46.0	42.5	41.2
No:									
	5.4	6.1	7.0	5.4	5.8	5.9	7.2	2.3	8.8
Indifferent:									
	73.3	31.6	43.5	55.3	56.8	49.2	46.8	55.2	50.0

Ethnicity:
$$\chi^2 \, (df = 6) = 55.01, \, p < .01$$
Age:
$$\chi^2 \, (df = 4) = 4.32$$
Gender:
$$\chi^2 \, (df = 2) = 9.65 \, p < .01$$

107. About how much do you feel an adequate funeral would cost?

	Cau.A.	Afr.A.	His.A.	Asn.A.	20–39	40–59	60+	Male	Female
0–$700:									
	9.1	10.8	6.9	21.6	10.0	10.0	9.6	8.1	11.3

Ethnicity, %				Age, %			Sex, %	
Cau.A.	Afr.A.	His.A.	Asn.A.	20–39	40–59	60+	Male	Female

107. About how much do you feel an adequate funeral would cost *(cont'd)*?

$701–$1400:

| 14.0 | 17.2 | 18.1 | 13.7 | 20.4 | 8.5 | 16.3 | 12.9 | 18.1 |

$1401–$2100:

| 6.1 | 12.9 | 17.0 | 13.7 | 13.0 | 9.2 | 14.1 | 11.4 | 13.1 |

$2101–$2800:

| 8.5 | 8.6 | 14.4 | 9.8 | 12.6 | 9.2 | 9.6 | 12.4 | 9.6 |

$2801–$3500:

| 18.3 | 11.8 | 18.6 | 9.8 | 13.5 | 25.4 | 12.6 | 21.9 | 12.4 |

$3501–$4200:

| 8.5 | 15.1 | 10.6 | 5.9 | 9.6 | 11.5 | 10.4 | 11.4 | 9.6 |

$4201–$4900:

| 16.5 | 8.6 | 7.4 | 5.9 | 8.3 | 14.6 | 9.6 | 9.5 | 11.0 |

More than $4900:

| 18.9 | 15.1 | 6.9 | 19.6 | 12.6 | 11.5 | 17.8 | 12.4 | 14.9 |

Ethnicity:

χ^2 (df = 21) = 48.67, $p < .01$

Age:

χ^2 (df = 14) = 24.71, $p < .05$

Gender:

χ^2 (df = 7) = 12.30

108. Would you want children under 10 years old to attend your funeral?

Yes:

| 47.9 | 68.4 | 57.6 | 40.4 | 58.7 | 52.6 | 49.6 | 55.5 | 53.6 |

No:

| 13.3 | 8.4 | 9.6 | 17.5 | 7.4 | 7.4 | 21.9 | 11.9 | 11.3 |

Indifferent:

| 38.8 | 23.2 | 32.8 | 42.1 | 33.9 | 40.0 | 28.5 | 32.6 | 35.1 |

Ethnicity:

χ^2 (df = 6) = 16.43, $p < .05$

Age:

χ^2 (df = 4) = 22.76, $p < .01$

Gender:

χ^2 (df = 2) = 0.35

109. Do you want a wake/reception to be held before the funeral service?

Yes:

| 27.7 | 70.6 | 56.5 | 18.2 | 47.7 | 42.6 | 46.0 | 46.0 | 46.4 |

No:

| 27.1 | 9.8 | 17.5 | 45.5 | 18.0 | 24.3 | 27.0 | 22.5 | 21.7 |

Indifferent:

| 45.2 | 19.6 | 26.0 | 36.3 | 34.3 | 33.1 | 27.0 | 31.5 | 31.9 |

	Ethnicity, %				Age, %			Sex, %	
	Cau.A.	Afr.A.	His.A.	Asn.A.	20–39	40–59	60+	Male	Female

Ethnicity:
χ^2 (df = 6) = 80.44, $p < .01$
Age:
χ^2 (df = 4) = 5.77
Gender:
χ^2 (df = 2) = 0.05

110. (If yes) Where do you want your wake to be held: at a funeral home, at a church, at your home, or someplace else?

Funeral home:

	40.3	57.7	26.5	14.3	25.2	36.8	59.0	37.7	37.3

Church:

	24.2	28.2	25.8	50.0	30.9	30.9	17.9	28.7	25.5

At own home:

	19.4	11.5	44.7	28.6	37.4	26.5	17.9	28.7	30.4

Someplace else:

	16.1	2.0	3.0	7.1	6.5	5.8	5.2	4.9	6.8

Ethnicity:
χ^2 (df = 9) = 53.27, $p < .01$
Age:
χ^2 (df = 6) = 25.67, $p < .01$
Gender:
χ^2 (df = 3) = 0.77

111. Do you expect that there will be some drinking of liquor during your wake/reception or funeral service?

Yes:

	30.3	32.0	39.6	18.9	37.4	28.6	28.8	38.5	29.5

No:

	69.7	68.0	60.4	81.1	62.6	71.4	71.2	61.5	70.5

Ethnicity:
χ^2 (df = 3) = 9.11, $p < .05$
Age:
χ^2 (df = 2) = 4.26
Gender:
χ^2 (df = 1) = 4.39, $p < .05$

112. Do you expect that others will take tranquilizers to keep calm during your wake/reception or funeral?

Yes:

	29.1	33.3	29.7	29.4	34.3	26.1	26.2	25.5	33.7

No:

	70.9	66.7	70.3	70.6	65.7	73.9	73.8	74.5	66.3

	Ethnicity, %				Age, %			Sex, %	
Cau.A.	Afr.A.	His.A.	Asn.A.	20–39	40–59	60+	Male	Female

112. Do you expect that others will take tranquilizers to keep calm during your wake/reception or funeral *(cont'd)*?
   Ethnicity:
   χ^2 (df = 3) = 0.59
   Age:
   χ^2 (df = 2) = 3.94
   Gender:
   χ^2 (df = 1) = 3.88, $p < .05$

113. Where do you want your funeral service to be held: at a funeral home, at a church, at your home, or someplace else?
   Funeral home:

30.6	4.2	31.5	41.5	20.5	29.5	36.6	34.6	21.9

   Church:

50.6	87.5	33.5	32.1	52.3	43.2	48.5	45.3	51.7

   At own home:

1.3	3.1	29.4	18.9	19.2	14.4	6.0	12.6	16.0

   Someplace else:

17.5	5.2	5.6	7.5	8.0	12.9	8.9	7.5	10.4

   Ethnicity:
   χ^2 (df = 9) = 142.03, $p < .01$
   Age:
   χ^2 (df = 6) = 22.71
   Gender:
   χ^2 (df = 3) = 10.40, $p < .05$

114. Would you object to having an autopsy performed on your body?
   Yes:

18.9	25.5	21.2	9.3	14.5	25.7	24.4	14.1	24.0

   No:

57.9	52.0	57.1	46.3	55.4	56.6	53.3	54.1	56.2

   Indifferent:

23.2	22.4	21.7	44.4	30.2	17.7	22.3	31.8	19.8

   Ethnicity:
   χ^2 (df = 6) = 15.72, $p < .05$
   Age:
   χ^2 (df = 4) = 13.37, $p < .01$
   Gender:
   χ^2 (df = 2) = 13.49, $p < .01$

115. Would you object to being embalmed?
   Yes:

21.5	13.3	22.0	20.8	16.2	19.9	27.2	17.9	22.1

   No:

56.4	75.5	53.0	20.8	52.7	58.8	55.1	51.8	57.6

	Ethnicity, %				Age, %			Sex, %	
	Cau.A.	Afr.A.	His.A.	Asn.A.	20–39	40–59	60+	Male	Female
Indifferent:									
	22.1	11.2	25.0	58.5	31.1	21.3	17.7	30.3	20.3

Ethnicity:
$$\chi^2 \, (df = 6) = 53.68, \, p < .01$$
Age:
$$\chi^2 \, (df = 4) = 13.16, \, p < .05$$
Gender:
$$\chi^2 \, (df = 2) = 6.81, \, p < .05$$

116. How would you like your body to be disposed of?

	Cau.A.	Afr.A.	His.A.	Asn.A.	20–39	40–59	60+	Male	Female
Buried:									
	38.1	71.4	67.5	29.6	54.7	54.0	56.4	57.9	53.1
Cremated:									
	28.8	14.3	12.5	46.3	14.8	28.9	26.3	21.7	21.7
Donated:									
	8.7	1.0	8.0	13.0	9.9	5.9	4.5	7.4	7.3
Indifferent/Undecided:									
	24.4	13.3	12.0	11.1	20.6	11.2	12.8	13.0	17.9

Ethnicity:
$$\chi^2 \, (df = 9) = 72.73, \, p < .01$$
Age:
$$\chi^2 \, (df = 6) = 19.90, \, p < .01$$
Gender:
$$\chi^2 \, (df = 3) = 2.45$$

117. At what age do you expect to die? (40–59/60+ collapsed)
20–39 years old: (*mean* years)

	Cau.A.	Afr.A.	His.A.	Asn.A.	20–39	40–59	60+	Male	Female
Male:									
	79.2	107.7	80.1	75.6					
	(16.5)	(18.6)	(18.0)	(6.8)					
Female:									
	83.2	86.8	76.6	75.8					
	(11.8)	(13.7)	(10.6)	(6.0)					
Total:									
	81.2	97.3	78.4	75.7	83.2			85.7	80.6
40+ years:									
Male:									
	88.7	89.5	85.8	74.2					
	(11.2)	(10.4)	(10.8)	(6.5)					
Female:									
	84.9	86.8	84.0	73.6					
	(11.0)	(11.1)	(9.6)	(4.8)					
Total:									
	86.8	88.2	84.9	73.9		83.5		84.6	82.3

	Ethnicity, %				Age, %			Sex, %	
	Cau.A.	Afr.A.	His.A.	Asn.A.	20–39	40–59	60+	Male	Female

118. Now, if you could choose, to what age would you like to live?
20–39 years old: (*mean* years, SDs in parentheses)
Male:

	Cau.A.	Afr.A.	His.A.	Asn.A.	20–39	40–59	60+	Male	Female
	290.2	112.0	182.7	60.6					
	(390.1)	(11.5)	(268.9)	(25.8)					

Female:

	Cau.A.	Afr.A.	His.A.	Asn.A.	20–39	40–59	60+	Male	Female
	89.7	94.5	86.0	65.0					
	(12.3)	(13.1)	(9.8)	(24.7)					

Total:

	Cau.A.	Afr.A.	His.A.	Asn.A.	20–39	40–59	60+	Male	Female
	190.0	103.3	134.4	62.8	122.6			161.4	83.8

40–59 years:
Male:

	Cau.A.	Afr.A.	His.A.	Asn.A.	20–39	40–59	60+	Male	Female
	156.7	98.3	91.6	76.5					
	(242.9)	(7.3)	(9.6)	(11.4)					

Female:

	Cau.A.	Afr.A.	His.A.	Asn.A.	20–39	40–59	60+	Male	Female
	89.2	88.1	88.3	74.3					
	(15.6)	(9.2)	(11.7)	(9.3)					

Total:

	Cau.A.	Afr.A.	His.A.	Asn.A.	20–39	40–59	60+	Male	Female
	123.0	93.2	90.0	75.4		95.4		105.8	85.0

60+ years:
Male:

	Cau.A.	Afr.A.	His.A.	Asn.A.	20–39	40–59	60+	Male	Female
	99.5	97.1	91.4	75.4					
	(14.9)	(17.0)	(8.6)	(6.1)					

Female:

	Cau.A.	Afr.A.	His.A.	Asn.A.	20–39	40–59	60+	Male	Female
	91.6	397.8	100.0	74.3					
	(9.3)	(465.7)	(11.3)	(9.0)					

Total:

	Cau.A.	Afr.A.	His.A.	Asn.A.	20–39	40–59	60+	Male	Female
	95.6	247.4	95.7	74.9			128.4	90.8	165.9

119. Where would you like to die?
At home:

	Cau.A.	Afr.A.	His.A.	Asn.A.	20–39	40–59	60+	Male	Female
	81.2	62.2	75.9	79.2	71.9	88.0	69.4	77.4	74.0

In a hospital:

	Cau.A.	Afr.A.	His.A.	Asn.A.	20–39	40–59	60+	Male	Female
	12.1	28.9	9.7	13.2	10.2	9.0	26.9	9.6	17.7

Other:

	Cau.A.	Afr.A.	His.A.	Asn.A.	20–39	40–59	60+	Male	Female
	6.7	8.9	14.4	7.6	17.9	3.0	3.7	13.0	8.3

Ethnicity:
χ^2 (df = 6) = 25.59, $p < .01$
Age:
χ^2 (df = 4) = 49.78, $p < .01$
Gender:
χ^2 (df = 2) = 8.22, $p < .05$

	Ethnicity, %				Age, %			Sex, %	
	Cau.A.	Afr.A.	His.A.	Asn.A.	20–39	40–59	60+	Male	Female

120. Do you feel people should be allowed to die if they want to?
Yes:

81.5	56.0	28.0	58.2	40.7	59.7	69.7	50.9	54.5

No:

18.5	44.0	72.0	41.8	59.3	40.3	30.3	49.1	45.5

Ethnicity:
χ^2 (df = 3) = 103.93, $p < .01$
Age:
χ^2 (df = 2) = 31.92, $p < .01$
Gender:
χ^2 (df = 1) = 0.63

121. (If yes) Under what circumstances should they be allowed to die?
In pain:

30.5	25.9	28.4	21.6	31.3	28.9	23.7	25.0	30.5

Dying anyway:

38.2	27.6	26.9	24.3	26.8	39.8	30.9	34.2	31.1

Unproductive/Unhappy:

2.3	1.7	4.5	0	2.7	1.2	3.0	5.0	0.6

No feelings or sensations:

3.8	12.1	7.5	24.3	8.9	8.4	9.3	7.5	8.4

Because they want to:

17.6	19.0	13.4	24.3	17.0	14.5	20.6	15.0	19.2

Other:

7.6	13.8	19.4	5.4	13.4	7.2	12.4	13.3	10.2

Ethnicity:
χ^2 (df = 15) = 29.45, $p < .05$
Age:
χ^2 (df = 10) = 7.15
Gender:
χ^2 (df = 5) = 7.87

122. (If no) Why do you feel this way?
Only God has the right to take life:

59.6	81.7	86.4	75.0	78.5	80.3	83.3	73.8	84.2

Sake of others:

10.6	2.8	1.9	4.2	5.5	3.0	0	3.3	4.1

Always hope:

8.5	8.5	9.1	16.6	9.8	9.1	9.1	12.3	7.6

Other:

21.3	7.0	2.6	4.2	6.1	7.6	7.6	10.6	4.1

Ethnicity:
χ^2 (df = 9) = 31.17, $p < .01$

	Ethnicity, %				Age, %			Sex, %	
	Cau.A.	Afr.A.	His.A.	Asn.A.	20–39	40–59	60+	Male	Female

122. (If no) Why do you feel this way *(cont'd)*?
    Age:
        χ^2 (df = 6) = 4.35
    Gender:
        χ^2 (df = 3) = 7.23

123. Have you ever considered that all human life might be eliminated from earth?

	Cau.A.	Afr.A.	His.A.	Asn.A.	20–39	40–59	60+	Male	Female
Yes:	73.3	48.9	34.4	47.2	58.3	43.3	45.4	49.3	52.1
No:	26.7	51.1	65.6	52.8	41.7	56.7	54.6	50.7	47.9

    Ethnicity:
        χ^2 (df = 3) = 55.02, $p < .01$
    Age:
        χ^2 (df = 2) = 10.00, $p < .01$
    Gender:
        χ^2 (df = 1) = 0.39

124. (If yes) How?

	Cau.A.	Afr.A.	His.A.	Asn.A.	20–39	40–59	60+	Male	Female
Nuclear explosion:	15.0	17.4	25.0	11.1	16.8	15.1	21.1	18.7	17.5
War (not nuclear):	4.4	0	0	0	2.8	1.9	0	0.9	2.8
Ecologically:	20.4	6.5	17.6	14.8	10.5	28.3	21.1	15.9	16.1
Cosmic natural event:	24.8	6.5	19.1	33.3	18.9	22.6	24.6	35.5	10.5
Other:	35.4	69.6	38.2	40.7	51.0	32.1	35.3	30.0	53.1

    Ethnicity:
        χ^2 (df = 12) = 30.24, $p < .01$
    Age:
        χ^2 (df = 8) = 16.09, $p < .05$
    Gender:
        χ^2 (df = 4) = 27.55, $p < .01$

125. What effect has this interview had on you?

	Cau.A.	Afr.A.	His.A.	Asn.A.	20–39	40–59	60+	Male	Female
Positive:	23.5	30.9	33.3	25.5	26.9	35.3	26.3	27.5	29.5
Neutral:	72.3	58.8	58.7	70.9	68.2	60.3	62.0	67.9	62.0
Negative:	4.2	10.3	8.0	3.6	4.9	4.4	11.7	4.6	8.5

Ethnicity, %				Age, %			Sex, %	
Cau.A.	Afr.A.	His.A.	Asn.A.	20–39	40–59	60+	Male	Female

Ethnicity:

χ^2 (df = 6) = 11.50

Age:

χ^2 (df = 4) = 11.04, $p < .05$

Gender:

χ^2 (df = 2) = 3.61

Appendix B

Chi Square Comparisons of Kalish and Reynolds' Study With the Present Study's Results on Selected Items

Experience With Death

16. How many persons that you knew personally died in the past two years?
    Overall χ^2 (df = 3): 11.72**
    Post hoc χ^2:
    | None | 3.09 |
    | 1–3 | 1.69 |
    | 4–7 | (df = 1): 4.34* |
    | 8 or more | 3.60 |

21. How many funerals have you attended in the past two years?
    Overall χ^2 (df = 3): 2.03

23. How many persons who were dying did you visit or talk with during the past two years?
    Overall χ^2(df = 2): 17.84**
    Post hoc χ^2:
    | None | (df = 1): 7.51** |
    | 1 | 1.84 |
    | 2 or more | (df = 1): 8.49** |

30. Do you actually know of someone who was dying in circumstances like these, so that a decision was made to tell him/her or not to tell him/her that he/she would shortly die?
    Overall χ^2 (df = 1): 1.12

91. Have you ever experienced or felt the presence of anyone after he/she had died?
    Overall χ^2 (df = 1): 3.36

*$p < .05$. **$p < .01$.

Attitudes Toward One's Own Death, Dying, and Afterlife

24. About how often do you think about your own death?
    Overall χ^2 (df = 4): 25.57**
    Post hoc χ^2:
Daily	(df = 1): 7.88**
Weekly	(df = 1): 8.83**
Monthly	(df = 1): 6.50*
Yearly/Hardly Ever	1.18
Never	1.18

29. If you were dying, would you want to be told?
    Overall χ^2 (df = 1): 20.52**
    Post hoc χ^2:
Yes	(df = 1): 4.60*
No	(df = 1): 15.92**

35. If you were told that you had a terminal disease and had six months to live, how would you want to spend your time until you died?
    Overall χ^2 (df = 5): 98.69**
    Post hoc χ^2:
With a marked change in behavior (quit job, etc.)	(df = 1): 6.20*
By withdrawing or focusing on Inner Life	(df = 1): 20.16**
By showing concern for others	(df = 1): 55.73**
By completing projects	0.51
With no change in behavior	(df = 1): 16.02**
Other	0.07

36. Would you tend to accept death peacefully or fight death actively?
    Overall χ^2 (df = 2): 139.88**
    Post hoc χ^2:
Accept	(df = 1): 33.07**
Fight	0.11
Depends	(df = 1): 106.70**

42. Would you try very hard to control the way you showed your emotions in public?
    Overall χ^2 (df = 1): 10.58**
    Post hoc χ^2:
Yes	3.22
No	(df = 1): 7.36**

55. I am afraid of what might happen to my body after death.
    Overall χ^2 (df = 2): 22.13**
    Post hoc χ^2:
Very important	(df = 1): 11.08**
Important	(df = 1): 6.53*
Not important	(df = 1): 4.52*

*$p < .05$. **$p < .01$.

56. I could no longer care for my dependents.
    Overall χ^2 (df = 2): 37.32**
    Post hoc χ^2:
Very important	(df = 1): 8.06**
Important	0.89
Not important	(df = 1): 28.37**

57. I am uncertain as to what might happen to me.
    Overall χ^2 (df = 2): 93.57**
    Post hoc χ^2:
Very important	(df = 1): 51.70**
Important	(df = 1): 4.82*
Not important	(df = 1): 37.05**

58. I could no longer have any experiences.
    Overall χ^2 (df = 2): 21.92**
    Post hoc χ^2:
Very important	(df = 1): 9.33**
Important	(df = 1): 5.33*
Not important	(df = 1): 7.26**

59. My death would cause grief to my relatives and friends.
    Overall χ^2 (df = 2): 65.75**
    Post hoc χ^2:
Very important	(df = 1): 28.95**
Important	1.12
Not important	(df = 1): 35.68**

60. All my plans and projects would come to an end.
    Overall χ^2 (df = 2): 1.58

61. The process of dying might be painful.
    Overall χ^2 (df = 2): 33.08**
    Post hoc χ^2:
Very important	(df = 1): 6.36*
Important	(df = 1): 5.50*
Not important	(df = 1): 21.22**

62. Some people say they are afraid to die and others say they are not. How do you feel?
    Overall χ^2 (df = 3): 267.88**
    Post hoc χ^2:
Afraid/Terrified	(df = 1): 8.51**
Neither afraid nor unafraid	(df = 1): 62.66**
Unafraid/Eager	(df = 1): 132.81**
Depends	(df = 1): 63.90**

70. Have you taken out life insurance?
    Overall χ^2 (df = 1): 4.72*
    Post hoc χ^2:
    　　Yes　1.69
    　　No　3.03

71. Have you made out a will?
    Overall χ^2 (df = 1): 19.49**
    Post hoc χ^2:
    　　Yes　(df = 1): 13.69**
    　　No　(df = 1): 5.80*

72. Have you made arrangements to donate your body or parts of it to medicine?
    Overall χ^2 (df = 1): 69.55**
    Post hoc χ^2:
    　　Yes　(df = 1): 60.08**
    　　No　(df = 1): 9.92**

73. Have you made funeral arrangements?
    Overall χ^2 (df = 1): 0.96

74. Have you paid for or are you paying for a cemetery plot?
    Overall χ^2 (df = 1): 0.42

75. Have you seriously talked with anyone about your experiencing death someday?
    Overall χ^2 (df = 1): 36.15**
    Post hoc χ^2:
    　　Yes　(df = 1): 22.26**
    　　No　(df = 1): 13.89**

86. Do you believe you will live on in some form after death?
    Overall χ^2 (df = 1): 140.03**
    Post hoc χ^2:
    　　Yes　(df = 1): 40.06**
    　　No　(df = 1): 99.97**

95. Other than during dreams, have you ever had the unexplainable feeling that you were about to die?
    Overall χ^2 (df = 1): 6.97**
    Post hoc χ^2:
    　　Yes　(df = 1): 5.36*
    　　No　1.61

98. How often do you dream about your own death or dying?
    Overall χ^2 (df = 3): 64.57**
    Post hoc χ^2:
    　　Never　　　　　　　　　　　　　　(df = 1): 27.55**
    　　Frequently/Sometimes/Rarely　(df = 1): 37.02**

*$p < .05$. **$p < .01$.

114. Would you object to having an autopsy performed on your body?
        Overall χ^2 (df = 2): 33.21**
        Post hoc χ^2:
            Yes   (df = 1): 6.57*
            No   1.44
            Indifferent   (df = 1): 25.20**

115. Would you object to being embalmed?
        Overall χ^2 (df = 2): 20.49**
        Post hoc χ^2:
            Yes   0.09
            No   (df = 1): 5.52*
            Indifferent   (df = 1): 14.88**

116. How would you like your body to be disposed of?
        Overall χ^2 (df = 3): 25.65**
        Post hoc χ^2:
            Buried   (df = 1): 6.71**
            Cremated   0.33
            Donated   2.49
            Indifferent/Undecided   (1): 16.12**

119. Where would you like to die?
        Overall χ^2 (df = 2): 34.25**
        Post hoc χ^2:
            At home   (df = 1): 10.81**
            In a hospital   (df = 1): 7.03**
            Other   (df = 1): 16.41**

125. What effect has this interview had on you?
        Overall χ^2 (df = 2): 34.92**
        Post hoc χ^2:
            Positive   (df = 1): 15.44**
            Neutral   (df = 1): 15.45**
            Negative   (df = 1): 4.03*

Attitudes Toward the Dying, Death, or Grief of Someone Else:

26. Should your friend be told that he/she is going to die?
        Overall χ^2 (df = 2): 72.97**
        Post hoc χ^2:
            Yes   (df = 1): 5.90*
            No   (df = 1): 49.18**
            Depends   (df = 1): 17.89**

28. Do you think a person dying of cancer probably senses he's dying anyway
    without being told?
        Overall χ^2 (df = 2): 51.91**

28. Do you think a person dying of cancer probably senses he's dying anyway without being told *(cont'd)*?
    Post hoc χ^2:
Yes	(df = 1): 4.41*
No	3.05
Depends	(df = 1): 44.45**

33. Did you ever tell someone that he/she was about to die?
    Overall χ^2 (df = 1): 6.96**
    Post hoc χ^2:
Yes	(df = 1): 6.41*
No	0.55

45. Would you be likely to kiss the body at any of the funeral services?
    Overall χ^2 (df = 1): 0.18

50. An infant's death (up to 1 year old), a child's death (around 7 years old), a young person's death (around 25 years old), a middle-aged person's death (around 40 years old), and an elderly person's death (around 75 years old). Which seems most tragic?
    Overall χ^2 (df = 5): 141.46**
    Post hoc χ^2:
Infant	(df = 1): 9.81**
Child	0
Young person	(df = 1): 35.28**
Middle-aged person	(df = 1): 13.51**
Elderly person	(df = 1): 5.63*
Depends	(df = 1): 77.23**

51. Which seems least tragic?
    Overall χ^2 (df = 5): 117.15**
    Post hoc χ^2:
Infant	(df = 1): 18.37**
Child	0.21
Young person	0.27
Middle-aged person	0.90
Elderly person	(df = 1): 5.80*
Depends	(df = 1): 91.60**

53. Which seems most tragic: Natural death, accidental death, suicidal death, homicidal death, or death in war?
    Overall χ^2 (df = 4): 161.51**
    Post hoc χ^2:
Natural death	0.80
Accidental death	0.28
Suicidal death	(df = 1): 61.58**
Homicidal death	0.31
Death in war	(df = 1): 98.54**

---

*$p < .05$. **$p < .01$.

78. To remarry?

    Overall χ^2 (df = 4): 246.44**

    Post hoc χ^2:

Unimportant to wait	(df = 1): 48.80**
1 week–6 months	(df = 1): 14.86**
1 year	(df = 1): 61.53**
2 years	0.11
Never/Depends	(df = 1): 121.14**

79. To stop wearing black?

    Overall χ^2 (df = 3): 85.72**

    Post hoc χ^2:

Unimportant to wait	0.63
1 day–4 months	(df = 1): 13.63**
6 months or more	(df = 1): 27.93**
Others/Depends	(df = 1): 43.93**

80. To return to his/her place of employment?

    Overall χ^2 (df = 3): 72.47**

    Post hoc χ^2:

Unimportant to wait	(df = 1): 5.37*
1 day–1 week	(df = 1): 4.00*
1 month or more	(df = 1): 7.46**
Other/Depends	(df = 1): 55.64**

81. To start going out with other men/women?

    Overall χ^2 (df = 4): 131.61**

    Post hoc χ^2:

Unimportant to wait	(df = 1): 19.57**
1 week–1month	(df = 1): 10.73**
6 months	(df = 1): 22.50**
1 year or more	2.54
Other/Depends	(df = 1): 76.27**

120. Do you feel people should be allowed to die if they want to?

    Overall χ^2 (df = 1): 2.47

121. (If yes) Under what circumstances should they be allowed to die?

    Overall χ^2 (df = 5): 20.2**

    Post hoc χ^2:

In pain	0.50
Dying anyway	(df = 1): 8.48**
Unproductive/Unhappy	0.30
No feelings or sensations	1.09
Because they want to	1.95
Other	(df = 1): 7.88**

References

Aries, P. (1981). *The hour of our death.* (H. Weaver trans.). New York: Knopf.

Baltes, P. B. (1968). Cross-sectional and longitudinal sequences in the study of age and generation effects. *Human Development, 11,* 145–171.

Barrett, R. K. (1993). Psychocultural influences on African American attitudes towards death, dying, and funeral rites. In J. D. Morgan (Ed.), *Personal care in an impersonal world: A multidimensional look at bereavement* (pp. 213–230). Amityville, NY: Baywood.

Becker, E. (1973). *The denial of death.* New York: Free Press.

Bengtson, V. L., Cuellar, J. B., & Ragan, P. K. (1977). Stratum contrasts and similarities in attitudes toward death. *Journal of Gerontology, 32,* 76–88.

Benoliel, J. Q. (1997). Death, technology, and gender in postmodern American society. In S. Strack (Ed.), *Death and the quest for meaning: Essays in honor of Herman Feifel.* Northvale, NJ: Aronson.

Berger, A. S. (1988). *Evidence of life after death: A casebook for the tough-minded.* Springfield, IL: Charles C Thomas.

Blumenfield, M., Levy, N. B., & Kaufman, D. (1979). The wish to be informed of a fatal illness. *Omega, 9,* 323–381.

Braun, K. L., & Nichols, R. (1997). Death and dying in four Asian American cultures: A descriptive study. *Death Studies, 21,* 327–359.

Brofenbrenner, E. (1977). Toward an experimental ecology of human development. *American Psychologist, 32,* 513–531.

Brown, H. A. (1990). Social work practice with the terminally ill in the Black community. In J. K. Parry (Ed.), *Social work practice with the terminally ill: A transcultural perspective* (pp. 67–82). Springfield, IL: Charles C Thomas.

Caldwell, C., McGee, M., & Pryor, C. (1998). The sympathy card as cultural assessment of American attitudes toward death, bereavement, and extending sympathy: A replicated study. *Omega, 37,* 121–132.

Cicirelli, V. G. (1998). Personal meanings of death in relation to fear of death. *Death Studies, 22,* 713–733.

Cloud, J. (2000, September 18). A kinder, gentler death. *Time,* 60–67.

Connelly, R. J. (1998). The medicalization of dying: A positive turn on a new path. *Omega, 36,* 331–341.

Corr, C., Nabe, C., & Corr, D. (2003). *Death and dying: Life and living.* Belmont, CA: Wadsworth.

Counts, D. R., & Counts, D. A. (1991). Conclusions: Coping with the final tragedy. In D. R. Counts & D. A. Counts (Eds.), *Coping with the final tragedy: Cultural variation in dying and grieving* (pp. 277–291). Amityville, NY: Baywood.

Cox, G. R. (2003). The Native American way of death. In C. D. Bryant (Ed.), *Handbook of death and dying, Vol. 2: The response to death* (pp. 631–639). Thousand Oaks, CA: Sage.

Crowder, L.S. (2003). The Taoist (Chinese) way of death. In C. D. Bryant (Ed.), *Handbook of death and dying, Vol. 2: The response to death* (pp. 673–686). Thousand Oaks, CA: Sage.

Davis, S. F., Martin, D. A., Wilee, C. T., & Voorhees, J. W. (1978). Relationship of fear of death and level of self-esteem in college students. *Psychological Reports, 42,* 419–422.

DeSpelder, L. A., & Strickland, A. L. (2002). *The last dance: Encountering death and dying* (6th ed.). Boston: McGraw-Hill.

DeVries, B., Lana, R. D., & Flack, V. T. (1994). Parental bereavement over the life course: A theoretical intersection and empirical review. *Omega, 29,* 47–69.

Doka, K. (1989). *Disenfranchised grief: Recognizing hidden sorrow.* Lexington, MA: Lexington.

Doka, K. J. (2000). Editorial: Challenging our understandings of grief and dying. *Omega, 41,* 3–4.

Enck, G. E. (2003). The dying process. In C. Bryant (Ed.), *Handbook of death and dying, Vol. 1* (pp. 457–467). Thousand Oaks, CA: Sage.

Feifel, H. (Ed.). (1959). *The meaning of death.* New York: McGraw-Hill.

Feifel, H. (1965). The function of attitudes toward death. *GAP Report Death and Dying: Attitudes of Patient and Doctor, 5,* 632–641.

Feifel, H. (1992). The thanatological movement: Respice, adspice, prospice. *Loss, Grief and Care, 6,* 5–16.

Feifel, H. & Nagy, V. T. (1981). Another look at death. *Journal of Consulting and Clinical Psychology, 49,* 278–286.

Fiero, A. (1980). A note on death and dying. *Hispanic Journal of Behavioral Science, 2,* 401–406.

Fenn, E. A. (1989). Honoring the ancestors: Kongo-American graves in the American south. In E. Nichols (Ed.), *The last miles of the way.* Columbia, SC: Dependable.

Florian, V., & Kravitz, S. (1983). Fear of personal death: Attribution, structure, and relation to religious belief. *Journal of Personality and Social Psychology, 44,* 600–607.

Florian, V., & Mikulincer, M. (1997). Fear of personal death in adulthood: The impact of early and recent losses. *Death Studies, 21,* 1–24.

Florian, V., Mikulincer, M., & Green, E. (1994). Fear of personal death and the MMPI profile of middle-aged men: The moderating impact of personal losses. *Omega, 28,* 151–164.

Fox, J. W. (1992). The structure, stability, and social antecedents of reported paranormal experiences. *Sociological Analysis, 53,* 417–431.

Franke, K. J., & Durlak, J. A. (1990). Impact of life factors upon attitudes toward death. *Omega, 21,* 41–49.

Frazier, E. F. (1966). *The negro family in the United States.* Chicago: University of Chicago Press.

Fry, P. S. (1990). A factor analytic investigation of home-bound elderly individual concerns about death and dying and their coping responses. *Journal of Clinical Psychology, 46,* 737–748.

Fulton, R. (Ed.). (1965). *Death and identity.* New York: Wiley.

Fulton, R. (Ed.). (1976). *Death and identity* (rev. ed.). Bowie, MD: Charles Press.

Fulton, R., & Owen, G. (1988). Death and society in Twentieth century America. *Omega, 18,* 379–395.

Gesser, G., Wong, P. T. P., & Reker, G. T. (1987). Death attitudes across the life-span: The development and validation of the Death Attitude Profile. *Omega, 18,* 113–128.

Grabowski, J., & Frantz, T. T. (1993). Latinos and Anglos: Cultural experiences of grief intensity. *Omega, 26,* 273–285.

Greyson, B. (1992). Reduced death threat in near-death experiences. *Death Studies, 16,* 523–536.

Harley, B., & Firebaugh, G. (1993). American's belief in an afterlife: Trends over the past two decades. *Journal for the Scientific Study of Religion, 32,* 269–278.

Hayslip, B., Guarnaccia, C., Radika, L., & Servaty, H. (2002). Death anxiety: An empirical test of a blended self-report and projective measurement model. *Omega: Journal of Death and Dying, 44,* 277–294.

Hayslip, B., & Hansson, R. O. (2003). Death awareness and adjustment across the life span. In C. D. Bryant (Ed.), *Handbook of death and dying, Vol. 1: The presence of death* (pp. 437–447). Thousand Oaks, CA: Sage.

Hayslip, B., Sewaty, H., & Guarnaccia, C. (1999). Age cohort differences in perceptions of funerals. In B. de Vries (Ed.), *End of life issues* (pp. 23–36). New York: Springer.

Hirayama, K. K. (1990). Death and Dying in Japanese culture. In J. K. Parry (Ed.), *Social work practice with the terminally ill: A transcultural perspective* (pp. 159–174). Springfield, IL: Charles C Thomas.

Irish, D. P., Lundquist, K. F., & Nelsen, V. J. (1993). Conclusions. In D. P. Irish, K. F. Lundquist, & V. J. Nelsen (Eds.), *Ethnic variations in dying, death, and grief: Diversity in universality* (pp. 181–190). Washington, DC: Taylor & Francis.

Kalish, R. A. (1981). *Death, grief, and caring relationships*. Monterey, CA: Brooks/Cole.

Kalish, R. A. (1986). Cemetery visits. *Death Studies, 10,* 55–58.

Kalish, R. A., & Reynolds, D. K. (1976). *Death and ethnicity: A psychocultural study.* Los Angeles: The University of Southern California Press.

Kamerman, J. B. (1988). *Death in the midst of life: Social and cultural influences on death, grief, and mourning.* Englewood Cliffs, NJ: Prentice-Hall.

Kastenbaum, R. (1978). Death, dying, and bereavement in old age: New developments and their possible implications for psychosocial care. *Aged Care and Services Review, 1,* 1–10.

Kastenbaum, R. J. (2001). *Death, society, and human experience.* Boston: Allyn & Bacon.

Kastenbaum, R., & Aisenberg, R. B. (1972). *The psychology of death.* New York: Springer.

Kastenbaum, R., & Costa, P. T. (1977). Psychological perspectives on death. *Annual Review of Psychology, 28,* 225–249.

Kastenbaum, R., & Herman, C. (1997). Death personification in the Kevorkian era. *Death Studies, 21,* 115–130.

Kearl, M. C. (1989). *Endings: A sociology of death and dying.* New York: Oxford University Press.

King, J. R. (1980). African survivals in Afro-American religion: Significant psychological factors in endurance. *Review of Afro-American Issues and Culture, 2.*

Kubler-Ross, E. (1969). *On death and dying.* New York: MacMillan.

King, J., & Hayslip, B. (2002). The media's influence on college students views of death. *Omega: Journal of Death and Dying, 44,* 37–56.

Laungani, P., & Young, B. (1997). Conclusions I: Implications for practice and policy. In C. M. Parkes, P. Laungani, & B. Young (Eds.), *Death and bereavement across cultures* (pp. 219–232). London: Routledge.

Leming, M. R., & Dickinson, G. E. (1994). *Understanding dying, death, and bereavement* (3rd ed.). Ft. Worth, TX: Harcourt Brace.

Lester, D. (1971). Attitudes toward death today and thirty-five years ago. *Omega, 2,* 168–173.

Lester, D. (1972). Studies in death attitudes, II. *Psychological Reports, 30,* 440.

Lester, D. (1992). The stigma against dying and suicidal patients: A replication of Richard Kalish's study twenty-five years later. *Omega, 26,* 71–75.

Lester, D., & Becker, D. M. (1993). College students' attitudes toward death today as compared to the 1930s. *Omega, 26,* 219–222.

Levy, N. (1973). Fatal Illness: Should the patient be told? *Medical Insight, 5,* 20–23.

Lund, D. A., & Caserta, M. S. (1998). Future directions in adult bereavement research. *Omega, 36,* 287–303.

Marris, P. (1958). *Widows and their families.* London: Routledge and Kegan Paul.

Marshall, V. W. (1980). *Last chapters: A sociology of aging and dying.* Monterey, CA: Brooks/Cole.

McGee, M. (1980). Faith, fantasy, and flowers: A content analysis of the American sympathy card. *Omega, 11,* 25–35.

McIntosh, J. L. (1999). Death and dying across the lifespan. In L. T. Whitman, R. V. Merluzzi, & R. T. White (Eds.), *Life-span perspectives on health and illness* (pp. 249–274). Mahwah, NJ: Erlbaum.

Middleton, W. C. (1936). Some reactions toward death among college students. *Journal of Abnormal and Social Psychology, 31,* 165–173.

Moller, D. W. (1996). *Confronting death: Values, institutions, and human mortality.* New York: Oxford University Press.

Moore, C. C., & Williamson, J. B. (2003). The universal fear of death and the cultural response. In C. D. Bryant (Ed.), *Handbook of death and dying, Vol. 1: The presence of death* (pp. 3–13). Thousand Oaks, CA: Sage.

Morgan, J. D. (1995). Living our dying and our grieving: Historical and cultural attitudes. In H. Wass and R. A. Neimeyer (Eds.), *Dying: Facing the facts* (3rd ed., pp. 25–45). Washington, DC: Taylor & Francis.

Mount, B. M., Jones, A., & Patterson, A. (1974). Death and dying—Attitudes in a teaching hospital. *Urology, 4,* 741–748.

Myers, J. E., Wass, H., & Murphey, M. (1980). Ethnic differences in death anxiety among the elderly. *Death Education, 4,* 237–244.

National Hospice Foundation. (2004). About NHF. http://www.nationalhospicefoundation.org.

Neimeyer, R. A., Dingemans, P., & Epting, F. R. (1977). Convergent validity, situational stability, and meaningfulness of the Threat Index. *Omega, 8,* 251–265.

Neimeyer, R. A., & Van Brunt, D. (1995). Death anxiety. In H. Wass & R. A. Neimeyer (Eds.), *Dying: Facing the facts* (3rd ed., pp. 49–88). Washington, DC: Taylor & Francis.

Nichols, E. (Ed.). (1989). *The last miles of the way: African American home-going traditions, 1890–present.* Columbia, SC: Dependable.

Nishi, S. M. (1995). Japanese Americans. In P. G. Min (Ed.), Asian American: *Contemporary trends and issues* (pp. 95–133). Thousand Oaks, CA: Sage.

Oken, D. (1961). What to tell cancer patients: A study of medical attitudes. *Journal of the American Medical Association, 175,* 1120–1128.

Oltjenbruns, K. A. (1998). Ethnicity and the grief response: Mexican American versus Anglo American college students. *Death Studies, 22,* 141–155.

Owen, G., Fulton, R., & Markusen, E. (1982). Death at a distance: A study of family survivors. *Omega, 13,* 191–225.

Palmer, J. (1979). A community mail survey of psychic experiences. *Journal of the American Society for Psychical Research, 73,* 221–251.

Pandey, R. E., & Templer, D. I. (1972). Use of the Death Anxiety Scale in an inter-racial setting. *Omega, 3,* 127–130.

Parkes, C. M. (1972). *Bereavement: Studies of grief in adult life.* London: Travistock.

Parkes, C. M. (1997). Conclusions II: Attachments and losses in cross-cultural perspective. In C. M. Parkes, P. Laungani, & B. Young (Eds.), *Death and bereavement across cultures* (pp. 233–243). London: Routledge.

Parkes, C. M., Laungani, P., & Young, B. (Eds.). (1997). *Death and bereavement across cultures.* London: Routledge.

Perry, H. L. (1993). Mourning and funeral customs of African Americans. In D. P. Irish, K. E. Lundquist, & V. J. Nelsen (Eds.), *Ethnic variations in dying, death, and grief: Diversity in universality* (pp. 51–65). Washington, DC: Taylor & Francis.

Post, P. (1997). *Emily Post's Etiquette* (16th ed.). New York: Harper Collins.

Pratt, L. (1981). Business temporal norms and bereavement behavior. *American Sociological Review, 46,* 317–333.

Pratt, C. C., Hare, J., & Wright, C. (1985). Death anxiety and comfort in teaching about death among preschool teachers. *Death Studies, 9,* 417–425.

Pyszczynski, T., Solomon, S., & Greenberg, J. (2003). In the wake of 9/11: The psychology of terror. Washington, DC: American Psychological Association.

Rambachan, A. (2003). The Hindu way of death. In C. D. Bryant (Ed.), *Handbook of death and dying, Vol. 2: The response to death* (pp. 640–648). Thousand Oaks, CA: Sage.

Raphael, B. (1995). The death of a child. In J. B. Williamson & E. S. Shneidman (Eds.), *Death: Current perspectives* (4th ed., pp. 261–275). Mountain View, CA: Mayfield.

Rees, W. D. (1975). The bereaved and their hallucinations. In B. Schoenberg (Ed.), *Bereavement and its psychosocial aspects*. New York: Columbia University Press.

Riegel, K. (1976). The dialectics of human development. *American Psychologist, 31,* 689–700.

Rogers, R. G., Hummer, R. A., Nam, C. B., & Peters, K. (1996). Demographic, socioeconomic, and behavioral factors affecting ethnic mortality by cause. *Social Forces, 74,* 1419–1438.

Rosenblatt, P. C. (1997). Grief in small-scale societies. In C. M. Parkes, P. Laungani, & B. Young (Eds.), *Death and bereavement across cultures*. London: Routledge.

Rosow, I. (1978). What is a cohort and why? *Human Development, 11,* 65–75.

Salcido, R. M. (1990). Mexican-Americans: Illness, death, and bereavement. In J. K. Parry (Ed.), *Social work practice with the terminally ill: A transcultural perspective* (pp. 99–112). Springfield, IL: Charles C Thomas.

Sanders, C. M. (1989). *Grief: The mourning after—Dealing with adult bereavement*. New York: Wiley.

Sanders, C. M., Manger, P. A., & Strong, P. N. (1985). *A manual for the grief experience inventory*. Blowing Rock, NC: Center for the Study of Separation and Loss.

Sanders, J. F., Poole, T. E., & Rivero, W. T. (1980). Death anxiety among the elderly. *Psychological Reports, 46,* 53–54.

Schaie, K. W. (1965). A general model for the study of developmental problems. *Psychological Bulletin, 64,* 92–107.

Schindler, R. (2003). The Jewish way of death. In C. D. Bryant (Ed.), *Handbook of death and dying, Vol. 2: The response to death* (pp. 687–693). Thousand Oaks, CA: Sage.

Shapiro, E. R. (1995). Grief in family and cultural context: Learning from Latino families. *Cultural Diversity and Mental Health, 1,* 159–176.

Sultan, D. H. (2003). The Muslim way of death. . In C. D. Bryant (Ed.), *Handbook of death and dying, Vol. 2: The response to death* (pp. 649–655). Thousand Oaks, CA: Sage.

Suzuki, H. (2003). The Japanese way of death. In C. D. Bryant (Ed.), *Handbook of death and dying, Vol. 2: The response to death* (pp. 656–672). Thousand Oaks, CA: Sage.

Thorson, J. A., Powell, F. C., & Samuel, V. T. (1998). African- and Euro-American samples differ little in score on death anxiety. *Psychological Reports, 83,* 623–626.

Tokunaga, H. T. (1985). The effect of bereavement upon death related attitudes and fears. *Omega, 16,* 267–280.

Travis, T., Noyes, R., & Brightwell, D. (1974). The attitudes of physicians toward prolonging life. *International Journal of Psychiatry in Medicine, 5,* 17–26.

Wagner, K. D., & Lorion, R. P. (1984). Correlates of death anxiety in elderly persons. *Journal of Clinical Psychology, 40,* 1235–1241.

Wong, P. T., Reker, G. T., & Gesser, G. (1994). Death Attitude Profile-Revised: A multidimensional measure of attitudes toward death. In R. A. Neimeyer (Ed.), *Death anxiety handbook: Research, instrumentation, and application* (pp. 121–148). Washington, DC: Taylor & Francis.

Wood, W. R., & Williamson, J. B. (2003). Historical changes in the meaning of death in the Western tradition. In C. D. Bryant (Ed.), *Handbook of death and dying, Vol. 1: The presence of death* (pp. 14–23). Thousand Oaks, CA: Sage.

Yamamoto, J. K., Okonogi, K., Iwasaki, T., & Yoshimura, S. (1969). Mourning in Japan. *American Journal of Psychiatry, 125,* 1661–1672.

Zusman, M. E., & Tschetter, P. (1984). Selecting whether to die at home or in a hospital setting. *Death Education, 8,* 365–381.

Index